BOYD LIBRARY
SANDHILLS COMMUNITY COLLEGE
PINEHURST, N.C. 28374

W9-BOP-381

The Public Administrator's Grievance Arbitration Handbook

HD
6972
.5
IP37
1983

The
Public Administrator's
Grievance Arbitration
Handbook

Lee T. Paterson / *Reginald T. Murphy*

Longman

New York & London

HD
6972
.5
.P37
1983

The Public Administrator's Grievance Arbitration Handbook

Longman Inc., 1560 Broadway, New York, N.Y. 10036
Associated companies, branches, and representatives
throughout the world.

Copyright © 1983 by Longman Inc.

All rights reserved. No part of this publication may be
reproduced, stored in a retrieval system, or transmitted
in any form or by any means, electronic, mechanical,
photocopying, recording, or otherwise, without the prior
permission of the publisher.

Developmental Editor: Irving E. Rockwood
Editorial and Design Supervisor: Ferne Y. Kawahara
Manufacturing Supervisor: Marion Hess
Composition: Weber & Stevens
Printing and Binding: Interstate

Cases from *Public Sector Arbitration Awards* © Labor
Relations Press, Fort Washington, Pa. Reprinted with
permission.

Cases from *Arbitration in the Schools* © American Arbitration Association, New York, N.Y. Reprinted with
permission.

Library of Congress Cataloging in Publication Data
Paterson, Lee T.
    The public administrator's grievance arbitration
handbook.
    Bibliography: p.
    Includes index.
    1. Grievance arbitration.   2. Public administra-
tion.   I. Murphy, Reginald T.   II. Title.
HD6972.5.P37   1983   350.1'76   82-17188
ISBN 0-582-28381-7 (pbk.)
ISBN 0-582-28382-5 (loose-leaf)

Manufactured in the United States of America

WITHDRAWN

To J. Michael Taggart,
our friend and colleague, whose untimely death
deprived the legal profession of a brilliant star
and diminished our personal world.

WITHDRAWN

Contents

Preface

This manual has been designed specifically for public agency managers, including public-school administrators. It emphasizes the pragmatic as well as the philosophical in its approach to grievance processing. The addenda to each chapter include checklists and forms easily reproduced for use by administrators, in addition to selected arbitration cases-in-point.

Although much has been written about grievance arbitration as a concept or as a contract clause, little has been produced to assist directly the manager on the firing line who must implement grievance procedures at the point of contact—the work location. This comprehensive manual attempts to fill the vacuum. It is hoped that this manual will prove valuable to *all* levels of public management.

The outline of this book is also an outline for a management training course in grievance administration. Chapter I provides the philosophic background for the public adminsitrator's approach to grievance procedures. Chapter II analyzes the important elements of a grievance policy from the management point of view. Chapter III provides the rules for processing grievances at the first step. Chapter IV discusses the rules for handling grievance appeals by higher-level managers. Chapter V provides an analysis of typical grievance issues, what the supervisor should look for, and suggestions for successful arbitration of these issues. Chapter VI discusses the steps management should take to prepare for the arbitration hearing and includes the transcript, the exhibits, and the decision of a real hearing. Chapter VII reviews the procedural and substantive rules and the criteria the arbitrator will use in reaching a decision. Finally, Chapter VIII offers techniques and an outline to be used to train various levels of management in effective grievance handling.

Lee T. Paterson
Reginald. T. Murphy

Introduction

The most significant recent development in labor relations in this country has been the spectacular growth and importance of collective bargaining in public-sector employment. When one notes that in 1946 there were 5.6 million civilians employed by government and that by 1975 there were 15.4 million, it is not difficult to understand the commensurate interest by unions in public employees. Each year of the 1960s and 70s has brought additional legislation and bargaining for public employee unions, including the acceptance of compulsory arbitration. Today there are over 7.8 million federal, state, and local government employees covered by collective bargaining agreements, most including grievance and arbitration procedures.

Marked population growth, increased social consciousness demanding a wide range of services, competitive labor market for professionals and semiprofessionals, the declining strength of unionism in the private sector, general public dissatisfaction with the status quo, and eagerness to challenge constituted authority have all contributed to revolutionary changes in employer—employee relations in the public sector. At first, many public officials were reluctant to acknowledge the impact of unionism in the public service. Today most public administrators recognize that the traditional methods of public-sector management have undergone a drastic revolution. The old concepts have yielded to approaches similar to those found in the private sector, but these very approaches have exacerbated personnel problems because of the decided differences that exist between the public and private sectors.

Two of the more significant areas of difference are: (1) in private enterprise, authority is clearly located at the top, whereas governmental authority is often diffused and shifts with political tides; and, (2) funding for public services is often unconnected with the recipients of the service, so that quality and quantity of service are frequently not reflected in the income of the agency. (The outstanding example of this is the continuation of income to public agencies even when they are closed due to strikes.)

Because of these developments, public administrators have come to realize that management is a profession in its own right, and today, those who would be successful in managing resources and people effectively must learn new skills, concepts, and approaches. The most direct impact of this changing environment in public sector employee relations has been on the first-line supervisor. No longer can the supervisor play the role of a benevolent father figure discussing the situation with "his people," via the "open door policy," while taking into consideration the "impact on the public," in a philosophy of being "fair and just to everyone."

Similarly, public employees have been changed by these new dynamics. In the past such employees were assumed to be "public servants" who were good-natured, dedicated, and nonaggressive. Low pay was in most cases justified by special benefits such as tenure, nondiscrimination, and stability of position. What the employee gave up in terms of incentive and paycheck was compensated for by job protection until the employee left the service on a public pension.

Under no circumstances was a public servant expected to be loud or aggressive, even if outraged by inefficient supervision or upset about the waste of public funds. Employees who didn't value stability and pension plans needed to look for other jobs. The idea that an employee or group of employees would challenge the system was unthinkable.

This traditional approach, when coupled with civil service and other statutory protections, worked well enough. Employees were generally protected against significant arbitrary actions. The supervisor, on the other hand, had the flexibility on minor issues to run the department as he/she saw fit.

The traditional system encouraged supervisors and department heads to identify closely with their employees. In many cases this identification created almost autonomous departments in which the supervisor and the employees worked together closely and guarded their independence. The supervisor became the advocate for the employees against top administrators and elected officials.

Today the respective stereotypes of the old-line public manager and employee are fading from the scene. The "paterfamilias" approach is giving way to a professional management orientation. Public agencies are beginning to use management systems, goal setting, and private-sector labor relations techniques to manage resources and people. At the same time, with the rise of militant unionism, public employees are demanding and receiving more input into decisions regarding their salaries, working conditions, and the services they provide. Public employee organizations have been willing to use whatever tools they have at hand, including political pressure, to acquire decision-making power.

The primary cause for the drastic change in agency personnel management has, of course, been the reality of militant public-sector unionism. As employee organizations have become more powerful they have pushed hard for restricting the authority of managers and supervisors to make unilateral decisions. Whereas the traditional system was established to cope with only major supervisory decisions such as hiring, discipline, promotion, and discharge, employee organizations are pushing for a system that will review and control all decisions affecting employees. In particular, unions and associations have fought to restrict the ability of the supervisor to make decisions based on subjective criteria. By negotiating personnel and working conditions, policies based on contractually defined standards such as seniority, and *most* significantly, by providing that violations of such policies are subject to grievance and arbitration procedures, employee organizations have been able to restrict severely the flexibility of supervisors.

In this new work environment, administrators attempting to make subjective decisions based on what they consider fair are a target for both sides. A public agency in which department heads make individual interpretations of either the collective agreement or personnel policies is vulnerable to "whipsawing" negotiation demands and/or grievances by employee organizations that want the most favorable interpretation of the contract or the policy. Similarly, the employee organization confronted with department heads making their own interpretation of language must respond to its members' demands for protection.

The end product of these changing circumstances has been a demand for a different type of public sector administrator to cope with the realities of contemporary labor management relations, one who can work as an effective member of a management team and who can recognize the need for relinquishing the autonomy of individual departments for the sake of a unified management approach.

The taxpayers have begun to realize that if the quality and efficiency of public institutions are to be maintained and improved, it must be done by people with the authority to get the job done, people with the training and experience to inspire, direct and lead others.

That is why public administrators are there, and that is why they are paid a premium over rank-and-file employees. It is for such a new-era public administrator that this book is designed.

Chapter II

Management's Attitude Toward Grievance Procedures

Too frequently public-sector administrators tend to view grievance procedures as essentially negative and antagonistic, or at the least as a disruptive nuisance. However, it is important for management to remember that there are positive elements in grievance procedures which should not be ignored, and which contribute effectively to the manager's function.

A valid and effective formal grievance procedure is the "heart" of any negotiated agreement, and it provides an orderly and peaceful redress for alleged violations of employee rights. A process for resolving differences is preferable to protracted legal action, disruptive tactics, confrontation or work stoppages initiated by a union. From the union standpoint, of course, the desirability of a functional grievance procedure is obvious. A grievance procedure can be a tension-relieving device among the union members, a quick, economical method of protecting contractual rights, and an alternative to costly strikes and picketing. The procedure can also be used as a weapon, of course. A manager who continuously fights the union can usually be broken by the filing of repeated grievances. If the pressure of the grievances doesn't get to the manager, the chief administrative officer will, because of the high costs of defending the suits. In addition, unions may use grievances during membership organizing drives. Some evidence of this can be seen in the following quote from the AFL-CIO:

> Many unions use the successful prosecution of a nonmember's grievance as a basic organizing tool. The successful handling of a grievance helps to answer the question "What can the Union do for me?" Even though the individual with the grievance may not join the union, some other nonunion workers may be persuaded to do so.

A positive, open management attitude best serves both management's own interest and that of the individual employee. Certainly there always exists potential for abuse where an overbearing, inflexible, and militant union leadership exists.

However, abuse of the grievance procedure is far more likely to be the exception than the rule. Management should keep in mind the valid reasons and benefits to management which exist in effective grievance procedures. Such benefits are best summarized as follows:

1. Contract provisions can be interpreted without recourse to a work disruption.
2. Employees have a safety valve with which to relieve tensions and voice complaints.
3. Management is alerted early to employee relations problems.

1. Contract Provisions Can Be Interpreted Without Recourse to a Work Disruption

Prior to the wide-scale use of grievance procedures, "self-help" was the common method of resolving grievances. At one time in American labor relations, unions resolved their members' grievances by assaulting and sometimes killing first-line supervisors. Even in the public sector, unions have used "self-help" when they have not had access to a grievance procedure. It is not unusual for public employee organizations to engage in work disruptions, political recall, blacklisting of supervisors and physical intimidation.

An example of the above actually occurred in one public agency where the employee organization, after losing a strike, began harassing the department head who had been the most effective in keeping his people at work. The union began making charges about him to the elected officials, claiming his employees worked under a dictator and were afraid of him. The agency officials were told the employees had numerous grievances which they couldn't talk about to the department head. The mayor called the department head in to discuss the charges. Even though the mayor gave the supervisor a clean bill of health, suspicions lingered. Within a year the department head left the city. A grievance procedure would have materially reduced the employee organization's credibility in using such tactics and probably would have precluded such character assasination.

A grievance procedure provides an alternative method for employees' organizations to resolve their problems. Without the grievance procedure, employee organizations are forced to accept the status quo or to use more dramatic methods of resolving problems. The cost of a grievance procedure in the long run may be far less than the cost of dealing with work stoppages, slowdowns and sabotage.

2. Employees Have a Safety Valve with which to Relieve Tensions and Voice Complaints

One of the most important reasons for a grievance procedure is to give employees a release for their work-related anxieties and problems. In many cases the existence of a grievance procedure is like having a fire station near your home — you don't expect to need it but its existence is reassuring.

In addition, employees and employee organizations often use management as a scapegoat for their own ills. Without a grievance procedure, management is vulnerable to this syndrome. With a grievance procedure, management can respond to the employee organization by saying, "File a grievance if you feel there is a legitimate problem."

Grievance procedures also protect management from the chronic complainer who stirs up problems in the back room. Sooner or later someone will challenge this employee to use the grievance procedure. Once the employee organization or an arbitrator drops the employee's complaint, the individual's credibility is gone and the person can no longer play the martyr role eliciting sympathy from co-workers.

An example of this chain of events occured in one large county welfare department. For a number of years one of the social workers had been a constant complainer about his supervisor and management in general. He had been the main force in organizing the employees for an international union. During the term of first contract no grievance procedure was put into the contract. For the next two years the employee agitated against management and the union. At the end of the contract he led employees into another union. In this contract there was a grievance and arbitration procedure. The employee immediately filed a series of grievances extending back for 10 years. The cases were consolidated before one arbitrator. After hearing the case the arbitrator issued his decision castigating the employee for wasting management's time with self-interested complaints. There were no further grievances and within a year the employee quit.

Establishing a grievance procedure, then, is really a cathartic device for employee morale. If management is effective, the procedure need not be used, but its very existence promotes good relations.

3. Management is Alerted Early to Employee Relations Problems

Finally, for the chief administrative officer and the elected officials, grievance procedures can provide an early warning indication of poor supervision. It is not unusual in public agencies to find a large number of grievances coming from one agency or facility. In some cases that is a function of the type of employee and/or of the union representative. In many cases, however, it is a function of the supervisor.

Employees should be able to have most of their problems solved without recourse to the grievance procedure. Where one supervisor has more formal grievances filed against him or her than other supervisors, higher-level supervision should check to see if supervisory problems are the basic cause of the grievances. Employees often file grievances for reasons other than those expressed on paper. Management needs to look beyond the formalities of the procedure to find out if there are other problems that need to be corrected.

In one public agency, the supervisor of the public works department over a period of 10 years had had a grievance filed by almost every employee in his department. Finally the union went to management and indicated that unless management did something about the problem there would be a strike the following year. Management checked into the problem and found that the supervisor had worked as a mine boss in South Africa for 15 years before he came to work with the agency. It appeared that he had never received any formal training either in supervision or labor relations since he came to the agency. The agency immediately put the supervisor into a formal training program. Within a few months the number of grievances began to drop, his employee retention increased, and departmental efficiency appeared to improve.

Another common problem is the inability of first-level supervisors to resolve formal grievances filed against them. At least 70 to 80 percent of all formal grievances should be resolved at the first step of the grievance procedure. If the supervisors are unable to settle grievances at the first step and continually buck them up to the next step, it may indicate that they need help in understanding their role in grievance processing. Supervisors often take grievances as personal attacks on themselves. If all of the supervisors are bucking grievances up, it indicates the need for management to inform and train supervisors on contract administration and grievance handling.

RULES FOR WORKING POSITIVELY WITH GRIEVANCE PROCEDURES

Maintaining a positive, open management attitude is much easier to describe than to implement, particularly at the first level of supervision. The mere processing of grievances under a formal grievance procedure is a major problem for many public managers. First-level supervisors faced with their first grievance over an overtime assignment are likely to take the grievance as a personal infringement of their rights. It is not unusual for first-level supervisors to ask "Why are you filing this grievance against me?" or to state, "If that's the way you guys are going to play it, so will I."

Effective managers accept grievance procedures as one of the realities of doing their job. Rather than fighting the system, they work within it to make the most out of the situation. The ineffective supervisor fights the system and in the long run is forced out.

The following are a few rules designed to help public managers work productively, effectively and positively:

1. Don't personalize the issues.
2. Reflect the attitude of the agency.
3. Distinguish between employees and employee organizations.
4. Work with employee organization representatives.
5. Evaluate the political role of the organization representative.
6. Be prepared to be overturned.
7. Support management.

1. Don't Personalize the Issues

Most supervisors faced with a formal grievance have an initial reaction of being under attack. They often feel that the grievance has been filed against them personally and that acceptance or rejection of the grievance will reflect on their abilities as supervisors. To some extent this is a normal reaction. However, supervisors have to realize that part of the responsibility of supervision is the risk of making mistakes. Good supervisors as well as poor supervisors make mistakes.

Grievances are not necessarily a reflection of poor supervision. In fact, in cases where a poor supervisor makes mistakes that are consistently in favor of employees or employee organizations, that supervisor will receive fewer grievances than the good supervisor who works "by the book."

Management has to depersonalize grievances and look at them from an organizational point of view. The first-level supervisor is a representative of the whole management team. Even in a perfectly run agency, the union will still have to file some grievances, if only to demonstrate its viability in the period between contract negotiations. Elected officials and public administrators should expect grievances to be filed — it's only when an abnormal number of grievances or no grievances at all are filed that the agency should consider whether the supervisor is part of the problem.

If supervisors accept grievances as a necessary part of a labor–management relations system, they can deal with them and respond to them effectively. If they look upon grievances as reflections on their ability, they will likely make mistakes that can cost themselves and the agency large sums of money and time.

2. Reflect the Attitude of the Agency

In handling labor relations problems public administrators often respond to employee relations problems from their own viewpoints. An agency supervisor with a conservative attitude about management rights would probably reject most grievances regarding subjective management decisions (e.g., employee performance evaluation, employee scheduling). If superiors and the elected officials share this attitude, the supervisor will have no problems. On the other hand, if the attitude of the deciding power in the agency tends to be acquiescent toward employee relations, the supervisor rejecting such a grievance is putting himself or herself on the proverbial limb which one of the superiors is sawing off.

Every agency has an attitude, implicitly or explicitly, toward labor relations problems. This attitude is usually set by key elected officials or by the chief administrative officer. In the best situations, the agency conducts periodic training sessions that make the attitude of the agency and the response expected from the administrator clear. In many instances, the administrators have to fend for themselves in discovering the agency attitude. In some cases this can be difficult because key decision makers in the agency may have different attitudes depending on the issue. It is not unusual, for example, for liberal elected officials to be indifferent about management's decision in selecting employees for overtime assignment, but to be extremely dogmatic about management's decisions in selecting and promoting women and minorities.

A public agency within the bounds set by law has the right to choose its own type of labor relations postures. Many elected officials and even line supervisors believe that unions are detrimental to public agencies and that their erosion of management power must be resisted at every step. On the other hand, there are just as many elected officials and public administrators who believe that unions should be given equal rights in terms of decision making in a public organization. Of course both of these attitudes are extremes and the vast majority of public agencies fall near the midpoint of these postures.

Serious labor relations problems for an agency don't come because of the posture the agency takes, but with the lack of consistency within management as a whole. This could be in the form of individual managers changing their posture on a day-to-day basis or inconsistent management decisions between different levels of supervision.

Whatever the attitude of the agency, it is important that the managers work within and reflect that attitude. Survival in labor relations requires the backing of higher-level supervision.

3. Distinguish between Employees and Employee Organizations

Management often makes the mistake of saying "the social workers are calling a strike" or "the janitors are demanding more money." A more accurate description would be that the social workers' union is calling a strike or that the association representing the janitors is demanding more money. By mentally combining employee organizations with their membership, management misses the point that employee organizations often have entirely different goals from their members.

An example of this occurred in one city where the city manager asked police officers to help out at a local charity show. The police officers were willing to do it but the union didn't want to agree because its sister local in a bigger city nearby was having a dispute about the same issue. If the city had lumped the employee organization together with the police officers, it would have given up in disgust. Instead, realizing the distinction, the city manager called a meeting with the police management group, explained the problem, pointed out the union's political motivation and suggested that the management group talk with the men. Within 24 hours almost every man on the police force had volunteered for the show.

4. Work with Employee Organization Representatives

Whatever the relationship of the public agency toward the employee organization, each individual supervisor will have his or her own relationship with the local employee organization representative. That doesn't mean that the supervisor won't reflect the attitude of the agency but rather that within that attitude he or she has to build individual credibility with the organizational representative. Even in the worst conflict-oriented situations such as strikes, no public administrator should place himself/herself in a personal one-on-one battle with union representatives. For example, in one strike a department head took it upon himself to taunt the picketers. After the strike he found that the union had tried to get him fired as part of the settlement agreement.

Working with the employee organization representative doesn't mean making concessions or even always reaching agreements. It does mean being able to communicate with the organizational representative about potential solutions to problems, being able to meet with the representative away from the representative's membership, and having the respect of the representative.

At the department level, the supervisor should make a point of having meetings with the local representative. In some cases, the meeting can consist of a cup of coffee in the supervisor's office. In other cases, it may mean going out to lunch with the representative. Whatever it takes, the supervisor needs a ready means of communication with the union representative before major problems occur.

One critical rule in dealing with unions and associations is *don't surprise the organization representative*. If supervisors anticipate a problem that may result in a grievance they should alert the representative to it. In some cases supervisors may alert the representative to problems that never occur, but in the majority of cases they will be getting their story in first before the representative hears the employee complaint. Particularly in the area of discipline and discharge, supervisors should fill in the union representative before taking action against the employee. Often union representatives in the first interview with employees can convince them to accept the management action rather than fight it. Once the employee files the grievance, the union's hands are tied because from that point on the union has to aggressively represent the employee.

At the top administrative level the chief personnel officer has to maintain a relationship with the head of the employee organization. Even where both management and the union have a militant attitude, there has to be some communication between the parties. Few public agencies and fewer employee organizations have the resources or the stomach to maintain continuous warfare over every management action. Often, matters that are serious grievances at the first level, when discussed at the top level in the context of the whole agency are not nearly as important and can be settled by both sides.

5. Evaluate the Political Role of the Organization Representative

Public administrators are often upset because union officials take seemingly illogical positions. It is not unusual to hear complaints by first-level supervisors because the union is supporting the grievance of a person who is obviously in the wrong. In trying to understand the union's or the association's point of view, the manager has to look at the organization's position from a political viewpoint.

Employee organization representatives are elected to office. To maintain their jobs they have to maintain the support of their constituents. Even where the employee organization representative understands the logical solution, that may not be good enough for the members. No one is less employable than the *former* head of an employee organization. Employee organization officers know that and often take illogical positions to win the support of their members. In the area of grievance procedures the union will often pursue a losing grievance knowing that it will be better to blame the loss on management or the arbitrator than refuse to handle the case.

6. Be Prepared to be Overturned

First-level supervisors expect and deserve line-management support for their decisions. However, implicit in a multi-step grievance procedure is the possibility of review and referral of the first-level supervisor's decision.

Generally, two reasons are given for reversing lower-level supervision: the first-level decision was patently incorrect, or, even though the decision was correct the overall results of litigating and winning the case aren't worth the cost to management and the impact on employer–employee relations.

Obviously, if a supervisor has made a mistake in interpreting a contract or his or her subjective judgment won't stand up to the standards set in the contract, the supervisor should expect to be overturned. The supervisor should also expect a full explanation of the reasons and, if necessary, training in how to deal with similar cases in the future.

The tough case for the first-level supervisor is the situation where he or she is right but the cost or the impact on labor relations is too great. In deciding to settle such cases management should carefully weigh supervisory morale as part of the settlement cost. Where the decision is made to settle because of other considerations the supervisor is entitled to an explanation of those considerations.

In reality, however, one of the purposes of a multi-step grievance procedure is that grievances can be settled at higher levels. All supervisors should be prepared to face the fact that their decisions, no matter how right they believe they are, will be reversed periodically at higher management levels.

7. Support Management

All of the above rules will help public administrators in dealing with employees and employee organizations. However, in the last analysis there is one rule that is paramount for the public administrator dealing in employee relations: *Support Management*.

Managers periodically try to substitute their judgment for that of the agency. For example, a department head may not agree that employees should be required to sign out when they leave the department. If the department head substitutes personal judgment for agency rules and doesn't require employees to sign out when they leave, this individual will weaken management's position in dealing with the union in other departments. In addition, this department head may promote grievances against other department heads who are trying to enforce the rule.

Similarly, in trying to establish a personal relationship with employees and union representatives, public managers are often tempted to ignore agency policies or the collective agreement and substitute their own concept of fairness to settle the grievance. In interpreting the language of a contract, arbitrators have to be guided by the meaning intended by the parties. One way of determining the meaning is to look at the practice of the parties. If the employee organization can get a few managers to substitute their own practices in areas covered by the contract, they can use those practices to get agency-wide interpretations of the language.

Every manager has the responsibility of making sure that all the rights that management has retained are preserved. Everything supervisors do in their job sets a precedent that may affect other administrators. Before settling a grievance or dealing with a labor relations problem, supervisors should ask themselves if they are supporting their fellow managers.

CONCLUSION

In the final analysis, grievance procedures can only be as effective as the parties that use them. If supervisors won't work with employees and employee organization representatives, the agency will be burdened with unnecessary grievances. If supervisors won't support management the agency won't have grievance problems but will lose everything they fought to retain at the bargaining table. If a public agency wants effective grievance handling, it must first negotiate a good procedure and secondly, train management to utilize that procedure.

Chapter III

Management Objectives in Grievance Policies

More than any other provision of a negotiated agreement, the grievance procedure is, or certainly should be, a reflection of the relationship between the parties. A management with a conciliatory or acquiescent philosophy of labor relations is going to have difficulty if it expects its first-line supervisors to work within the so-called literal –legalistic approach to contract implementation. Prior to the time management begins to write a proposed grievance procedure, it should make an assessment of its basic employee relations philosophy and an assessment of its relationship with the employee organization.

Grievance procedures are probably the single most difficult policy to negotiate — not only because they are complicated, but because every word in the grievance procedure may at a later date have an effect on the interpretation of other agency policies. Management negotiators should not begin negotiating grievance procedures until they have addressed the critical question of whether the proposed procedure will promote or detract from the agency's labor relations program objectives. A poorly drafted grievance procedure will fail to accomplish these objectives, and by virtue of this failure tends to destroy all of management's efforts to evolve effective personnel policies.

MODEL GRIEVANCE PROCEDURES

The processing of grievances follows a sequential pattern similar to that illustrated in Addendum II-1. Although this typical public agency grievance process is found with great frequency, there are myriad approaches to the actual handling of grievances. As previously noted, such handling must reflect the personnel relations policy of the agency. However, for simplicity we can reduce these approaches to three basic models:

1. The literal contract approach.

2. The human relations approach.
3. The moderate or compromise approach.

1. The *literal contract approach*. A legalistic approach to grievance handling which holds that grievance procedures are only designed to interpret the language of the master contract between the parties. This view reflects an attitude that management is conducting a holding action against the erosion of its prerogatives by both employee organizations and arbitrators.
2. The *human relations approach*. A humanistic approach which holds that a grievance procedure should be a relief valve for employee dissatisfaction. This approach also reflects the view that the master contract is only an outline of the basic relationship between the parties, and that a grievance procedure is needed to provide continuous refinement and interpretation.
3. The *moderate or compromise approach*. An approach that attempts to realistically combine the better parts of the literal—legal contract and the humanistic approach by providing a broad definition of grievance with specific exclusion of management rights issues. In this approach, management welcomes resolution of employee complaints over basic issues, such as salaries or working conditions which directly affect the employee, but resists intrusions of an arbitrator into management rights areas such as agency goals or the budget. These latter are areas of concern unique to public sector employee organizations. A model for this moderate approach to grievance procedure is illustrated in Addendum II−2.

Whichever approach to grievance procedures management selects, the admonition stated earlier that it should be reflective of the basic agency philosophy is still the critical criterion. Any grievance procedure that does not reflect this basic philosophy of the agency constitutes a time bomb waiting to explode. For example, the literal contract philosophy is not compatible with blue sky definitions of grievances, nor are administrators who are devoted to the literal contract orientation compatible with elected officials advocating the humanistic approach to labor relations. Indeed, any public administrator attempting to negotiate a literal—legalistic contract grievance procedure for a human relations-oriented agency is a perfect setup for an "end run" by the employee organization.

ELEMENTS OF GRIEVANCE PROCEDURES

Grievance procedures can be separated into five key elements:

1. Definition of grievance.
2. Definition of the grievant.
3. Procedural steps for processing the grievance.
4. Procedural limitations on processing a grievance.
5. Role of the third-party neutral.

There is nothing unique or radically different for public agencies in the major concepts underlying grievance procedures. Indeed, public management has traditionally worked within a pattern of successive management review steps in handling employee complaints. In grievance procedures the steps are simply more formalized with more precise procedural requirements. In addition, many public sector jurisdictions have merit or civil service commissions who function as grievance review boards for employee complaints. It must be noted, however, that with the advent of collective bargaining and its emphasis on third-party neutral as the final step of a binding grievance arbitration procedure, civil service commissions are losing their prestigious role as a major court of appeal for aggrieved employees. Nevertheless the procedural and tactical aspects of a typical merit commission hearing are not significantly different from those utilized in an arbitration hearing.

Grievance procedures became popular in the private sector on the premise that arbitration was a quicker and less expensive method of resolving disputes than work stoppages. Time and human nature have certainly eroded the validity of that premise. Today the average grievance runs five to six months from occurrence to arbitration decision. The cost of an average arbitration to management now runs $8,000 to $10,000 in lost time, arbitrator's fees, hearing costs (witnesses, transcripts, etc.), and legal fees.

1. Definition of Grievance

One of the major issues between management and labor organizations in negotiating the grievance procedure revolves around the definition of the grievance itself: that is, the determination of what types of claims may be processed through the procedure. Employee organizations feel strongly that agreements reached at the table are only useful if they can be enforced. From the union perspective, this means that enforcement depends upon grievance procedures and the definition therefore becomes a critical element.

There are four basic categories of grievance definitions in common usage:

a. Broad. In the broad grievance definition, a grievance is anything that affects employees in their work. A broad definition reflects the humanistic approach to employee relations. Some examples of grievances brought under the category of broadly defined are: Unfair treatment of other employees by management; benefits given to other employees; attitudes of managers toward employees; hiring practices.

A typical broad category grievance procedure definition would be:

A grievance is any dispute between employee and the agency.

or

A grievance is a written complaint filed by an employee with his supervisor.

or

A grievance is a professional problem between employee and the agency.

Unions prefer the broadest definition of grievance in order to encompass not only alleged violation of the agency's policies, but also claims of a breach of past practice, administrative procedures, and of course any terms of the master contract. By including such terms as "controversy, dispute or disagreement" in the definition, the question of arbitrability is rendered moot because the employee association does not have to prove that a contract violation, for example, is involved. Thus, the third-party neutral (e.g., arbitrator) can proceed directly to the substance of the employee's complaint. On the other hand, employers argue that subjecting any management decision to the grievance procedure has the practical effect of including all policies and procedure, both written and unwritten, in the master agreement negotiated by the parties. This would of course include a multiplicity of subjects never brought to the table for bargaining, or proposals that the employee union actually lost at the bargaining table.

b. Narrow.   In the narrow grievance definition, a grievance is limited to only specific violations of those items negotiated between the parties at the table. A narrow definition reflects the literal–legalistic contract approach to employee relations. None of the examples cited above in the broad category definition would normally be defined as grievances under the narrow definition. Only such complaints as refusal to pay negotiated wages, violations of layoff provisions, or failure to distribute overtime as provided in the master contract would be considered acceptable under the narrow definition.

From a management perspective the narrow definition of grievance prevents misuse of the grievance procedures, particularly where a third-party neutral review is involved. The premise underlying this perspective is that grievance procedures are not designed to make equitable decisions about every problem in the public agency or to make changes in agency policies, but rather to preclude inequitable application of the master contract. From a management point of view, the ideal definition narrows grievances to alleged violations of specifically expressed terms of the master contractual agreement as negotiated.

A typical narrow grievance definition would be:

A grievance is an alleged violation of a specific provision of this agreement which adversely affects an employee covered by this agreement in his employment relationship.

or

Grievance as used in this agreement is limited to a complaint or allegation by an employee which involves the interpretation or application of, or compliance with, an expressed term of this agreement.

Management negotiators seeking to obtain a narrow grievance definition such as the above would, of course, be operating under what we have defined as the literal–legalistic approach to grievance procedures. The full implementation of this approach would involve more than the mere definition. The basic purposes and objectives that negotiators would be pursuing for management under such an approach are illustrated in Addendum II-3. This approach has its counterpart from the union side of the table as shown in Addendum II-4.

c. Compromise.   Most negotiated agreements today adopt a halfway approach between the narrow legalistic–literal and the broad ''blue skies'' definition. In this category of grievance procedure, employees may grieve not only negotiated master agreement language, but also any adverse action taken by management which affects their individual wages, hours or working conditions. Typical grievances allowed by such a compromise definition which would not be permitted under a narrow definition would include unfair promotions, alleged sex discriminations, unsafe working conditions, and allegedly punitive transfers.

A typical compromise or moderate grievance definition would be:

> A grievance shall mean any alleged violation, misinterpretation, or inequitable application of the existing agreement, or of the written rules, procedures, regulations or administrative orders of the agency, or of any state or federal law which adversely affects the grievant.

d. Special limitations. In some cases, management may try to limit the grievance procedure; one reason is that there are multiple forums for litigation in the public service. (See discussion on multiple forum problems at end of this chapter.) The purpose of such limitations is usually to reduce the possibility of the union using the procedure as a bargaining ploy or tool for harassment. Following are some of the more common limitations, which may be considered under the heading of management rights:

> The selection or the assignment of supervisory employees is the sole responsibility of the agency and shall not be subject to the provisions of Article _____, Grievance Procedures.

or

> A probationary employee may be discharged at any time with or without cause and shall not have recourse to the provisions of Article _____, Grievance Procedures.

2. Definition of the Grievant

With respect to determining who the complaining party (i.e., grievant) may be, the basic categories of broad or narrow are generally applied:

a. Broad. A broad definition of the grievant enables the employee organization, as well as one or more employees, to file grievances. Employee organizations usually demand the right to initiate grievances on the ground that the organization represents the rights of all employees.

A typical broad definition of a grievant would be:

> A grievant is the person or persons, including the union or representatives thereof, making the claim.

Under such a broad definition of a grievant, groups of employees can file a class action or the union can process a grievance on its own regardless of whether an employee files a grievance or not. Management should and usually does strongly resist such an all-inclusive definition.

For example, in one city the police department had agreed to strict seniority for promotions within the detective staff. When the chief detective position opened up, all of the detectives agreed it should be filled from the outside. When the city did so the union filed a grievance. The arbitrator held that under the city's broad definition of grievant the union had the right to prosecute the case even though none of their members would file a grievance.

A similar type of grievance is the class-action grievance. In this situation, an employee or the union files a grievance on behalf of an entire group of employees regardless of their individual position on the issue. In one city, management had a contract provision giving all employees a 30-minute lunch period. For years water department employees had eaten on the job and only worked a 7½-hour day. Six months after the contract was signed the union filed a class action grievance on behalf of all of the water department employees for half-hour back pay. Over the city's objection the arbitrator ruled the union had a right to file one grievance for all of the employees regardless of what the individual employee's particular position on the issue might be.

As stated above, management should resist this category of definition on the premise that the primary purpose of a grievance procedure is to provide a reasonable method for the resolution of individual employee dissatisfactions with their working relationships. Frequently the employee organization seeks to use the grievance machinery to provide itself with a forum in which it can demonstrate its ability to fight for employee rights, and often it will actually create grievances in an effort to build its own militant image, particularly during the negotiations process or a certification election. Ideally, the union seeks a broad definition of grievant to enable it to:

1. Initiate grievances in the name of any employee unilaterally.
2. Grieve over violation of association rights.
3. Unilaterally appeal a grievance once initiated.
4. Control entry into the third-party review procedure.
5. Be present at all stages (i.e., steps) of all grievances.
6. Be consulted about all grievance adjustments before management renders a decision.

b. Narrow. The other category of grievant definition is the narrow definition in which the right to file grievances is restricted to individual employees only, who allege their rights have been infringed as a result of a specific violation of the master agreement. Narrow definitions are therefore reflective of the literal contract approach.

Management's reasons for insisting in negotiations on a narrow definition of the grievant are:

1. The purpose of the procedure is to resolve individual employee problems and dissatisfactions.
2. The procedure should not be abused by allowing the union to utilize it as a harassment technique, or as a vehicle to gain that which they could not achieve by good faith bargaining at the table.

A typical narrow definition of grievant is:

A grievant may be any city employee who is a member of the bargaining unit covered by the terms of this agreement.

3. Procedural Steps for Processing the Grievance

Grievance procedures characteristically provide a series of steps in which the employee initially presents his/her grievance to the immediate supervisor and, if unresolved, to successive administrative levels up the chain of command. The rationale for this standard procedure is the need to expedite resolution of the grievance. With arbitrators taking four to six months to render a decision, it is preferable to resolve employee grievances at the earliest administrative stage. In addition, delay has a tendency to polarize the positions of the respective parties and to inhibit resolution as the process becomes more formalized.

The number of steps will vary depending upon the size of the particular public agency. Characteristically, management desires multiple steps in order to maximize communications within the management team, and provide as many opportunities as possible for resolving the grievance short of the time-consuming arbitration process. The union, on the other hand, considers two levels of administrative review as the limit. The reasoning behind this position is that the grievant who was unsatisfied after a second review should be allowed to go directly to arbitration for resolution of his or her concerns. However, most negotiators will agree on a procedure with successive steps which gives both management and union a chance to evaluate the grievance from a tactical as well as a resolution-oriented perspective. Such steps are described below.

Step one: informal conference with immediate supervisor. Many grievance procedures provide, as a first step, an informal conference between the employee and the immediate supervisor only. The informal conference is important because it is here that the grievant and his/her supervisor should attempt to resolve the problem while their positions are still flexible. In theory and practice, when the written or formal grievance is filed, the parties' positions become more rigid and it is more difficult to resolve the grievance. Most capable supervisors will resolve their grievances prior to the onset of formal procedures. Poor supervisors will often create more problems for themselves even in the informal procedure.

Typical contract language for an informal conference would be:

> The employee shall first discuss the matter in an informal conference with the supervisor with immediate administrative responsibilities for the position to which the employee is assigned.

One major problem with informal conferences is determining time limits before and after the conference. Some agencies have negotiated contracts providing for time limits from the informal conference; for example, "The immediate supervisor will give an answer to the grievance within ten (10) days after the informal conference." Since supervisors have continuous meetings with employees, many of them over work problems, it is often difficult to pinpoint the day when they had an informal conference. Employees themselves are often confused and feel they have entered the grievance procedure because of a brief conversation that they subsequently want to define as an "informal conference." If management has a strict grievance deadline, for example, "Grievances must be discussed with the immediate supervisor within ten (10) days after their occurrence," it is very difficult to enforce when the time limit is related to the informal conference. It is better in such cases to make the time limit related to the second step of the procedure, for example, ''Grievances must be filed in writing at the second step within fifteen (15) days after their occurrence.''

Step two: formal presentation of a written grievance to the immediate supervisor. If the informal step fails to resolve the grievance, the next step is normally a formal grievance presented in writing on a form provided by management, to the employee's immediate supervisor. At this step, the first-level supervisor is put on notice that the grievance is serious and, if unresolved, the employee or the employee organization will appeal the matter up the chain of command. Typical master contract language for a first formal step is:

> If the matter is not resolved at the informal conference, the employee may present his grievance in writing on the form provided to the supervisor with immediate administrative responsibility for the position to which the employee is assigned.

A question that often arises in writing the first step of the grievance procedure is, what should happen when the subject of the grievance, or the remedy sought, is beyond the scope of responsibility of the immediate supervisor? Examples of such grievances would be complaints concerning rates of pay, paycheck shortages, and union rights. Some agencies handle this problem by allowing such grievances to be filed at higher levels (e.g., ''Grievances relating to city-wide matters may be filed at Step 3.'') In allowing this, however, management is subverting the administrative chain of command and surrendering its right to review, and preferably resolve, the complaint at the lowest level. Since the grievance is filed against the agency, and since first-level supervisors have to be the representatives of the agency with their subordinates, it is preferable to have all grievances commence and be formally filed with first-level supervisors.

The majority of grievances should be settled at the first step of the procedure. Those appealed beyond the first step often reflect poor supervision or relate to broader areas of employee relations than just the individual's grievance.

Successive steps: appeals through administrative channels. The next steps of the grievance procedure are appeals through higher levels of management. The procedure usually provides:

> If the grievant is not satisfied with the decision of the immediate supervisor he may within five (5) working days after receiving the decision of the administrator appeal the grievance in writing to his department head.

Normally the administrative appeals process ends in review with the chief executive officer of the agency. However, the agency's lay board, for example, Board of Education, may also be the final step of administrative appeal.

4. Procedural Limitations on Processing a Grievance

All grievance procedures contain some form of limitation on the processing of grievances. The most common restrictions concern:

a. The time limits for filing and answering grievances.

    b. The role of the employee organization representative (i.e., representation rights).

    c. The required format for filing written grievances.

    d. The question of confidentiality.

a. Time limits. Both employee organizations and management want time limits on grievances to ensure that evidence is still available on the issues, and to ensure prompt remedial actions. Generally employee organizations want a long period of time for the initial filing of a grievance and then short time limits for the actual processsing. Sometimes this is to their advantage — sometimes not.

Normally, a grievance procedure will have time restrictions on: (1) the period of time in which grievances can be filed, for example, "Grievances must be filed within ten (10) working days after the event giving rise to the alleged grievance occurred" (restrictive) or "Grievances must be filed within ten (10) working days after the employee knew, or should have known, of the event giving rise to the grievance" (broad); (2) the periods of time that a supervisor has in which to answer the initial grievance; (3) the time periods for response at higher appeal steps; and (4) the periods of time that the employee or his representative has in which to appeal an unfavorable answer by a supervisor. Most procedures also provide that both parties may waive the stated time limits by mutual written agreement.

While time limits are very important, management staff must realize that most agency lay boards, particularly Boards of Education, are not supportive when staff rigidly enforces time limits. In addition, arbitrators will do almost anything to avoid throwing a grievance out because it was untimely. Time limits must be written clearly and without ambiguity so the arbitrator can't create his or her own interpretation of the meaning. First-level supervisors have to be cautioned not to answer an untimely grievance on its merits alone. If it was not filed within the prescribed time limits, such a failure to raise the timeliness question at step one often waives the agency's right to argue that issue before the arbitrator at the final step.

b. Organization representative. Another common procedural limitation is protecting the employee's right at the outset to present his or her own grievance rather than automatically filing grievances through the organization representative. In private sector law and some states' statutes, an employee has a legal right to file grievances on his or her own, at least up to the arbitration level.

A typical management master agreement proposal on this subject would be similar to the following:

> Any employee with a grievance who desires to appeal the step one decision of his immediate supervisor shall do so in accordance with procedures of this section. Representatives of the association may be present at the step two conference.

After the first step, some procedures provide that the employee has to initiate any appeal. However, most procedures allow either the employee or the employee's organization to appeal the grievance.

Just as associations want released time for negotiating, they also want released time for association business such as grievance handling. One difficulty with this is that grievance handling takes time away from work. In some agencies, union representatives take from one to two hours a day off to handle grievances or alleged grievances. In fact, some representatives actually enjoy the time off from duty and use the excused time to generate grievances. Many negotiated agreements include provisions regarding time off for organization representatives who are involved in processing grievances. These clauses may be in the portion of the agreement dealing with the grievance procedure or they may be contained in other parts of the contract, such as employee organization rights. Many agreements provide organization representatives with time off to participate in grievance conferences and appeal and arbitration proceedings. Some contracts provide additional time off to investigate grievances.

One common type of provision requires notification and permission from the supervisor prior to being released.

> A steward, upon application to, and permission from, his immediate supervisor shall be permitted to devote reasonable time during his working hours without loss of pay:
>
> 1. To investigate or process a grievance or dispute as his or her assigned work location at the request of an employee.
>
> 2. To confer with the Chief Steward with regard to an alleged grievance or dispute.
>
> 3. Upon request from the union to the agency to attend grievance hearings and arbitrations where he/she is directly involved.

Some contracts place specific limitations on the amount of paid time the union can use.

> The union may use up to a total of ten (10) hours of paid time per month for processing grievances.

One problem in some agencies is that the union appoints so many grievance representatives, they start to compete with each other to find grievances. One way to control this is to put limitations in the contract on the number of grievance representatives the union may appoint.

> The union may appoint one steward for every 25 employees in the unit. The stewards' names and areas of responsibility shall be furnished to the personnel office by the association.

A few contracts even put limitations on union representatives generating grievances themselves. Such provisions are obviously difficult to enforce.

> No union representatives or officers may solicit grievances from employees.

c. Written grievances. Another common issue is whether the grievances should be filed in writing. Some master contracts are silent on this subject. Generally, the smaller the organization and/or the better communications between management and the union, the less likely it is that management will insist that grievances be presented in written form only. Prevailing practice, however, provides that all formal grievances and appeals be in writing. Example of forms utilized for this purpose will be illustrated in the Addenda to Chapter III.

d. Confidentiality. Another procedural limitation that often arises is the question of confidentiality. Although it is again difficult to draft master contract language to cover the subject effectively, management needs to be alert to the advantage that the union enjoys in being able to "go public" whenever it so desires. Because management is the initiator of personnel actions, it most frequently bears the burden of not being able to discuss such personnel actions without inviting ethical if not statutory censure. Therefore, some restriction on disclosure and a requirement for confidentiality of the subject matter should be included in the grievance procedure in order to at least share this burden of responsibility with the union once a grievance has been filed.

5. *Role of the Third-Party Neutral*

An impartial review by a neutral third party is the critical denominator in a grievance procedure. In the absence of such an independent party to review management and employee organization interpretations of master contract language and related problems, the grievance procedure becomes only as good as the general relationship between the parties. It is true that such third-party review, even when advisory, causes public management to lose part of its control over interpretation of policies and procedures. However, with such review, both parties are cognizant in the early steps of the grievance process that failure to settle the grievance will eventually force it to an outside review.

For example, if a school district were to negotiate contract language stating that "all teachers shall have a duty-free lunch period," and some teachers then volunteered to give remedial instruction to minority children during the lunch hour, most administrators, board members, and possibly even union teachers would feel that the spirit of the language had not been violated. An arbitrator, however, might look at this language as an absolute requirement that teachers have totally free time in the middle of their teaching day. He/she might very well order the district not to allow teachers to use school facilities for volunteer instruction of pupils regardless of the latter's need and the teachers' desire to do so.

There are a number of methods of third-party review. The two most common types for public agencies are:

    a. Advisory arbitration.
    b. Binding arbitration.

a. Advisory arbitration. Factfinding with recommendation is a process in which the third party is asked to go beyond the basic facts and to make a recommendation for the resolution of the grievance. Advisory arbitration is rare in the private sector, but is frequently found in public agencies wherein lay boards of control are accountable to the taxpaying electorate for policy making, including fiscal decisions. The real impetus behind an advisory arbitration decision is the logic behind the arbitrator's rationale and the weight of public and employee opinion behind the recommendations.

b. Binding arbitration. This is a method of grievance resolution in which the third party is asked to substitute his/her judgment for that of the employer and the grievant. Since the U.S. Supreme Court legitimatized binding arbitration for private industry in the Steelworkers trilogy cases of 1960, [1] binding arbitration has become the predominant method of adjudicating grievances in the private sector. In the public sector, there continues to be strong resistance to the concept of binding arbitration. Most local public agencies are reluctant to divest themselves of their discretionary authority without specific statutory authority. However, such statutory authority is more frequently the case today, and even in its absence courts have a tendency to rule that public agencies may enter into contracts with binding grievance arbitration clauses. [2] As previously noted, the employee union's position is one of vigorous advocacy of binding arbitration. Indeed, most union leaders feel that without the built-in enforcer of final and binding arbitration in the master agreement, any grievance procedure is nearly worthless.

Limitations on arbitrator's authority.   Any restriction the agency or the employee organization wishes to place on an arbitrator's authority must be expressly stated in the master contract. Most grievance procedures have a general limitation on the arbitrator's authority using language such as the following:

> The arbitrator shall have no power to add to, subtract from, or modify the terms of this agreement.

In addition, some contracts specifically limit an arbitrator's power to interpret certain specific clauses of the contract.

> Issues arising out of the exercise by the city of its responsibilities delineated in Article 3, Management Rights, Article 9, Promotion, and Article 12, No Strike, including the facts underlined in exercise of such discretion shall not be subject to arbitration.

> The fees and expenses of the arbitrator in the hearing shall be equally borne by the County and the grievant. All other expenses shall be borne by the party incurring them.

Another excellent method of discouraging frivolous grievances and encouraging early resolution is to require the loser to pay all fees and expenses. This is usually a difficult item to persuade an employee organization to accept.

> The arbitrator's fees and expenses, cost of any hearing room, and the cost of the transcript, if any, shall be borne by the losing side of the arbitration. The arbitrator will be requested to specify the loser. The arbitrator may also award legal expenses to the winning party.

Selection of arbitrators.   The normal sources of selection of third-party neutrals are referral lists maintained by the Federal Mediation and Conciliation Services, local bar associations, American Arbitration Association, State Conciliation Services, or County and State Superintendents of Schools. However, many

---

1. *Steelworkers v. American Manufacturing Co.,* 363 U.S. 564 (1960); *Steelworkers v. Enterprise Wheel & Car Corp.,* 363 U.S. 593 (1960); *Steelworkers v. Warrior & Gulf Navigation Co.,* 363 U.S. 574 (1960).

2. *Dayton Classroom Teachers' Assn. v. Dayton Board of Education,* 41 Ohio St. 2d 127, 323 N.E. 2d 714 (1975).

grievance procedures provide for a single named arbitrator, for selection by a local professional organization, or for selection from a limited group of people (e.g., taxpayers, community leaders). In a few agencies, both management and the association have become dissatisfied with new arbitrators for every grievance, and have agreed to name a "permanent umpire" to sit as the arbitrator on every case.

THE MULTIPLE FORUM PROBLEM

A special problem for public sector agencies in an agreement with grievance/ arbitration procedures is the possibility that management has given the grievant more than one method of collecting from the agency. Normally in Anglo-American law, when a person is sued in one court (e.g., state court) and loses, he or she cannot file another suit on the same subject in a different court (e.g., federal court). This principle is called "Res Judicata." In fact, under this principle, a person is required to state at one time all claims that can be litigated by the court between two parties, and if the individual fails to do so, all nonstated claims are waived. The major purpose of such a rule is obviously to limit the number of lawsuits both for the courts and for the defendants.

Prior to 1974, one of the benefits to employers in negotiating grievance procedures was the exclusion of more expensive and time-consuming court actions. In the Steelworkers trilogy cases of 1960 the Supreme Court had held that arbitration was the exclusive remedy available to employers and unions once they had included it in a collective bargaining agreement. In a more recent case the United States Supreme Court held that employees had the right to file a grievance and to file a complaint with the Equal Employment Opportunity Commission.[3] In this case, a terminated employee filed a grievance against the company, alleging racial discrimination. The arbitrator ruled in favor of the company and dismissed the grievance. The employee then pursued a claim under the Civil Rights Act for the same termination. The Federal District Court and the Court of Appeals held that the employee was bound by the Arbitrator's decision and having lost, could not bring up the same issues in a court action. The Supreme Court, however, disagreed and reversed the decision.

In addition, the problem for public sector managers is magnified beyond the problem faced in the private sector. So far, state courts in public sector cases have not clearly followed the Supreme Court's lead of judicial deferral to arbitration. Therefore, an arbitration decision in the public sector is still subject to serious judicial scrutiny. In addition, there are numerous protective statutes for public employees which supercede the collective agreement in the area of discipline and termination. Adding an arbitration provision, therefore, provides the serious risk that an employee can pursue multiple cases against the employer, taking the best of all decisions for himself or herself.

The public sector negotiator has three choices in dealing with this problem:

1. Limit the grievance procedures.
2. Require an explicit waiver of all other remedies.
3. Accept the possibility of multiple litigation.

3. *Alexander* v. *Gardner-Denver Company,* 415 U.S. 36 (1974).

1. Limit the Grievance Procedures

It is not unusual in the public sector to find explicit limitations on the use of grievance procedures. A common provision is:

> It is expressly agreed and understood that disciplinary proceedings that are reviewable by the Civil Service Commission are excluded from these procedures.

A broader provision would be an attempt to eliminate any claim from arbitration which might be the subject of another legal procedure. Such a clause in the contract would state:

> ...provided, however, that this procedure is not applicable to any matter which is otherwise reviewable pursuant to law, or pursuant to any rule or regulation having the force and effect of law.

There is a two-fold problem with such limitations in a grievance procedure:

a. Management may prefer resolving the matter in arbitration rather than a public court proceeding. It is conceivable that an employee could have even three or four potential suits against an employer all stemming out of the same management decision.

b. Many grievances cannot be differentiated clearly between subjects relating to the law and matters relating to the contract.

If this is a serious problem for the public agency, then it should consider one of the other alternatives.

2. Require an Explicit Waiver of All Other Remedies

Another option is to require that an employee wishing to use the arbitration clause must first agree to make it the only remedy. Such an agreement could be a clause in the contract requiring a written agreement by the employees prior to requesting arbitration. For example:

> If the grievant is not satisfied with the answer of the City Manager, he may request arbitration by filing with the personnel department a statement of his objection along with a statement that the grievant voluntarily waives all other legal and administrative actions arising from the grievance and agrees to be bound by the decision of the arbitrator.

Or the procedure could include language that grants the employee the choice of remedies:

> If the grievant is not satisfied with the step IV answer he may either 1) Exercise whatever legal or administrative remedies that are available, or 2) Accept arbitration as the final and binding resolution of all disputes arising out of the actions leading up to the grievance.

So far there are no cases reporting the feasibility of forcing the grievant into this option. For the employer who is worried about a double bite from the employee this is the one way of cutting down the options.

3. Accept the Possibility of Multiple Litigation

The majority of public and private sector employees have chosen to accept the risk of multiple litigation. Since suits are filed by an extremely small percentage of employees, this risk is probably reasonable. For those few employers with high legal fees and a number of suits, a renegotiation of the contract language may be more attractive.

CONCLUSION

The grievance procedure, reflecting as it does the relationship and philosophical perspectives of the parties, is the single most important article of agreement. Loose and poorly drafted language in other clauses of the agreement can result in management losing a favorable interpretation of that particular clause; poorly drafted language in the grievance arbitration procedure can cause the agency to lose disputes over any or all articles of the master agreement. In addition, the public agency under such circumstances can find itself forced into accepting positions it never negotiated at the table. It therefore behooves management staff and elected officials of public agencies to insist that the number one priority in negotiations be a grievance procedure reflective of the agency's personnel relations policies, with precise language, specific procedural steps and limitations, and appropriate protection for the agency's discretionary authority.

TYPICAL PUBLIC AGENCY GRIEVANCE PROCESS

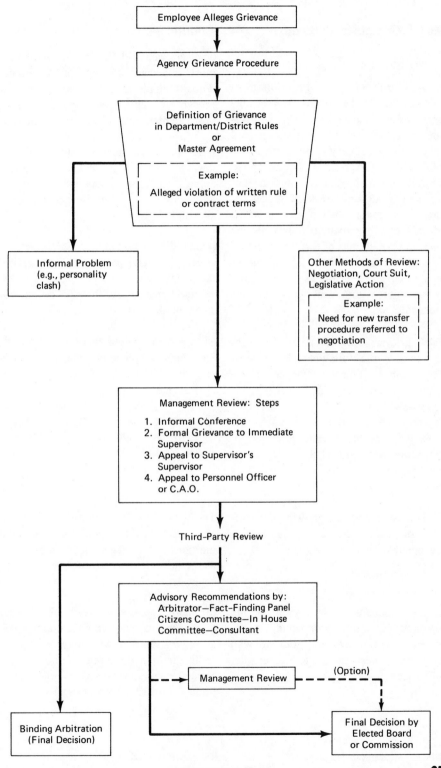

Model Grievance Procedure

1. *Definitions*

A. A grievance is an allegation by a grievant that he has been adversely affected by a violation of _____*_____. Actions to challenge or change the general policies of the agency as set forth in the rules and regulations or administrative regulations and procedures must be undertaken under separate legal processes. Other matters for which a specific method of review is provided by law, by the rules and regulations of the Civil Service Commission or by the administrative regulations and procedures of this agency are not within the scope of this procedure.

B. A grievant may be _____. Insert one of the following: Example 1. Any nonmanagement employee of the agency covered by the terms of this agreement. Example 2. Any employee or group of employees covered by the terms of this agreement. Example 3. Any employee, group of employees or the employee organization covered by the terms of this agreement.

C. A day is any day in which the offices of the _____ are open.

D. The Immediate Supervisor is the lowest level administrator having immediate jurisdiction over the grievant, who has been designated to administer grievances.

Commentary

The grievance definition is the single most important element of the procedure. It should reflect management's approach to employee relations (e.g., broad human relations; narrow contract).

Grievance definitions should avoid giving an employee "another bite at the apple" where he already has one method of review (e.g., Civil Service Commission hearing).

It should be assumed throughout the procedure that grievances are filed against the agency, not against individual supervisors. If necessary, this can be emphasized in the definition.

Management should insist that "outsiders" such as executors, widows and children not be allowed to file grievances against the agency.

The right to file class grievances and the right of the organization to file grievances is usually a major trade-off item for management in negotiations.

The word "day" is confusing in public agencies because of public holidays and multiple shifts. The policy either should use calendar days or define days as suggested.

In many cases employees take formal grievances to quasi-administrators, such as payroll clerks, who may attempt to settle them in the name of the district. Formal grievance practices should be limited to designated supervisors.

---

* Insert appropriate language (e.g., "the specific provisions of the agreement").

ADDENDUM II−2

2. *Informal Level*

Before filing a formal grievance, the grievant should attempt to resolve it by an informal conference with his immediate supervisor.

Informal grievances are easier to resolve since the parties are less likely to take fixed positions.

3. *Formal Level*

A. *Step One*

Within ten (10) days after the occurrence of the act or omission giving rise to the grievance, the grievant must present his grievance in writing on the appropriate form to his immediate supervisor.

This statement shall be a clear, concise statement of the grievance, the circumstances involved, the decision rendered at the informal conference and the specific remendy sought.

Grievance has to be presented promptly so that evidence may be presented, and so that grievances can't be "saved up" to dump on management all at once. Formal grievances should be in writing so that all parties know the matter is serious, the issues are defined, and the issues cannot be changed.

B. The supervisor shall communicate his decision to the employee in writing within ten (10) days after receiving the grievance. If the supervisor does not respond within the time limits, the grievant may appeal to the next level.

Management should respond to the grievance within a reasonable time frame. Failure to respond gives the employee a right to appeal. Be careful of proposals which state "failure to respond results in settlement in favor of the employee."

C. Within the above time limits either party may request a personal conference.

A personal meeting is the most effective way to discuss and resolve grievances.

D. *Level II*

In the event the grievant is not satisfied with the decision at Level I, he may appeal the decision on the appropriate form to the _____*_____ within ten (10) days. This statement should include a copy of the original grievance, the decision rendered, and a clear, concise statement of the reasons for the appeal.

The second level of review should be a division level or agency level person who can review the grievance from a broader operational perspective and settle it if appropriate. Management should not allow grievances to jump from the bottom of the administrative chain to the top (e.g., foreman to agency director). The grievance should move up the organizational structure. Anything else breaks down mid-level management authority.

* Insert appropriate title.

E. The _____*_____ shall communicate his decision within ten (10) days after receiving the appeal. Either the grievant or the Assistant Director may request a personal conference within the above limits. If the Assistant Director does not respond within the time limits, the grievant may appeal to the next level.

F. *Level III*

If the grievant is not satisfied with the decision at Level II, he may within ten (10) days appeal the decision on the appropriate form to the Chief Executive Officer or his designee. This statement shall include a copy of the original grievance and appeal, the decisions rendered, and a clear, concise statement of the reasons for the appeal.

G. The Chief Executive Officer or his designee shall communicate his decision to the grievant within ten (10) days. If the Chief Executive Officer or his designee does not respond within the time limits provided, the grievant may appeal on the next level.

H. *Level IV*

If the grievant is not satisfied with the decision at Level III, he may within five (5) days submit a request in writing to the Chief Executive Officer for (advisory) arbitration of the dispute. Grievant and the agency shall attempt to agree upon an arbitrator. If no agreement can be reached, they shall request the American Arbitration Association to supply a panel of five names of persons experienced in hearing grievances in public agencies. Each party shall alternately strike a name until only one name remains. The remaining panel member shall be the (advisory) arbitrator. The order of striking shall be determined by lot.

Sometimes employee organizations and management bluff each other to the top of the grievance procedure without either party being sure the case is appropriate for arbitration. Formal notice sometimes gives both parties a chance to reevaluate their positions.

ADDENDUM II−2

I. The fees and expenses of the arbitrator and the hearing shall be borne equally by the agency and the grievant. All other expenses shall be borne by the party incurring them.

J. The (advisory) arbitrator shall, as soon as possible, hear evidence and render a decision on the issue or issues submitted to him. If the parties cannot agree upon a submission agreement, the arbitrator shall determine the issues by referring to the written grievance and the answers thereto at each step.

K. The arbitrator will have no power to add to, subtract from or modify the terms of this agreement.

L. Issues arising out of the exercise by the administration of its responsibility referred to in Article _____ (Management Rights) including the facts underlying its exercise of such discretion shall not be subject to this procedure.

M. After a hearing and after both parties have had an opportunity to make written arguments, the (advisory) arbitrator shall submit in writing to all parties his findings and recommendations (which shall be final).

N. *Level V*

In the event that either party is not satisfied with the recommendation of the arbitrator, he may appeal the decision in writing within ten (10) days to the Civil Service Commission.

Optional clause for advisory arbitration procedures. With this clause the decision of the arbitrator is final unless appealed.

O. The council alone has the power to render a final and binding determination of a grievance. The recommendation of the arbitrator shall only be advisory and if, upon review, the Civil Service Commission determines that it is unable to render a final determination on the record, it may reopen the record for the taking of additional evidence.

Optional clause for advisory arbitration procedures. This clause states clearly that the procedure is advisory to the agency.

P. The arbitrator's fees and expenses, the cost of any hearing room and the cost of a transcript shall be borne by the losing side of the arbitration. The arbitrator will be requested to specify who is the loser. Each party will pay the cost of their own witnesses.

Most procedures specify who pays. A few require the agency to pay everything. Most require the arbitrator's fees and costs be split equally. Witness fees are particular problems since the union could call 30 "witnesses" who sit at the hearing for a day or two. "'Loser' pays" makes both sides think twice about going to arbitration.

TYPICAL MANAGEMENT PURPOSES AND OBJECTIVES
FOR GRIEVANCE PROCEDURES

1. Only actual misapplications or violations of the Ordinance, Contract, Rules, or Agreement.
2. No binding arbitration. Advisory, if at all.
3. Final decision by agency management.
4. Preservation of agency's prerogatives and rights.
5. Decisions not applicable agency wide.
6. Only individual employee grievances.
7. Numerous steps within and "through channels."
8. Extended time limits for steps.
9. Costs shared, or loser pays all.
10. Actual processing after the working day.
11. Immediate initiation of grievance.
12. Only written grievances to be processed.

TYPICAL ASSOCIATION PURPOSES AND OBJECTIVES
FOR GRIEVANCE PROCEDURES

1. Any employee dissatisfaction is grievable.
2. Any misapplication of Rules, Policy, Regulation, or the Agreement is grievable.
3. Binding arbitration.
4. "Test Cases" to change Agency Policy.
5. Association and/or group grievances (Class Actions).
6. Automatic appeal to next level of procedure.
7. Organization representation rights.
8. Written response by management first step.
9. Few steps maximum of two.

Chapter IIII
Grievance Processing —
The First Step

The initial handling of employee grievances is the most critical step in the grievance procedure. Consequently, no other individual in the agency is more important to positive employee relations than management's spokesmen at the outset or birth of the grievance (i.e., the immediate supervisor). In the grievance process, he/she is the first agency representative with whom the employee must deal, and is therefore the agency's first opportunity to resolve the problem. It is the school principal, for example, who is in the best position to resolve most problems before they reach the formal stage of a grievance per se. Once launched on the formal track of grievance processing, it becomes more difficult to resolve the initial complaint to the mutual satisfaction of the parties. This is why resolution of grievances at the first level is considered both a major responsibility and challenge for the immediate supervisor. The attitude displayed in meeting this challenging responsibility will largely determine whether the grievance can be effectively resolved.

Higher morale and better employee attitudes are obvious when the initial handling of employee complaints and just plain "gripes" is done well. Equally evident is the increased militancy and negative employee attitudes generated by indifferent, weak, or poor disposition of such complaints at the outset. Another critical factor to be considered in today's collective bargaining environment is that weak handling of first-stage grievances often forces the agency's negotiator to deal with so-called "rights" disputes at the bargaining table. The latter deal with the interpretation or application of the master agreement itself. Such disputes should not be allowed to reach the bargaining table, or to be converted into so-called "interest" questions, which deal with basic terms and conditions of employment and do legitimately belong at the bargaining table. Expedient and effective management action at the first step keeps these "rights" questions where they belong, inside the adjustment (i.e., grievance) procedure, and away from the bargaining table.

Today most public agencies have some kind of grievance procedure, and the immediate supervisor is expected to assume the responsibility of working with subordinates and union representatives to implement that procedure fairly and effectively. However, for many supervisors grievance handling is a new and disturbing responsibility imposed on them by higher levels of management. One can understand how many supervisors have a feeling of being more in the middle than ever before, and at times, living in a "no man's land" in which they are expected to be a human relations expert, psychiatrist, diplomat, "mini" contract administrator, and first-line supervisor all at once. As a consequence, a supervisor faced with his/her first grievance often succumbs to one of the following stereotypes:

1. *Low-priority syndrome:* "I make only big decisions."

   Some supervisors treat grievances as if they did not have time for such minor matters. Because the supervisor considers grievance handling to be a minor, low-priority responsibility, he or she often shuffles grievances to the bottom of the pile or reacts too quickly to get rid of them. This type of supervisor is often under pressure from higher management to complete other work assignments within a restricted time frame. Faced with these deadlines, the supervisor is impatient and reluctant to sit down and discuss employee grievances in an unhurried and attentive manner.

2. *Front-line warrior syndrome:* "I'll get even."

   Supervisors sometimes view grievances as frontal attacks upon their entrenched positions in the agency. Such supervisors react aggressively, if not downright hostilely, to grievances, regardless of whether this reflects on their own actions or the actions of other supervisors in the agency. Employees under such supervisors are often afraid to file grievances, and are more likely to let them smolder than get them out in the open where they can be resolved.

   In many cases, this supervisor generates a false, but attractive image to higher level management, because he/she doesn't appear to have problems. It is only when a labor relations crisis occurs (strike, sick-out), that the festering resentment emerges and top-level management realizes what has been smoldering below the surface for so long.

3. *The good guy syndrome:* "It's not me."

   Supervisors, particularly those appointed from the ranks, often regard top-level management with a quasi-adversary attitude. When an employee brings in a problem, rather than resolve it there, this supervisor will blame top-level management for the employee's troubles. With this approach, the supervisor builds substantial, if short-lived, credibility with his or her subordinates. Of course, in the long run, when everyone recognizes the good guy syndrome in action, the supervisor loses support from both management and employees.

4. *Pacifier syndrome:* "I'll buy you off."

   Some supervisors fear that once a subordinate files a grievance, upper management will begin to question that supervisor's adequacy or ability to do the job properly. This type of supervisor tries to bury problems quickly by settling at any cost. Often he/she makes settlements that are contrary to agency policy. Once again, this type of supervisor maintains a short-lived conciliatory relationship with employees, but his/her own immediate supervisor is soon alert to the pacifier's game. In the meantime, this stereotype of supervisor makes life exceedingly difficult for his/her fellow first-line supervisors who are sincerely trying to enforce the master agreement and agency policies.

In order to avoid being one of the above stereotypes, supervisors handling grievances at the first step must remember four basic attitudinal concepts:

1. *Grievance resolution is a primary responsibility.*

   Employees' morale is directly related to the quick and fair resolution of their complaints. A supervisor faced with a grievance does not have to drop everything else in order to resolve it. However, the supervisor certainly cannot put it at the bottom of the pile and expect it to "go away" or resolve itself. He or she need only act reasonably and set up a meeting within the time limits to discuss the grievance at a more convenient time and in an atmosphere conducive to resolution. It is well for the supervisor to remember that others including his or her superiors and third-party neutrals, such as arbitrators, do not expect the supervisor to be infallible. However, they do have a right to expect him or her to be reasonable.

   It is important that the initial meeting with the employee be scheduled as soon as possible, and obviously, within any time lines stipulated in the master agreement. Delays for no apparent reason in the scheduling of such meetings by supervisors generally serve only to frustrate employees. Once the grievant has raised the issue, the supervisor cannot, and should not, avoid the problem by delay. Rather, the supervisor should make resolution of the grievance within agency policy and the master agreement, if any, a primary goal.

2. *Don't treat the grievance as a personal attack.*

   While it is true that employees and employee unions sometimes use grievance procedures to embarrass, and even to attack management, the supervisor has to treat each grievance objectively and look upon it as a positive opportunity to resolve problems. The supervisor cannot afford to become defensive before he/she even discusses the matter with the individual employee. Oftentimes, supervisors expect too much from the employee organization in terms of disciplining its ranks or weeding out seemingly antagonistic grievances. Employees pay dues to their union to protect and defend their rights, and not to be criticized or denied representation to which they feel entitled. The union position in this regard is basically that they are an employee organization, not a religious sect.

3. *Don't pass the buck.*

   It is temptingly easy as a first-level supervisor to blame problems on higher-level management. The supervisor, however, is the representative of that higher level management, at the point of most direct employee contact. If the supervisor fails, the entire management system fails.

First-level supervisors, such as school principals, are often in a position from which they cannot see the reasons for district or agency-wide policies. However, the supervisor must remember that by its very nature, his/her position requires implementation of management-established policies that may or may not coincide with the supervisor's personal or professional views, but which nevertheless must govern daily operations. In daily dealings with employees, the supervisor must consistently support management positions, or in good conscience resign.

4. *Don't treat grievances as black marks.*

If a supervisor is doing the job, and making decisions, there are going to be grievances from employees. Even the best supervisors have grievances filed against them. Indeed, a supervisor against whom no grievances have ever been filed may be either lucky or incompetent. Even the union recognizes this as a somewhat unnatural state of affairs. It is interesting to note that the National Education Association, in its guidelines for grievance handling, suggests something may be wrong if grievances *never* come from a particular school. The contention that "everything is fine at my school — we had no grievances this year" is not, in the NEA's view, based on reality. No complaints at all, according to the NEA, should be regarded as a sign that the school should be checked because the employee representatives may not be doing the job.

A good supervisor knows the key to resolution of both grievances and human relations problems is tact, self-control, and good judgment. The supervisor who exhibits these traits can eliminate most grievances before they become formalized.

EVOLUTION OF THE GRIEVANCE

Most employee complaints go through a series of stages before they become full-blown formal grievances.

The initial stage begins when an individual is irritated by some job-related problem. Perhaps he or she didn't get the transfer or shift he or she wanted, the classroom teaching assignment that was preferred, or feels that the supervisor is showing favoritism in the assignment of extra paid work. Possibilities are innumerable, but the key concept for the supervisor to remember always is that the problem or irritation is very important to the employee. Indeed, the actual facts themselves are not as consequential or significant as how the employee *perceives* them. The skilled manager develops an ability to anticipate problem situations, to locate and resolve them before they become formal grievances.

The next stage occurs when the employee begins to complain about the problem, either to the superior, to other employees, or to the union representative. At this stage, the employee is trying to resolve the problem by getting responses from other people. It is during this stage that the "grapevine" or the supervisor's own "radar" signals that trouble is brewing, and that an effort should be made to resolve this employee's problem immediately, if at all possible.

The final stage is reached when the employee becomes so disturbed he or she takes specific steps, and in effect, "demands" a solution to the problem. The employee may consult with the union representative, consult with the supervisor, file a written formal grievance, or indeed, may do all three. At this point, the supervisor is often the only management person who can peacefully resolve the problem, or at least offer some compromise solution. If the supervisor shirks this responsibility, the problem can only escalate and grow worse.

Techniques for Handling Grievances at the First Level

In a formal grievance procedure it is customary in the first step for the employee, with or without the union representative, to present his or her grievance to the immediate supervisor. It is important for the supervisor to remember that the employee organization places a high priority on grievance advocacy and many organization representatives are highly skilled in processing grievances. The supervisor must be equally skilled and alert to processing requirements and techniques. For this reason many supervisors use a checklist such as is shown in Addendum III—1.

While there is no magic formula that will guarantee the immediate superior will be able to resolve the complaint to the employee's satisfaction, the following practices have been used successfully by supervisors to help resolve problems in the first step of the grievance procedure:

1. Let the employees tell their story.
2. Get the facts.
3. Give a timely response.
4. Follow up.

1. Let the Employees Tell Their Story

One of the most frequently heard complaints by employees is that their superior "doesn't listen" to them. It is easy to forget that employees want to feel someone is willing to listen to their problems. Very often the most productive way to solve minor gripes is just to "let the employees get it off their chests." If other pressures cause the supervisor to adopt a defensive posture toward employees each time there is a complaint, the supervisor frustrates the employee's need for a sympathetic ear and, in the long run, creates a situation in which employees will refuse to discuss problems with the supervisor. Experience shows that employees will then turn to the sympathetic ear of an organization representative.

When an employee comes in to express a gripe or complaint, the way or manner in which the supervisor handles the problem is often the key to whether it eventually becomes a formal grievance. It is imperative at this point that the supervisor adopt a positive problem-solving approach and encourage the employee to tell his/her story. Above all, the supervisor must *listen* so there can be a full understanding of the employee's meaning. As stated previously, the supervisor must not personalize the issue, or use so-called "fighting words" such as "foolish," "ignorant," "disagree," or "uninformed." Such dogmatic words and statements can only raise barriers to the resolution of the problem and aggravate relationships. The supervisor should concentrate on using only objective questions such as: "When did this happen? When did it start? How do you feel this should have been handled?

How can I help straighten this out? Is there anything else I should know about the problem?''

It is clearly established now that employees are entitled to a representative of their choice in initial grievance hearings. In some procedures the union has waived this right. Failing an explicit waiver, however, the supervisor has to agree if the employee requests that a representative be present.

In asking questions, the supervisor must concentrate on the presentation of the grievance. Often a supervisor allows constant interruptions by phone calls and other employees, and the employee feels he or she never really has the full attention of the supervisor. Under all circumstances the manager must stay calm and objective even though the employee or the organization representative may become abrasive and angry. Organization representatives will often deliberately bait or attempt to irritate supervisors in the hope the latter will make some prejudicial remark that may later be used against the agency.

Many times employee gripes or complaints can be settled just by letting the employee get them out in a frank, open discussion. The basic problem may be the employee is upset, not by what was done but by the way it was done. The first-level supervisor should settle the problem with an apology. Apologizing does not imply the supervisor is going to change what was done, but it does reflect the supervisor's interest in good personnel relations. This is the only case in which management should give an immediate answer to the grievance.

If this approach is not successful, the immediate supervisor should then take pencil in hand and ask the employee to go back over the story while the supervisor takes some notes to make certain that "I have the facts as you stated them." Many supervisors use a format for notations like the sample shown in Addendum III-2. The supervisor should write down all the critical facts about the grievance, including names, dates, times, places, the particular section of the agreement, board policy, or administrative regulation which the employee feels has been violated, and the specific remedy which the employee seeks. Quite often employees are vague about the specific remedy they are requesting. This is particularly true if the remedy would negatively affect another employee. Often too, the employees have never really thought through the consequences of the remedy they seek and when they realize, for instance, that another employee would have to be removed from a position, they often decline to pursue the matter.

After getting all the facts in writing, the supervisor should then restate the grievant's story in his or her own words and ask the grievant to confirm whether or not the story has been correctly restated. Listening to the grievance restated in someone else's words often gives the employee the chance to evaluate the reasonableness of the grievance and to back down from all or part of it. In addition, it guarantees the supervisor a clear understanding of the grievance and the remedy desired by the employee.

In restating the grievance, the manager may discover whether the employee is stating the *real* cause of the grievance. Often employees will push a purported problem or a complaint even though their real complaint is hidden and relates to another issue.

As the last step in the initial interview, supervisors should make an appointment with employees for a future meeting, at which the employees will get an answer to the grievance. Giving the employees a specific appointment reassures them of management's good faith and gives them something definite to count on. Failure to give them a specific date for an answer leaves them confused and in doubt and may lead to more difficulty in settling the grievance.

2. Get the Facts

When the first-level supervisor is *absolutely certain* of the facts, knows the proper answer, and feels that an immediate reply will resolve the matter, then a quick reply to the employee is proper. A good test to determine whether to respond immediately is, "Would I be willing to live with my mistake if I am wrong?" Ninety-nine percent of the time it is better to think about the matter for at least a couple of hours.

The place to start in analyzing a grievance is with the definitions of a grievance and a grievant in the master agreement. Many procedures restrict grievances to specific violations of the agreement, agency policy, or administrative regulation — any other problem is a gripe or complaint to be worked out between the employee and the superior and is not subject to any kind of appeal. The supervisor should also determine if the employee is the proper grievant. The supervisor should next check the grievance policy for time limits. Most procedures have a limit on the number of days the employee can wait to file a grievance. At the same time the immediate supervisor can check the time limits to the answer. After checking the grievance procedure, the supervisor should check the agreement and agency policy — particularly the management rights clause and the specific clause(s) the employee alleges have been violated. Also the department practice should be compared to the agency *policy* in regard to the employee's grievance — very often practice and policy are not the same! It is not unusual to find an individual supervisor using a practice or procedure that is not in conformity with an agency policy. Therefore, managers have to check not only whether they have been following the agreement or agency policy but whether their peers are following the policy.

The first-level supervisor should check all appropriate records, such as payroll time cards, overtime records, sick leave records, safety records and other materials which will provide documented facts on which to base an answer and possible defense in an arbitration hearing. If there were witnesses, they should be identified and interviewed.

The supervisor should ask the agency personnel office about the disposition of similar grievances in other departments. In doing this, the supervisor may find that the resolution of other grievances has already set a pattern for a decision in the grievance at hand.

3. Give a Timely Response

After fully investigating the facts, the first-level supervisor is in a position to respond to the grievance. At this point most experienced administrators make a preliminary decision and then check it out with their superior or the personnel representative. Consultation with other supervisors after fully investigating the facts and reaching a tentative decision is not a sign of weakness but the mark of a prudent manager. Interaction with other managers ensures bilateral communication and consistent interpretation of the rules or master agreement.

Whatever decision is made the supervisor should make every effort to respond promptly and within the time limits set by rule or master agreement. If the supervisor develops a reputation for quick and fair resolution of grievances, he/she is more likely to settle grievances at the first step.

In responding to the employee, the supervisor should call the employee in, explain that he/she has fully investigated the facts and has consulted with other people. The supervisor should then give the employee a full response to the grievance. If the grievance is justified, the supervisor should be positive about it and try to achieve whatever credit is possible from granting the remedy sought.

If the supervisor rejects the employee's grievance, the former should explain the reasons for this rejection carefully. The supervisor should try to convince the employee of the correctness of the decision. If the employee is still dissatisfied, it is a good practice to explain the grievance procedure for the next steps to make sure the employee understands his or her right to appeal the decision to a higher level.

While a detailed oral explanation should be given to the employee, any written response required should be short and concise. However, the response should be formalized enough to establish the nature of the grievance, remedy sought, and time limits for the record. A typical step one response format is illustrated in Addendum III−3. A well-drafted standardized form for filing and responding to grievances can be an extremely useful tool in effective grievance processing. The format of such a form would be influenced by the grievance language in any collective bargaining master agreement or by agency rules. A suggested format is shown in Addendum III−4.

After the interview, the supervisor should collect all notes and records and write up a report for the file. If he/she has used a format such as the one illustrated in Addendum III−2, this would suffice for the record in the event of an appeal; on the other hand, if the grievance is settled, the settlement may become a precedent for other settlements in the future, and it will be important to have a record on file.

4. Follow Up

One of the key elements in grievance processing is to follow up on grievances. The supervisor owes it to the grievant to check to make sure the things promised have been accomplished.

One sure way to encourage grievances is to back down at the threat of an appeal. Once the supervisor has made a decision, it should be adhered to and carried out. If the employee organization realizes a supervisor is unsure or will give in to pressure, its members know they can single out that supervisor as one against whom grievances can be accumulated as a pressure tactic. After the answer is given, any alterations should come only from higher levels of management and within the grievance procedure.

Dealing with the Employee Representative

As noted earlier, the relationship between the employee organization representative and the first-line supervisor is a critical cornerstone of a successful grievance procedure. Without daily contact between these two individuals, the efficiency of the agency's operations is impaired and the grievance procedure becomes choked at higher levels with problems that should have been solved at the work location itself. A constructive working relationship between the two of them ensures that preventive measures can be taken early enough to be effective. There are two basic aspects or categories of the relationship between the first-line supervisor and employee representatives:

1. Representation rights within the grievance procedures.
2. Representation rights exclusive of the grievance procedures.

1. Representation Rights Within the Grievance Procedures

Every collective bargaining master agreement, and many agency personnel procedures, will call for representation of the employee by an individual of his or her choice during the various steps of the grievance procedure. Depending on the language of the particular master agreement or rule, the representation can be by the exclusive bargaining agent, any employee organization, or any individual. It is, of course, most often the on-site union representative who acts as the spokesman for the grievant. Whenever the employee organization representative is to be involved, whether the latter is the equivalent of the private sector "shop steward," and therefore an employee of the site, or a paid field representative from union headquarters, the supervisor is well-advised to recognize and accept some fundamental realities in the relationship.

First, the supervisor should understand that the union representative is a political personality. The latter needs to maintain the stance of competency and status, and above all to avoid losing face in front of the client, the grievant. For this reason, it is sometimes desirable for the supervisor to meet with the union representative on a one-to-one basis, either before or after the step one grievance conference, depending on the circumstances, and of course, the individual union representative. If the representative is a reasonable and cooperative individual, it is to the supervisor's advantage to insure that the representative maintains status and credibility with the grievant. Supervisors gain little by demeaning the union representative in front of the employee, and potentially have a great deal to lose. Unless the union representative becomes overtly abusive or insulting in the conference, the supervisor is well-advised to maintain the cool, polite, courteous, but firm attitude of an attentive listener. An occasional smile, and a pertinent question directed to the union representative is generally well received and makes for a more productive conference. Most experienced union representatives do not expect an immediate answer at the step one conference, and will react positively to an indication that the supervisor is going to investigate and review carefully the information presented in this conference.

Next, it is important for the supervisor to establish clearly beforehand where the meeting will be held, as well as the date and time, the latter preferably being off worktime for the employee, and exactly who the attendees will be. For example, if any personnel other than the grievant, the union representative, and the supervisor are to be permitted to attend the step one conference, it should be clearly established beforehand; indeed, the supervisor may wish a witness of his or her own to be present. Also, the supervisor should be alert to signs of larger or more basic issues than the employee's personal "gripe"; the union will frequently seek "test cases" to bend or interpret the contract in their favor. If the supervisor senses this, he/she should notify higher management levels immediately, so the agency's position may be reinforced at each level of the grievance procedure. If, on the other hand, the supervisor discovers through information presented at the conference by the union representative, and verified by the supervisor's subsequent communication with higher levels of management, that he/she has misinterpreted the contract or rule, this is the time to make an adjustment. If the supervisor feels the facts justify an adjustment or change of decision, he or she will gain stature by admitting this and making the necessary adjustments at the first level.

The union representative at the work location who is also an employee is in effect exercising a dual role. This duality often causes supervisors some difficulty in determining exactly how to handle this particular employee. Here again, some basic ground rules may be helpful.

a. When acting solely as an employee, this individual is subject to the same standards of behavior as any other employee at the work location.
b. When functioning solely as a union representative, this employee has more latitude so long as his or her actions are concerned with union business, such as investigating and processing grievances, and do not violate the limits of proper conduct and reasonable behavior.

While it is often difficult to identify the exact line between union representative and employee roles, supervisors should always be prepared to take strong measures with any union representative who interferes with work or sets such a poor example it results in other employees violating the master agreement or agency rules.

2. Representation Rights Exclusive of the Grievance Procedures

Since representation rights during the grievance process are usually clearly delineated in collective bargaining agreements and/or agency rules, the entitlement question does not often present itself. However, this is not the case in those problem areas such as investigatory interviews, which lie outside the grievance procedure and for which employees often request representation. Frequently the employee's request for representation is based on the alleged belief that some disciplinary action might result from a conference called by the supervisor. The basic question, of course, is whether or not an employee has the right to request that union representatives be present at any meeting called by his or her superiors.

First, supervisors should know there is almost unanimous agreement by arbitrators and other third-party neutrals that union representation is *not* required every time management wishes to speak to an employee. However, the right of an employee to have representation when subject to investigation is an expanding right in the private sector under our current legal system. In fact, the question of representation rights in private employment has reached the U.S. Supreme Court. The National Labor Relations Board was upheld in its view that employees were entitled to representation when they had reasonable grounds to believe action to be taken by the employee could lead to discharge. In supporting the N.L.R.B. the court established the principle that even if representation was not explicitly provided in the agreement, when the employee reasonably believes an investigatory interview may result in disciplinary action, he or she is entitled to union representation. (*J. Weingarten, Incorporated* v. *N.L.R.B.*, 420 U.S. 251 [1975]. As a consequence, some public employee organizations are pressuring public employers for expanded representation rights even though a particular agreement does not call for or authorize such a right to representation. First-level administrators therefore should be alert to requests for representation at conferences that involve disciplinary actions or union activities of union employees. The courts and state local agencies are inclined to adopt and extend such rationale to public employment, and in at least one state this has already occurred.

The Michigan Employment Relations Commission adopted the doctrine established in the *Weingarten* case in an unfair practices hearing involving employees at the University of Michigan. The Commission held that an employee is entitled to union representation during an interview with an employer under circumstances where disciplinary action can reasonably be expected.

For the first-line supervisor, the following guidelines to representation rights at nongrievance conferences may be helpful:

a. If the conference is to deal with the union activites of the employee, or if it constitutes a formal disciplinary action to be taken by the supervisor, representation should be granted.

b. If the conference deals with the employee's performance of duties, recommendations for improvement, non-disciplinary corrections, or any other routine subject matter, the request for representation should be denied.

Although the right to representation is expanding, it should never be allowed to interfere with legitimate management prerogatives in directing employees. The supervisor, for example, always remains free to terminate any interview and to continue his or her investigation by other means. Also, the employee representative's right to participate in the conference is severely limited if it is not a grievance step. The union representative can be required to restrict his/her participation to only a clarification of the facts. Also, the supervisor has the right to insist on the employee's version of the facts of the matter, not that of the union representative.

It is important to remember that the exact parameters of representation in nongrievance conferences have not been firmly established for public sector labor relations. However, since it is an expanding, rather than a restricting, right of the employee, better employee morale will usually result if the supervisor adheres to the above guidelines in determining representation at conferences.

CONCLUSION

The critical role of the first-line supervisor as the key management figure in resolution of grievances cannot be overemphasized. Effective handling, including a positive attitude by the first-line supervisor can resolve an employee complaint at the outset, thereby preventing it from escalating into a formal grievance confrontation with a potentially adverse impact on management policies. In today's problem-solving environment, management cannot afford some of the negative stereotypes of the past. Public sector labor relations today calls for a first-level supervisor who is capable of either preventing problems and gripes from becoming formalized into grievances, or, where they are appealed, is able to establish by actions and decisions, a firm management position which can be supported all the way through the grievance process up to and including arbitration. This includes the vital area of being able to work effectively with the local employee organization representatives, recognizing that such representation is an expanding employee right today.

A summary of the basic do's and don't's for today's first-line supervisor in handling grievances is shown in Addendum III-5.

CHECKLIST FOR HANDLING GRIEVANCE AT INITIAL STEP

I. Determine the Problem

_____ Let the grievant tell his or her story (listen).

_____ Don't personalize the issues.

_____ Take notes, keep a record.

_____ Ask the grievant to repeat his or her story (look for hidden complaints).

      _____ Get names.

      _____ Get dates and times.

      _____ Get locations.

      _____ Get the section of the contract allegedly violated.

      _____ Get the remedy desired.

      _____ Repeat the essentials of the grievance to the employee in your own words.

II. Get the Facts

_____ Check the agreement, policies and regulations.

_____ Check the time limits.

_____ Check grievability.

_____ Check policy and practices.

_____ Check previous grievance settlements for precedent.

_____ Check the experience of others in similar cases.

_____ Seek advice if necessary.

III. Give a Timely Answer

_____ Reach a preliminary decision and check it with your superior or a personnel representative.

_____ Settle the grievance at the earliest moment that a proper settlement can be reached.

_____ In deciding, give the benefit of the doubt to management.

_____ Write a simple answer to the grievance.

_____ Explain your position orally.

_____ Explain the employee's right to appeal.

IV. Follow Up

_____ Make sure any action you promised was carried out.

_____ Know your employees and their interests.

_____ Once it is made, stick to the decision.

_____ If you have done all of the above, expect management's support.

Sample: SUPERVISOR'S NOTATIONS
GRIEVANCE RECORD

Date of Entry:	September 1, 1984
Employee(s) Involved:	Will Gripe
Union Representative:	Egar Tusu
Complaint:	Gripe and Tusu came into my office on 7/29 at 10:00 a.m. and complained that Gripe should have been placed on the 8/1 overtime work list. Tusu said that Gripe had not been getting equal overtime along with other employees.
Remedy Sought:	Gripe wants to be assigned to overtime tonight. Tusu agreed but thought Gripe should get some money for the overtime lost.
Alleged Violation of:	Article 8, Section I—Master Agreement
Grievance Filed Within Time Limits:	Yes.
Facts Investigated:	I reviewed Gripe's file and found he was given equal chance at overtime but turned it down on 1/1, 2/15, 3/4 and 5/12. If he had accepted overtime those days he would be equal with other employees in his classification.
Answer Given:	I met with Gripe and Tusu on 8/1 at 8:30 a.m. and reviewed times Gripe had turned down overtime. Told Tusu I had to deny grievance. Tusu said they would think about it.
Action Taken:	None.
Follow Up:	None except to work with Gripe on future overtime assignments so he knows he is getting equal chance.

Sample: STEP 1 RESPONSE FORMAT

March 30, 1984

Mr. Mal Content
Tranquility High School
Serenity, California

Dear Mr. Content:

This will acknowledge receipt of your grievance dated April 1, 1984, and received by me on April 3, 1984. Your grievance alleges a violation of Section 1, Article 1, of the master agreement and asks as a remedy that you be appointed chairman of the faculty Human Relations and Liaison Committee. You will recall our Step 1 conference was held on April 5, 1984, in my office in accordance with the requirements of Section 2, Article 8. In attendance at that conference were Mr. I.M. Vice, Assistant Principal, and your representative, Mr. Tommy Hawk, of the STA.

After considering the information which you brought to my attention and other related materials, it is my decision that:

> there has been no violation of the contract provisions as alleged, and I must therefore deny your remedy as sought.

The above constitutes my decision and statement of position in response to your grievance and terminates Step 1 of the grievance procedure under Article 8 of the master agreement.

You may, if you wish, appeal this decision in accordance with Section 3 of the grievance procedure.

Very truly yours,

I.M. Wright

cc: Personnel Office/ Step 2 Supervisor/ STA Representative/File

Sample: GRIEVANCE FORM FOR STEP 1

CITY OF _____ Original: Immediate Supervisor
Copy 2: Immediate Supervisor
Return to Grievant
Copy 3: Department Head
Copy 4: Grievant's File

GRIEVANCE FORM—STEP 1

Submission of Complaint — All portions of this section must be completed by the grievant.

Employee Name _____ Work Location _____

Statement of Grievance _____

_____

Specific Contract Violation Alleged _____

Remedy Sought: _____

_____

_____   _____
    Date   Signature

Upon completion of this section, grievant shall present original and copies #2 and #3 to immediate supervisor. Copy #4 should be retained by grievant.

_____

Immediate Supervisor's Response: _____

_____   _____

_____

_____   _____
    Date   Supervisor

Upon completion of this section, immediate supervisor shall retain original, present copy #2 to grievant, and forward copy #3 to personnel.

ADDENDUM III—4

SUPERVISOR'S DO'S AND DON'T'S
FOR HANDLING GRIEVANCES

1. Investigate All Grievances

Investigate and handle each grievance as though it eventually may result in a hearing. When the grievance initially is discussed with you, you do not know whether it will go all the way through the process. It is better to treat it carefully and properly at your level than to wish you had done so after it has been appealed to a higher level.

2. Identify Violation

Always require the employee to identify the specific contract provision allegedly violated. Ask: (1) What provision is allegedly violated? and (2) How did the agency violate this provision?

3. Give Full Hearing

Regardless of whether the grievance appears to be legitimate within the definition, always give the employee a good and full hearing on the issue.

4. Make Employee Prove

In most grievance cases, the employee is the moving party, the one asserting a claim, and therefore it is up to the employee to present clear evidence supporting a claim. (When a grievance is due to an action taken by you, you should be prepared to explain why you took the action.)

5. Determine the Solution Sought

Always require employees to state clearly what they are seeking as a solution to the grievance. The cost of the solution or the precedent involved may be major factors in determining how to handle the grievance.

6. Do Not Let Grievance Processing Interfere with Operations

Do not interfere with agency operations to facilitate grievance processing. The grievance procedure generally is intended to facilitate the investigation and resolution of grievances in a manner that interferes as little as possible with orderly and efficient operations. However, informal grievances should be discussed as promptly as possible.

7. Correct Your Mistakes

If the grievance brings out the fact that you have violated a contract provision, admit you are wrong and provide the correct remedy to the situation. Admitting your mistakes will improve your credibility with employees. Also, it is easier to admit mistakes and correct them yourself than to have them corrected by higher management.

ADDENDUM III–5

8. Tell Employee of Corrective Action

If, after considering a grievance, you determine that a mistake has been made and corrective action should be taken, make sure you advise the employee of the corrective action you intend to take. Your willingness to correct an error gives you a real opportunity to win employee respect and confidence. Do not lose the opportunity.

9. Enforce Time Limits

Enforce and comply with the time limits set forth. An informal grievance must be initiated within reasonable time after the event or circumstance occasioning the grievance, and written complaints and appeals must be filed within five days. If the grievance is filed after the time limits have passed, deny it on the basis that it is un-timely. The purpose of the time limit is to keep stale complaints out of the grievance procedure. If grievances denied as untimely are appealed to higher levels, they will be reviewed on a case by case basis to determine whether there are gross inequities, and under certain circumstances they may be adjusted. This policy is intended to ensure continuing compliance with the time limit provisions of the agreement.

10. Comply with Time Limits

Make sure you comply with the time limits which apply to your handling of the grievance. An immediate supervisor has ten work days in which to give a decision or response to the grievance.

11. Do Not Cause Grievant to Be Untimely

Do not do anything to cause the employee to fail to comply with the time limits. Do not deny the grievance as untimely if the untimeliness is caused by you.

12. Allow Latitude But Do Not Take Abuse

Permit the employee reasonable latitude in presenting the grievance. However, do not permit the employee or the employee's representative to abuse or demean you or other management personnel. If the employee or the representative uses language that is inclined to threaten or provoke you, adjourn the meeting until the parties are in a better frame of mind to discuss the issues. You are not obligated to endure language that exceeds that normally used on the job.

13. Be Serious And Sincere

Most grievances are a serious matter to the individual concerned. It is important that you be utterly serious and perfectly sincere at all times in handling grievances. Do not misrepresent anything in connection with a grievance. Do not make a joke out of a grievance.

14. Do Not Lose Your Temper

Never let yourself get baited into losing your temper. If you find yourself losing your temper, continue the meeting at some other time.

ADDENDUM III–5

15. Have One Spokesman

In handling grievances, each side should have only one spokesman. This practice expedites discussion and minimizes the possibility of misunderstanding.

16. Keep Discussion on the Point

Do not let the discussion become bogged down in irrelevant side issues. The grievance at hand is the only issue.

17. Past Practices

Never admit to the binding effect of a past practice.

18. Agency Right to Make Rules

A grievance which claims the agency is without the right to promulgate a rule or rules must be denied, unless it violates a contract provision. The agency does have the right to make rules consistent with the agreement. The agency will not be able to plan effectively and carry out its operation if its legitimate right to make rules is ever seriously compromised.

19. Examine Contract Provisions

When the employee claims a violation of particular contract provisions, always examine those provisions and any other provisions which you believe are related to the issue at hand. If the provisions are unclear or are inconsistent, get an interpretation from higher management.

20. Visit the Work Area

If the physical location or condition of the work place has anything to do with the grievance, make sure you personally visit the work area so you can see for yourself what the conditions are.

21. Question Other Employees

If the grievance involves a case of questionable facts or information, question other employees to get information and views.

22. Determine if Agency Has Been Consistent

If the grievance involves the manner in which the agency has interpreted and applied a provision of the contract, determine whether the agency's application has been consistent. Has one administrator or office applied the provision in one manner while another administrator or another office has applied it in another manner? If so, guidance from your immediate supervisor should be sought before proceeding.

23. Look into Prior Grievance Settlements

If you are dealing with an issue with which you are unfamiliar, determine whether any prior grievance settlements relate to the issue, such as:

    a. If the identical issue was raised in a prior grievance and resolved by mutual agreement or other means, the current dispute should be in accord with that prior settlement.

    b. If the identical issue was raised in a prior grievance but denied by management and not appealed further by the employee, the current grievance should be denied.

    c. If a similar issue was raised and resolved, the principles and theories utilized in handling the matter may provide helpful guidance.

24. Obtain Records

Secure any records that bear on the case and review them carefully. Hold them for safe keeping.

25. Record Results

Record all results of your investigation! Make a full record of the agency's position, arguments, witnesses, evidence, and participants in discussions.

26. Do Not Decide While in Doubt

Do not settle a grievance while in doubt. If you are in doubt, investigate and review the matter further.

27. Definition Determines Scope of Grievance

Resolve grievances on the basis of fact, not emotion. If an employee cannot find a provision in the contract to support the grievance, he or she may make the appeal that it is only "fair" to give him the relief he is seeking. The employee should be treated fairly, but the settlement of a grievance must be based on objective data.

Settling grievances out of the contract because it is fair can be emotionally very appealing, but you have to resist the temptation. Such broadening of the scope of grievances is not in the best interest of the agency or of all employees.

28. Do Not Negotiate

Do not negotiate with the employee on matters not covered by present contract provisions. If a matter is not covered, then no violation has taken place.

29. Do Not Give the Employee Veto Power

Never make "mutual consent" agreements regarding future action. Never agree to a procedure where you can take action only if the employee consents to it. On the other hand, it often is desirable to advise the employee in advance of taking an action.

30. *Make No "Deals" Inconsistent with Policies or Regulations*

When dealing with employees, never make "deals" or individual agreements that are inconsistent with contract provisions that apply to the employee.

31. *Advocate Management's Position*

When discussing grievances, if you find yourself sympathizing with the positions and opinions of the grievant, you have a responsibility and obligation to present management's position vigorously and affirmatively. You hurt your position as an administrator if you disassociate yourself from the management or the management position. Do not belittle your position.

32. *Sell Your Decision*

If a contract provision gives a clear answer, quote it. Also state the common sense of the situation. It is critical to good employee relations that the employee understands your viewpoint. This cannot be overemphasized. Employees will often accept a decision they are unhappy with if they can see there is good reason for the decision.

33. *Be Aware that Employee Associations Have Internal Pressures*

Do not forget that the interests of the employee may be different from the interests and goals of the association. Keeping this in mind may help explain why certain grievances are pressed, though they appear to have little merit, or are pressed with vigor far beyond the apparent importance of the issue involved. Association representatives are subject to pressures from their "constitutents." Keeping this in mind may help you to look at grievances more objectively, with less inclination to see the grievance as something directed at you personally.

34. *Do Not Be Pressured into a Decision*

Do not be pressured into making a decision on the spot. The reason for time limits in the contract is to give both parties a chance to consider the facts.

35. *If Agreement Is Reached, Stop Discussion*

If, during a meeting on a grievance, you arrive at a mutually satisfactory solution, terminate the discussion. Many deals fall apart because the parties keep talking.

36. *Keep Grievance Denials Brief*

Generally, do not give long written grievance answers. If you must deny the grievance, it is usually better to do so orally, then follow up with a brief denial statement (if the grievance is at the written step).

37. *When Sustaining Grievance, Tell Why*

If you are going to sustain a formal written grievance, in full or in part, make sure that your written decision is clear and succinct. In sustaining the grievance, point out the specific provisions that allow you to grant the remedy. This helps limit the remedy to the grievance at hand. Do not let it appear that you agree with all the reasons cited by the employee to support the grievance.

38. Recommend Changes to Troublesome Provisions

If you come across a policy or regulation during a grievance that makes it difficult for you to supervise and manage your unit, make a record of it and let higher management know, so that an effort can be made to change the troublesome provision.

39. Do Not Abdicate to Employee Organizations

Do not transfer your authority to the employee organization. If you have an employee problem, you solve it.

40. Use Grievance Procedures to Resolve Disputes

If individual employees refuse to follow orders because they believe the order violates a policy or regulation, advise them that they have the right to use the grievance procedure to resolve the dispute, but that in the meantime they are obligated to obey orders. It is a commonly accepted rule that employees are obligated to obey instructions (assuming the instructions do not require the employees to jeopardize their health or safety or to commit illegal acts or the like). The rule is "obey first, grieve later." This allows operations to continue in an orderly manner while the employee still maintains the right to resolve the dispute through the grievance procedure.

41. Understand Why Your Decision Might Be Changed at a Higher Step

Occasionally your decision might be changed at a higher step. If this happens, realize there are reasons for it, such as additional facts were not available to you or you slipped up in collecting or weighing facts.

Chapter IV

Management Procedures in Grievance Appeals

Most grievance procedures provide for three to five appellate steps from the first-level supervisor up through line management to a top-level administrator. Typical grievance review processes of this nature are illustrated in Addendum IV −1.

Some procedures even provide for grievances being appealed by higher levels of employee organization officials, starting with the work location representative or departmental representative and going up as high as the president or executive secretary. In either case, the number of appeal steps varies, depending upon the size and needs of the public institution and the employee organization involved.

At the outset, it is important to distinguish among the various appeal procedures that exist in public agencies. For example, many public agencies have civil service commissions, or personnel boards, with rules providing for employee appeals for review of "adverse actions," for example, suspension, demotion, or discharge. There is usually a time limit imposed during which the employee must file a timely appeal after the notification of action. The full commission, a member of the commission, or a hearing officer appointed by the commission or board will often hear the case. The hearing officer or board then makes a decision based on the facts presented. A hearing officer's recommendation is usually returned to the full commission for ultimate action. The decision of the commission is binding on the agency. On occasion, however, the commission or board's decision is appealed to the courts. These types of appellate process are outside of the grievance procedure itself, and therefore are not the subject of our attention here.

In previous chapters, we have emphasized the critical importance of a positive management attitude as a factor in any successful grievance procedure. A basic requirement for effective grievance processing, including appeal and review, is the full, continuing, and active support of top management. We all recognize that conflicts are inherent in employer −employee relations because supervisors are required to give directions and orders; subordinates must learn to accept them, and carry them out, if the public institution is to serve the taxpayers. A vital part of this relationship between employee and supervisor is the feeling on the part of the individual employee that he or she is free to express complaints without fear of discrimination, and with the opportunity at higher management levels for a review of complaints that seem justified, but were denied by the immediate administrator.

In a theoretical sense, we might suggest such higher appeals should not be necessary since the union representative should speak for his/her organization, and the supervisor for management. As a practical matter, however, the appeals process provides both parties several opportunities to reconsider their positions, and with luck resolve the disagreement. In addition, the appeals process subjects the grievance to scrutiny from successively broader perspectives; it also enables management and the employee organization to retract diplomatically from a losing grievance situation and avoid the expense, involvement, and potential penalties of arbitration.

THE MANAGEMENT PERSPECTIVE

From a management point of view, the appeals process should provide an opportunity to consolidate the management position and policy, and an opportunity for reviewing the issues and adjusting the management position, including a reversal of the first-line supervisor's decision, if necessary.

An important facet of the management position at the appellate level is the distinction necessary between grievable and nongrievable subjects. Oftentimes, the first-level supervisor accepts a subject as a grievance when the latter is not a grievable item. In these situations, it remains for the next level supervisor at the appellate stage to indicate that part of the management position is that the subject matter is nongrievable. This is particularly important with respect to ''interests'' and ''rights'' disputes. The former are those concerned with the negotiation or modification of the terms of the master agreement. They are, in effect, unresolved issues in contract negotiations. Rights disputes, on the other hand, arise during the term of a master agreement and involve the interpretation and application of that agreement. The grievance procedure, therefore, should deal only with rights disputes, and management needs to insure that this is tightly controlled. When a question of misapplication of the master bargaining agreement or of the agency's rules and regulations is raised by the employee or the union, it is appropriate for a grievance to be filed in order to clarify the issue. If, however, the union or employee is concerned about a matter on which the agency policy and regulations are silent, that concern should be channelled to the bargaining table and not through the grievance procedure. Management, particularly at the appellate level, needs to insure that the grievance procedure is not being used to challenge or change the rules and regulations of the agency per se. This is one of the reasons why it is important for the first and second-line supervisors to maintain close communications on grievances. The appellate level of management needs to be informed regarding any and all attempts to exceed the terms and provisions of the master contract or expand the rules and policies of the agency by filing grievances.

In addition to the above, it is important for the management representative at the appellate level to insure good communications are maintained with the exclusive representative. In that regard, the second-level administrator needs to be well acquainted with the leadership and organizational positions and goals of the union, particularly if it is the exclusive representative. If there is more than one employee organization operating, it is incumbent upon the second-level supervisor to insure that the exclusive representative is notified of any grievances that may be working their way up the grievance ladder. Much will depend on the agency rules or the provisions of the master agreement. In any event, notification to the exclusive bargaining agent is almost always required, and is a highly recommended management technique. In addition, second-level management needs to reinforce the prerogatives of the on-site administrator to manage the agency's enterprise and to pursue with vigor management's overall rights.

THE AGENCY PERSONNEL DEPARTMENT

Personnel staff in public agencies usually play a key role in the appeals process. Many master agreements require the personnel department to review grievance disputes at one or several levels of the appeal procedure. Because the major responsibility for handling grievances rests with line management, personnel staffs should be oriented to provide assistance and support as a resource to line management. Any attempt to interpose themselves as part of the decision-making process only serves to confuse and weaken the basic management position in the resolution of grievances.

PROCEDURES FOR REVIEWING GRIEVANCES
AT THE APPEAL LEVELS

Just as there are no "magic formulas" for resolving first-level grievances, there are none at the appeal levels. There are, however, some techniques worth considering here to facilitate effective processing. This includes a checklist for handling the appeal as is illustrated in Addendum IV–2.

First, it is imperative that the second-level supervisor be in touch with the immediate administrator who made the step one, or first-level, grievance judgment. This bilateral communication should be part of the ongoing management communications process, but in any event, it is imperative in the grievance procedure that these levels of management communicate. Not only is it necessary for the next level of management to have adequate information in order to support a level-one decision, but if the level-one administrator is not to be supported, it is even more imperative that communications take place beforehand. In that regard, there are occasions when the first-level administrator feels he or she cannot make a judgment and either refers to the next level, or actually desires the next level to reverse the judgment. For example there may be a dress code issue on which the first-line administrator feels he or she must take an outmoded stand in order to be responsive to the community. Although the supervisor may recognize that times have changed and employees cannot be held to a rigid dress code, he or she may wish to have the next level of management make that declaration in order to maintain credibility with the community.

Although there may not be any magic formulas, there are some attitudinal considerations very similar to those discussed for the level-one supervisor, which the appellate-level administrator would do well to cultivate. The latter's attitude as a management representative should be positive and nonthreatening, but firm and consistent. In an ideal sense, the second-level administrator's action should be characterized by: fairness, reasonableness, flexibility, cooperation, trust, and respect for the employee organization.

In addition to the personal characteristics noted above, the following are some procedures which, if followed at the appeal level, will help find a compromise if one exists:

1. Coordinate with management levels.
2. Hold a personal conference with the grievant.
3. Investigate thoroughly.
4. Respond to the appeal.
5. Follow up.

1. Coordinate with Management Levels

It is imperative that the appellate-level supervisor communicate both up and down the management chain of command. This is particularly important in terms of the first-level supervisor. The mid-level supervisor needs to understand clearly what actions the immediate administrator took, the decision he or she made, and the rationale behind that decision. Also, it may be necessary to clarify agency policy interpretation with upper level management. Generally, the mid-level supervisor can obtain all of the information required from the immediate administrator, or the latter's notations. However, it is not advisable for the appellate-level supervisor to include the first-level supervisor in any conferences with the grievant. This often serves only to generate polarization and confrontation.

2. Hold a Personal Conference With the Grievant

After receiving the grievance appeal, the next-level supervisor should arrange a conference with the grievant and the organization representative. Oftentimes, union representatives misunderstand the basic facts behind a grievance; bringing the employee and the representative in to meet with the next-level supervisor can often have a salutary effect by clarifying the facts. Much of the success of this conference will depend upon the attitude and listening skills of the second-level administrator. He or she needs to manifest an attitude communicating that the most important function of the conference is to identify and correct dissatisfactions, and that as a mid-level manager, he or she is more concerned with what is right than with who is right. There also needs to be reassurance to the employee that the agency does not intend to make any entry or file any papers in the personnel file for the employee's involvement in a grievance, except as may be required to implement a decision in the matter. Even though most master agreements delineate this very clearly, it is important to reassure the employee and the union representative.

The employment of effective listening skills by the mid-level administrator becomes imperative and promotes a complete account of the employee's story. At this conference, the supervisor should listen to the employee and the representative to determine the pertinent facts behind the grievance. Being a good and effective listener requires the administrator to wait before responding, to eliminate as many outside distractions as possible, and to repeat verbatim what the grievant or representative says, oftentimes rephrasing, but maintaining the content and feeling of what the employee's dissatisfaction actually is. The supervisor should try to identify the important themes by seeking the real meaning beyond the mere words articulated. After listening carefully, the reviewing supervisor should go over the facts, and record them in a format similar to that used by the level-one administrator illustrated in the previous chapter (Addendum III−2). Such notations should include the essential facts, including the remedy the grievant is seeking, and the provision of the master agreement, rule, or policy which has allegedly been violated.

3. Investigate Thoroughly

Once the mid-level manager has obtained basic data from the grievant and the union representative, contact should be established with the first-line supervisor. The purpose for this communication is to insure the mid-level supervisor has a complete grasp of the record as transcribed by the step-one administrator, including elaborations. In accumulating and organizing the data, the mid-level supervisor may wish to use a format similar to that used at step one, and illustrated in Addendum IV−2

At this point the appeal-level administrator must make a concerted effort to discover all relevant facts and to separate the latter from opinion, conjecture, speculation, or assumption. He or she will therefore want to acquire pertinent documentation. Records such as payroll time cards, case load, inspection records, attendance records, and performance evaluations are typical items of documentation which play a vital part in a thorough investigation. The mid-level supervisor should also consult any potential witnesses, or other employees who may contribute to a clarification of the facts of the matter. It is particularly important at this phase of the grievance process to insure nonmanagement personnel are contacted if they have a contribution to make to the investigation. As part of this investigation, the reviewing administrator should also visit the work location to insure he or she has a grasp of the physical conditions surrounding the complaint.

The investigation should also include a determination of whether any procedural errors have been committed. The time limits should be reviewed to determine that there was compliance on the part of the grievant, and the subject matter of the grievance should be verified as grievable, or in other words, within the definition of a grievance under the master agreement or agency rules. If the subject is determined not to be grievable, that decision should be made and enunciated at this level in order to protect management's right to argue grievability.

After completing a thorough investigation, the mid-level supervisor should contact the next level of management in the chain of command and indicate what his/her tentative solution is to be. At that time, verification can establish that the solution is within management policy objectives, and can be supported at higher levels, if necessary. Also, there may be ramifications of the grievance unknown to the administrator at this level with consequences for the agency's bargaining position at the table. All of this can be determined once bilateral communication is opened up between the second-level administrator and higher-level management.

4. Respond to the Appeal

The same basic guidelines apply for answering the grievance at the appeal level as were applicable for the first-line supervisor. The response should be as early as is practical after the thorough investigation and within the time limits. A typical step two management response is shown in Addendum IV–3, assuming the agency has a form for responding at the appellate level. If it does not, a letter as is illustrated in Addendum IV–4 can be used. It should be noted the response in written form is fairly succinct and direct, and does not open wide areas for discussion. However, there is nothing to preclude the mid-level supervisor from contacting the grievant and his or her representative and providing oral elaboration or clarification of the basic decision. Oftentimes, this may be desirable for morale purposes.

5. Follow Up.

Once a grievance is appealed beyond the first level, it is likely there will be subsequent appeals. One of the most effective ways to reduce the number of the second-level appeals is to follow up with a departmental management case conference of the particular grievance. Such a case conference should include recommended methods for handling similar grievances in the future. A discussion of this sort builds the concept of management teams, trains lower-level supervisors, and promotes a consistency of management actions in handling the grievances.

The training of first and second-level management in proper grievance procedures should be a top management priority and responsibility. Many public agencies run formal grievance training programs for all levels of management, with particular emphasis on the first-line supervisors. Unfortunately, there are some agencies where grievance training consists solely of reprimands for poor handling, rather than formal training in positive techniques. A more detailed discussion with recommendations for programs will be found in Chapter VIII, on the subject of management training programs.

THE EMPLOYEE'S EXPANDING REPRESENTATION RIGHTS

Representation rights in grievance procedures are usually clearly delineated in collective bargaining master agreements and/or agency rules, and entitlement to representation is well established, especially at the appeal level. However, the questions can sometimes arise in ill-defined problem areas such as investigatory interviews which lie outside the grievance process. The subject of such representation rights per se has been discussed in Chapter III. The guidelines delineated there are also applicable at the next level of management review. It will suffice us here to note that such representation is an expanding right and management should proceed with caution in denying representation.

CONCLUSION

The appellate level is critical to an effective grievance procedure. Both from the standpoint of employee morale, and consistency of management interpretation and policy, it is a vital element in good employer–employee relations. It is important for the second-level administrator to make a thorough investigation of the matter, including a hearing for all parties concerned, and then to insure his or her decision coincides with management policy and equity for the employee. This second or appellate level in the grievance process is usually the last opportunity for resolution this side of arbitration. Subsequently the parties become polarized and more deeply entrenched in their respective positions. Top management must also realize that whether the first-level supervisor's decision is sustained or reversed, a management conference on the subject matter is an important tool for solidifying the management team in improving grievance handling procedures.

TYPICAL GRIEVANCE PROCEDURE

TIME LIMITS   EVENT

STEPS

Step 1   Within ten calendar days from   GRIEVANT →   ┌─────────────────────────────┐
         event.   │ EMPLOYEE INFORMALLY MEETS   │
                                                                │ AND DISCUSSES GRIEVANCE   │
                                                                │ WITH SUPERVISOR   │
                                                                └─────────────────────────────┘

1-a   Within 5 calendar days following   IMMEDIATE   ⬡ IMMEDIATE
         meeting with grievant.   SUPERVISOR →   SUPERVISOR'S
                                                                  ORAL
                                                                  RESPONSE

Step 2   Within 7 calendar days of   GRIEVANT →   ┌─────────────────────────────┐
         Supervisor's Response.   │ EMPLOYEE INITIATES   │
                                                                │ FORMAL WRITTEN   │
                                                                │ GRIEVANCE   │
                                                                └─────────────────────────────┘

2-a   Within 15 calendar days from   →   ⬡ FIRST
         Employer's Grievance Appeal,   LEVEL OF
         supervisor shall meet with   REVIEW'S
         grievant.   WRITTEN
                                                                  RESPONSE

Step 3   Within 7 calendar days from   GRIEVANT →   ┌─────────────────────────────┐
         First Level of Review Response   │ EMPLOYEE   │
                                                                │ APPEALS   │
                                                                │ GRIEVANCE IN WRITING   │
                                                                └─────────────────────────────┘

3-a   Within 15 calendar days from   →   ⬡ SECOND
         Employee's Grievance Appeal,   LEVEL OF
         Bureau Head or designee shall   REVIEW'S
         meet with grievant.   WRITTEN
                                                                  RESPONSE

Step 4   Within 7 calendar days from   GRIEVANT →   ┌─────────────────────────────┐
         Second Level of Review Response.   │ EMPLOYEE   │
                                                                │ APPEALS   │
                                                                │ GRIEVANCE IN WRITING   │
                                                                └─────────────────────────────┘

4-a   Within 30 calendar days from   →   ⬡ THIRD
         date arguments are submitted.   LEVEL OF
                                                                  REVIEW'S
                                                                  WRITTEN
                                                                  RESPONSE

Step 5   Within 7 calendar days from   GRIEVANT AND   ┌─────────────────────────────┐
         Third Level of Review   UNION JOINTLY →   │ EMPLOYEE   │
         Response.   │ APPEALS   │
                                                                │ GRIEVANCE IN WRITING   │
                                                                └─────────────────────────────┘

5-a   Within 7 calendar days from date   ⬭ ARBITRATION
         list of arbitrators is provided
         by Employee Relations Board.

┌──────────┐
│   │   Employee Action
└──────────┘

⬡   Management Action

Sample: GRIEVANCE APPEAL FORM

CITY OF _____

Original: Personnel
Copy 2: Return to Grievant
Copy 3: Immediate Supervisor
Copy 4: Grievant's File

GRIEVANCE FORM—STEP 2

Appeal to Personnel — All portions of this section must be completed by the grievant. Copy #2 of completed Grievance Form—Step 1 must be attached.

Article alleged to have been violated & remedy sought are as stated in Step 1.

Reason for appeal: _____

_____

_____

_____   _____
Date   Signature

Upon completion of this section, grievant shall present original and copies #2 and #3 to the personnel department. Copy #4 should be retained by grievant.

_____

_____

Respondent's Response _____

_____

_____

_____   _____
Date   Signature

Upon completion of this section, assistant superintendent shall retain original and forward copy #2 and copy #2 of completed Grievance Form — Step 1 to grievant, and copy #3 to grievant's immediate supervisor.

ADDENDUM IV−2

CHECKLIST FOR HANDLING GRIEVANCE APPEALS

I. Confer with the Grievant

_____ Hold a personal conference with the grievant.

_____ Listen intently as the employee repeats his or her story.

_____ Get the union representative's position.

_____ Get important facts.

_____ Take notes.

_____ Repeat the grievance in your own words to grievant and the grievant's representative.

_____ Get the remedy requested.

II. Investigate the Facts

_____ Check with immediate supervisor of employee.

_____ Check time limits.

_____ Check grievability.

_____ Visit the work location.

_____ Check facts from both sides.

_____ Seek advice if necessary.

_____ Reach a preliminary decision.

_____ Check your preliminary decision with your supervisor or personnel representative.

III. Answer the Grievance

_____ Answer as soon as possible.

_____ Explain your position orally.

_____ Write a succinct and understandable answer to the grievant.

_____ If necessary, give the benefit of the doubt to management.

_____ Explain the employee's right to appeal.

_____ Once it is made, stick to your decision.

IV. Follow up

_____ Make sure any action you promised was carried out.

_____ Train your supervisory employees to reduce grievances.

_____ Support management.

_____ If you have done all of the above expect the support of top management.

October 20, 1984

Mr. Henry Meany
Union Teachers Association

RE: MR. MAL CONTENT v. _____ UNIFIED SCHOOL DISTRICT

Dear Mr. Meany:

This letter constitutes the response required by Section 2.0, Article VI, Step 2, of the current Master Agreement.

Thank you for meeting with me as Mr. Content's representative at the Step 2 conference held in my office on October 18, 1984. During the conference you reviewed your reasons why you believed Mr. Content was entitled to supplemental pay. You stated he had assumed the responsibility for another teacher's class on a field trip and was therefore entitled to the extra pay per Section 3.0 of Article XIV.

I have reviewed the initial complaint, the Step 1 response, the applicable Master Agreement section, and considered the forthright presentation made by you on behalf of Mr. Content. I have also evaluated the information provided by Mr. Content himself and others involved.

I am unable to find a basis upon which to justify granting the remedy you request. It is, therefore, my decision to sustain the Step 1 decision. Consequently, the remedy that Mr. Content requests cannot be granted.

Sincerely,

I. M. RITE
Assistant Superintendent

IRR/ap

cc: Mr. M. Content
    Principal
    Files

Chapter V

Typical Grievance Issues

Since the essence of an employee grievance is essentially the perception by the employee of a problem or justifiable complaint, it is important for management to have an awareness of the issues that most frequently give rise to grievance filing. There are a number of reasons why it is important to assess the nature of these issues, not the least of which is that they may ultimately go to the arbitration level and become the subject of an arbitrator's ruling that will either bind the agency in its future procedures or at least have a significant impact on the evolution of agency policy. Arbitrators and other third-party neutrals are essentially specialists in master agreement interpretation, or rule interpretation of the agency. Based on an analysis of such issues, management can evolve its paramount considerations in negotiating grievance procedures. A typical list of such management-oriented grievance proposals is found in Addendum V–1.

Such an analysis of primary grievance issues also enables management to assess its own errors and take the necessary corrective measures, such as in-service training, which will be discussed in more detail in Chapter VIII. Furthermore, a study of key issues yields insight into the arbitrator's criteria, the subject of Chapter VII. It is important that management have a keen awareness of what subject matter is most frequently grieved, and not only what the basic issues are, but how they are identified by the union. For example, a study of major grievance topics yields a clue to the employee organization's criteria for what it considers major issues.

From an employee organization's standpoint, all problems are not necessarily issues. For a problem at the work location to be a major issue, and therefore grievable, it usually must meet the following tests:

1. It must be a fixed issue. That is, it must be localized to the extent that it can be identified and employees can readily relate to it within a confined situation or classification.
2. It needs to be immediate: something that is occurring close at hand, and not in the nation's capital.
3. It must be specific (i.e., real, visible, and concrete, not ideological.)

4. It must be controversial.
5. It must have potential for success: unions cannot afford to become involved in issues that are potential losers for them. The latter does serious damage to the organization's credibility, in addition to its financial capabilities.
6. It must be the proper size. The union will generally prefer a smaller issue, pivoted on a work-located problem, to going for a larger stake and losing. Containing the size of the problem makes it more winnable from the union's standpoint and builds credibility for the local union representative among his or her peers.

PROMINENT GRIEVANCE ISSUES

It is an axiom of labor relations that every agreement, rule, or policy is subject to interpretation. In the absence of a collective bargaining environment, such interpretation lies exclusively with management. However, in today's collective bargaining setting, and particularly where a master agreement exists, management interpretation is subject to challenge by the union. As we have noted previously, the vehicle for this challenge is, of course, the grievance procedure. However, most responsible unions are not interested in flooding the system with trivia. Using criteria similar to that noted above, most employee organizations in the public sector and private sector will seek to channel their grievance filings in the direction of what they consider to be major issues. In these areas, the union does not deny management's right to act, but essentially wishes to preserve its right to react and bring the challenge before a third-party neutral (i.e., an arbitrator). The private sector experience reflects issues that are basically wages and working conditions: salary demands, overtime, safety, supervision. These issues also surface in the public sector grievance arena, but there is a broader spectrum of concern among public employees in areas that approach the policy level. Many public employees are professionals with serious concerns about policies that affect their duties and responsibilities. For that reason, public sector management needs to be more alert to the potential difficulties in certain areas.

Issues which first-line public management may expect to be frequent subjects of grievance by employees and unions include the following:

1. Disciplinary actions.
2. Excessive absenteeism.
3. Insubordination.
4. Union rights.
5. Incompetency.
6. Off-duty misconduct.
7. Dress and grooming.
8. Procedural concerns.
9. Recrimination charges.
10. Employee performance evaluations.

In addition to the above areas, public school management is faced by some issues that are more typically teacher personnel subjects. These teacher issues are supplemental to the ones listed above, and include the following:

1. Utilization of the preparation period.
2. Duty-free lunch time.
3. Teacher evaluations: due process.
4. Assignment of cocurricular duties.
5. Teaching assignments or displacement.

Another source of grievance stimulation today lies in the area of employee benefits. The basic economic package of wages and medical benefits contained in nearly all public agency master agreements is rapidly being supplemented by other fringe benefits and improved working conditions. These benefits, which deal with days and hours of work, holidays, vacations, sick leave, overtime pay, employee promotion, and termination rights now appear with increasing frequency in the vast majority of agreements. As this area of employee benefits expands, there is a commensurate increase in rights disputes that generate grievance issues. It is necessary then to consider these working condition benefits as issues in a category of their own.

As an aid to the first-line administrator in organizing and preparing for these potential grievances, sections of this chapter are also devoted to:

1. Overtime and extra duty assignments.
2. Vacations.
3. Paid holidays.
4. Leaves of absence.
5. Emergency conditions.
6. Merit pay and incentives.
7. Promotions.
8. Nondisciplinary reductions and demotions.
9. Other working conditions.
10. Work or "plant" rules.

1. Disciplinary Actions

The issue of disciplinary action against employees evolves principally around the question of "just cause" for such management action. Given the tenure rights and job security features of public employment, it is imperative that public sector management have a firm rationale and due process procedure inherent in its disciplinary policy. In any grievance brought against management for taking disciplinary action, the arbitrator will wish to address the basic principles of "just cause" before rendering an award. The fundamental test, of course, is whether management acted fairly in enforcing agency rules, policies, or the provisions of the master agreement when it took disciplinary action against the grievant.

Although the precise criteria will vary with the arbitrator and the mertis of a particular disciplinary case, there are certain fundamental questions that most arbitrators will pose as necessary to establish the just cause provision. These will generally include the following:

a. Did the employee understand the consequences of his or her actions? Was management's action sufficient to put the employee on notice (e.g., a written warning)?

b. Can it be shown that the policy or rule invoked by management was a reasonable one (i.e., job related)?

c. Did management conduct a fair, impartial, and thorough investigation before taking the disciplinary action?

d. Did management's investigation produce substantive proof by a "preponderance of evidence" of the employee's guilt in the matter? It should be noted here that the term "preponderance of evidence" has significance in an arbitration hearing.

e. If a rule violation, was there in fact a rule, was the rule published to the grievant, was it enforced? Were the rules or policies in this particular case applied in an even-handed manner by management? It should be noted here that lack or discriminate enforcement of rules by management provides a very persuasive defense (i.e., grievance base) for the employee in such cases.

f. Was the disciplinary action or penalty invoked against the employee too great a deterrent for the alleged misconduct? In this regard, management needs to take into consideration the employee's past record as well as current infraction.

Some experts estimate as much as 70 percent of arbitration cases are predicated on disciplinary issues. When management loses such grievances in arbitration, it is generally because of a failure to meet the just cause criteria noted above, or failure to process the grievance itself properly. Generally, it is not so much a loss on the merits of the particular case as it is an error on the part of management personnel by reacting emotionally, and therefore too quickly in making disciplinary moves against the employee. Management is generally better advised to move cautiously and not surprise the employee with sudden disciplinary actions. In other words, discipline should be progressive and well-founded. This concept of progressive discipline is a key one in employer–employee relations. One of the most succinct and accurate definitions of the meaning of progressive discipline was contained in a recent public sector arbitraton award that describes the process as one designed to improve employee performance, not a punitive device, and moving from verbal warnings to written documentation so as not to have the employee surprised by the degree of discipline invoked.

For typical cases-in-point, see Addenda V–2 and V–3.

2. Excessive Absenteeism

There is little question among arbitrators or other objective observers that a chronic absentee is an unsatisfactory employee, and indeed may be subject to discharge for such absence. The problem, of course, lies with the definition of excessive. Before management can successfully claim an employee has a record of chronic absence, attention needs to be given to such factors as the duration of time over which the employee has been an absentee, the reasons offered for this absence, the particular duties performed by the employee, and the consistency of the agency's attendance policies with respect to all employees in the job classification. A grievant who claims to have been unreasonably disciplined or penalized for absenteeism will generally predicate his or her defense on the following premises:

a. There was no written or enunciated agency policy on attendance.
b. The supervisor applied the standards of attendance unevenly, and in the grievant's case discriminatorily.
c. The grievant was never given a warning by the supervisor of what would happen if the absenteeism continued.

If grievants can successfully demonstrate any of the above, they will probably be successful in having their grievance sustained and the penalty removed. A lesser argument is often advanced by the grievant with respect to the nature of his/her duties. It will be argued the absenteeism may have been above average, but did not greatly impair the efficiency of the department or agency to perform services. For example, in the case of a teacher, the availability of substitute teachers is often raised as a defense by chronically absent teachers. In addition, arbitrators have a tendency to deny the relevancy of pupil safety in the absence of the teacher for whom a substitute has been provided.

Again, the paramount importance of proper and early warning to an employee when the supervisor feels the former is exceeding reasonable limits of absence contrary to a promulgated agency policy should be noted.

For cases-in-point, see Addenda V-4, V-5, and V-6.

3. Insubordination

The standard cliché in the private sector of "obey now, grieve later" is also applicable to public-sector employees. Most arbitrators will sustain management's right to require compliance with an order that an employee may question, but cannot disobey, assuming the order meets the test of reasonableness. Again, there are factors that most third-party neutrals will consider in determining whether or not such an order was reasonable. These factors fall under the broad ambit of the just cause and due process requirements. In order to meet the test of whether insubordination was present, management must show the following:

a. The supervisor's instructions were clearly stated and included the possible penalty for failure to comply.
b. There was an overt refusal, not just a failure to carry out a direction, on the part of an employee.
c. The warning of consequences to the employee was very explicit, preferably in front of witnesses.

Often, the question of abusive language is raised with regard to so-called insubordination. The key factor is whether or not profane language is commonplace at the work location. Also, caution should be exercised by supervisors in disciplining union representatives, particularly if they claim they are acting in their official capacity. This feature of employee discipline will be discussed later in this chapter.

In our contemporary society, there is often a question raised by an employee as to whether they must answer questions during an investigation. As discussed in previous chapters, the rights of an employee during an investigation process are expanding with regard to representation. The question here might well be whether the employee can refuse to answer under penalty of a charge of insubordination by the employer. In this regard, most arbitrators are unanimous in upholding the right of management in the public sector to give an employee under investigation the choice of either answering the question during investigation, or alternatively, being discharged for failure to answer such questions. In this regard however, caution must be taken not to create the appearance of a coerced confession. Management is probably better advised to discipline an employee on a charge of willful failure to comply rather than on the narrow definition of insubordination. Most hearing officers will concur in the premise that a willful failure to recognize authority renders the employee subject to disciplinary action.

For applicable arbitration decisions, see cases-in-point in Addenda V−7 and V−8.

4. Union Rights

There is a broad and somewhat subjective area included under the term Union Rights. Unless union rights are explicitly and unambiguously spelled out in a master agreement or agency rules, the issue of antiunion animus can be a major one in grievance proceedings. Since most master agreements use somewhat ambiguous language such as "reasonable" access, and "no recrimination," there does exist a wide area for challenging certain management actions where union activities are involved. There is an even more specific area of challenge where the grievance procedure provides language precluding recrimination against an employee for actually filing a grievance. This can be a troublesome area for management, and is quite frequently the subject of grievances. This is especially so where an informal conference is called for prior to the filing of a formal grievance, but is not explicitly described as a step in the grievance procedure. That is, oftentimes, an employee feels he or she has entered the grievance process, whereas the immediate supervisor is under the impression it is merely an informal discussion occurring as a routine matter. This can be a particularly difficult area with respect to the charges of recrimination being subsequently brought against the supervisor, alleging that the latter is retaliating for the employee's initiating a grievance. For the first-line supervisor, there are some safeguards that should be observed in order to reduce, if not eliminate, such accusations.

Generally speaking, the most troublesome aspects of this issue (i.e., antiunion animus or recrimination) arise when the language of the master agreement is not carefully and specifically drafted on the subject of union rights. Also, it should be noted that a problem can surface if management denies to the union or the grievant information necessary to the preparation of an ongoing grievance case. Often this may be hard to define, but most arbitrators will support the union's request for at least a reasonable amount of information on the subject matter of a grievance. On the other hand, arbitrators are inclined to reject any union accusation of discrimination which is predicated upon an inference or conjecture, rather than clear evidence or overt acts of recrimination or antiunion animus. Management should therefore proceed with caution in this area also, being alert that it may give rise to a major grievance issue.

For cases-in-point, see Addenda V−9 and V−10.

5. Incompetency

Another irksome area for public management with respect to grievance potential is the question of employee competency. Frequently, supervisors take disciplinary action against employees on the basis of the latters' inefficiency or incompetency. The problem here is that most arbitrators will not consider incompetency per se to be a disciplinary problem since the due process requirements are not remedial. That is, the employee who is truly incompetent is more likely to be corrected by retraining, transfer, or demotion, than he or she is by direct disciplinary action. Therefore the caution public management must exercise is to insure that in an incompetency situation, an overly drastic remedy is not resorted to by the first-line supervisor. This is not to say that the unproductive employee has to be retained. However, management needs to exhaust the above possibilities, retraining, and so on, before taking any overt direct action that may be grievable as a claim of unreasonable disciplinary action. Generally, arbitrators will support management's actions as long as the same basic ingredients, substantial proof, adequate warnings, nondiscriminatory and even-handed treatment, are in effect.

For case-in-point, see Addendum V–11.

6. Off-Duty Misconduct

For the public sector employer, the question of misconduct off the job constitutes a more sensitive issue than is the case in private employment. Since employees are retained by the taxpayers, and are generally expected to obtain a higher standard of conduct off-duty as well as on, management efforts to exert disciplinary action in this area trigger grievance issues of unreasonableness.

The issue lends itself to a ready accusation by the union that management is imposing itself on the personal life of an employee and cannot be judging morality on its own standards. However, most arbitrators will agree that management has a responsibility in the public sector to invoke discipline when an employee's off-duty conduct can be correlated with his or her job performance. In other words, criteria for sustaining management action involves an establishment of proof that the employee is not able to perform the job effectively (e.g., the employee may be confined to jail). Arbitrators will also be responsive to the argument that the public agency, especially in highly visible jobs, may be harmed in its public image by immoral or criminal conduct on the part of the employee while off-duty.

Inherent here, then, is the premise that such off-duty misconduct must be directly correlated with the effective or orderly conduct of the public agency's functions and responsibilities with regard to the public. The same criteria is applicable with respect to the individual employee; the misconduct must impact directly on the employee's ability to function in his or her assigned duties.

For case-in-point, see Addendum V–12.

7. Dress and Grooming

Closely related to the off-duty misconduct issue as a typical subject for grievances is the related question of proper dress and grooming. Again, public agencies often find themselves suffering from a tarnished public image because of inappropriate dress and grooming by their employees. Again, probably the most sensitivity is shown by the public with respect to school teachers whom they expect to set a positive image of deportment and grooming for their children. However, this is an equally difficult area for public management to control in the face of an ever-changing public standard of acceptable attire. What was at one time considered to be in gross poor taste or at least offensive may today have become the fashion standard, or a manifestation of individual freedom. For this reason, public management also must proceed with caution and, as in the off-duty misconduct issue, must be able to show that the unsatisfactory dress and grooming to which management has taken exception correlates directly with the respective employee's job performance and efficiency and/or the agency's public image. In addition, the grooming standard must be clear, related to contemporary mores, and consistently enforced.

Dress and grooming regulations based upon safety, health, or comfort in a particular job classification or environment are objectively ascertainable and therefore reasonably enforceable. Regulations designed to promote the agency's reputation or image with the public are more difficult to ascertain and therefore to enforce. In private industry, the need to satisfy customer expectations of employee appearance is recognized as valid. The public employer also has a reputation and image to maintain with the public, even though it may be for different reasons than the private entrepreneur; this is particularly recognizable in the case of public employees who deal directly with the taxpayers, or with their children. Proof of the standards necessary to satisfy the public's expectations is of course much less objective than the proof of safety dress standards. Proof must be made in the same manner as proving an employee's conduct or lack of courtesy is offensive to the public as a whole. First-line supervisors would be well-advised to operate within the safeguards noted above and to acknowledge that this is an area in transition and inevitably involves some subjectivity. The challenge to management is to reduce that subjectivity to a minimum in order to have the regulation successfully sustained before a third party review of management's judgment.

For cases-in-point, see Addenda V−13 and V−14.

8. Procedural Concerns

By its very nature, any grievance procedure is itself exposed to challenges of application and interpretation. In other words, the meanings of terms contained within the grievance process, particularly the definition of a grievance, become in themselves major issues of grievance. The most common are the disputes over whether the particular item is within the ambit of the definition of a grievance, and whether the grievance itself was filed in a timely manner.

With respect to definition, most arbitrators will look to a strict interpretation of the master agreement language, or the agency regulation defining a grievance. If, for example, the agency has negotiated in the master agreement a definition that limits the grievance to the "express terms of this agreement," the agency will generally be sustained if it argues that a grievance brought on a subject outside the master contract contents is not grievable. However, if the definition is a so-called "blue sky" definition in which any employee dissatisfaction or objection to employee relations can be defined as a grievance, there is little hope of success for management to find that any particular subject is nongrievable. Arbitrators will look at the master agreement or rule language carefully, then consider the parol evidence reflecting what the intent of the parties were at the bargaining table. Generally, this will give the arbitrator sufficient basis upon which to render a decision of grievability.

The next most frequent procedural challenge within the grievance procedure comes with respect to the enforcement of time limits. The theory underlying delineation of time limits is the need to expediently settle grievances because failure to do so has an adverse affect on employee morale. Here again, if the agreement contains clear, unambiguous time limits for filing and processing grievances, the arbitrator will generally dismiss grievances in which the grieving party has failed to observe the deadlines. However, there is no unanimity of opinion on how strictly time limits should be enforced. Many arbitrators are inclined to sacrifice the time limit for the sake of providing an employee with "his or her day in court." Also, there are recognized exceptions to a strict construction of time limits. The most common error on the part of management in this regard is its failure to make an objection to an untimely filing at the earliest stage. As we discussed in Chapters II and IV, it is important for management in Steps I and II to state that the grievant has not filed in a timely manner if this is going to be a management position in subsequent steps. Also, there are extenuating circumstances wherein the grievance itself might not have been known until some time after the event occurred. In the latter cases, most arbitrators will rule that the time limit does not begin until the employee is aware of the circumstances giving rise to the grievance. If the act is an ongoing one by management, occurring day after day, arbitrators will generally hear the case on a continuing complaint basis.

It should be noted here that public sector supervisors have a unique problem in the procedural areas. For most agencies, the final, if not the ultimate steps in the grievance procedure include review by the agency's lay board of control, for example, a board of supervisors, or board of education. Such boards or commissions are particularly sensitive to political pressure and public input. As a consequence, most board members tend toward rendering a decision in a case based upon what they consider "fairness," or the merits of the case rather than the "inhuman" and apparently literal nitpicking by an inflexible management personnel anxious to invoke the letter rather than the spirit of grievance regulations. For this reason, it is better for the front-line supervisor in the public agency to include a substantive rationale for denying grievances along with declaring timeliness as cause for nonarbitrability. The immediate supervisor, if possible, or if necessary the mid-level manager who reviews the grievance, when faced with an employee who has failed to meet the time limits, should proceed as follows:

a. Deny the grievance on the procedural error, for example, failure to meet time limits.
b. Also prepare a substantive argument denying the grievance on meritorious grounds as well.
c. Continue to prepare management's position as though the grievance were destined for arbitration on the merits.

By adhering to the above guidelines, management runs minimal risk of finding itself with a case to prepare on short notice after having been denied the procedural argument of timeliness for grievability. In addition, many arbitrators prefer to hear the merits of the case at the same time as the procedural arguments. They will then rule on both at the time of the award.

For cases-in-point, see Addenda V−15 and V−16.

9. Recrimination Charges

Most contracts will call for some informal attempt on the part of the supervisor and the grievant to resolve the complaint prior to initiating the formal process itself. This is often characterized as a good faith attempt at resolution in a less polarized atmosphere than in later stages of the grievance process. Often such conferences do not include representation rights for the employee. The rationale for this is the need to reduce the dialogue to the lowest denominator and maintain the informality of the setting. It is hoped that such an informal atmosphere will facilitate the supervisor and employee's reaching an agreement that will resolve the complaint at the outset. The advantages and desirability of such a conference from the management stand-point have been discussed in Chapter II. These include more positive employee–employer relations, reduction of cost and inherent trauma to the formal grievance procedures, and the opportunity for management to make some concessions at a lower level to prevent losing at a more consequential stage of the grievance. Also, the employee is able to release some of his or her pent-up frustrations in a nonthreatening setting which is often both therapeutic and efficacious.

However, it should be noted there is at least one disadvantage that can grow out of this informal provision unless management is alert. Most master agreements provide a nonrecrimination clause in the grievance article. Such clauses generally specify there shall be no recriminatory action taken against an employee for invoking the grievance procedure per se. If the informal conference is or may be construed under the master contract as a step in the grievance procedures, there is the danger that a supervisor may be involved in the grievance process after the fact. For example, an informal conference that the supervisor considered to be routine problem solving may subsequently be declared by the employee to have been the informal step in the grievance procedure. Under those circumstances any action by the supervisor following the alleged informal conference may then become the subject of another grievance citing recriminatory action. Thus, it is essential the first-line supervisor determine the nature of the conference he or she is having with the employee. This is often made more difficult by the fact that employees are not always sure themselves if they have entered the grievance process. In order to preclude later accusations of recrimination, the supervisor should develop a technique for ascertaining and verifying the nature of the contact with an employee on any complaint.

When an employee asks for a conference with the supervisor to discuss a problem, the latter should be alert for key words or phrases during the conference which would signal a grievance-type complaint. If the employee uses such phrases as "grievance," "adjustment procedure," "contract violation," "contract interpretation," "arbitration," or "impasse," the supervisor should consider the meeting as an informal conference under the grievance machinery.

If the employee uses any of these terms, it would be appropriate and desirable for the supervisor to make a direct inquiry as to whether the employee considers the conference as initiating the grievance procedure. Obviously an affirmative reply settles the question in the supervisor's mind and the latter should proceed accordingly to the contract requirements.

However, even if the employee replies "no" to the question, but has been using these terms, the supervisor should assume the conference at least has potential for being declared an informal conference under the grievance machinery. In that event, the supervisor would be wise to adopt such techniques as the following:

a. Listen carefully to the statement of the problem by the employee and try to resolve it informally.

b. Immediately after the conference, whether or not a resolution has been accomplished, send a short informal note to the employee thanking him or her for coming in to discuss the concern. Carefully avoid any reference to the word "grievance" or "informal."

c. If subsequently the employee files a request for a step one conference with the supervisor, the latter should respond to the effect that no informal conference has taken place, stress the desirability of having the informal conference, and schedule one as soon as possible.

Although the above measures will not guarantee protection for the supervisor against subsequent allegations of recrimination, they will reduce the confusion in the minds of sincere employees over the nature of the "informal" conference, and reduce the possibility of entrapment of the supervisor. Such alertness on the part of the immediate supervisor should also discourage harassment techniques and efforts to intimidate by malingering employees who wish to hide behind the panoply of the grievance procedure by misusing it.

For cases-in-point, see Addenda V−17 and V−18.

10. Employee Performance Evaluations

Modern management control and fairness to employees in many situations require appropriate, accurate evaluation of the employee's performance. Evaluations may be necessary to sustain management's overall impression and treatment of the employee or to sustain future disciplinary action. The frequency, scope, content, and procedure by which the employee is advised of the results of evaluations are often codified. The volume of work and detail required sometimes causes the evaluator to skip details, leading to a grievance challenging the evaluation on procedural grounds. To avoid or at least prepare for such grievances, evaluators should check to determine whether: (1) the procedural steps required, including timeliness, were followed, (2) procedures for evaluation and conferences with the employee were held, documented in writing and preferably verified by the employee's signature. If not, the situation should be remedied immediately. A management action based upon a procedurally inadequate evaluation (especially disciplinary actions) substantially weakens management's case and may even indicate the need to "back off and start over."

Though substantive challenges by grievants to the evaluation itself are possible, management's legitimate rights to carry out its objectives gives it the right to set standards of performance subject only to reasonable, nondiscriminatory, nonarbitrary, uniform standards of evaluation. Evaluations are stronger if the standards and expectations of management have been clearly made known in advance. The more complete the documentation of incidents, of course, the stronger the evaluation will be against challenge.

For case-in-point, see Addendum V–19.

SCHOOL-BASED ISSUES

As noted earlier, there are certain issues peculiar to the schools which frequently become the subject of grievance complaints by teachers and other school employees. Classified employees of the school district generally file complaints involving those issues noted above common to other public agencies' employees, and which may be said to be pivotal on working conditions. However, teachers, by the nature of their profession, have issues organic to the teaching process and/or professional responsibility itself. The following are such school-related and teacher-oriented issues.

1. Utilization of the Preparation Period

Generally a preparation period, sometimes called the conference period, is considered to be a fringe benefit. In some decisions it has been held to be available to all teachers, even nonclassroom teachers. It has been applied to vocational teachers. However, in other cases where the contract language restricted eligibility for preparation periods to teaching employees, it was held that librarians who performed teaching assignments at the library voluntarily were not classroom teachers and hence not entitled to a daily preparation period.

Arbitrators differ as to whether a teacher may be required to stay with students during their preparation period. In at least one case it was held that the master agreement was not violated by requiring elementary classroom teachers to stay with students when they were scheduled to be in the instructional media centers; the teachers assigned to such duties were not considered as teachers within the classifications selected for preparation periods.

The preparation period has generally been understood to mean a free-from-duty time. For this reason, the ability of teachers to circulate freely within the school building and to exercise their discretion as to how to best professionally utilize their unassigned periods has been considered an employee benefit.

Most arbitrators subscribe to the concept that unless the master agreement clearly specifies otherwise, duty free implies no obligatory service can be required except in preparation of class-related activities.

Consequently, school negotiators are well-advised to incorporate into master agreement language a firm basis for the use of teacher preparation time as needed for supervision and school activities as well as emergency conditions. Absenting this specificity, arbitrators will have a tendency to interpret the preparation time as noted above (i.e., "duty free").

For cases-in-point, see Addenda V –20 and V –21.

2. Duty-Free Lunch Time

Most school districts and many state laws designate a minimum time that must be allocated to teachers for lunch during which no supervision duties can be assigned. As might be expected, most grievances issued on this subject also focus primarily on the nature of such a "free-from-duty" lunch period. However, the duration of such a lunch period may vary.

For example, in one case it was held teachers were not deprived of a duty-free lunch when their lunch period was not equal in duration to the time students were free for lunch. It has also been held that teachers could not be required to perform nonteaching duties during this period. It has been found proper for the school districts to require teachers to instruct students for a half-hour during the student lunch period even though the master contract called for no lunch duty. These teachers were required to conduct instructional education classes during this period but were then given a later duty-free lunch period.

The question of whether teachers can leave the school campus often generates grievances against administration's attempts to limit this either by number or duration. In at least one case where past practice had permitted high school teachers to leave school premises during the duty-free lunch period the arbitrator found it was an error for the district to require teachers to remain at the school. However, he also found with another group of teachers where there had been no such past practice the requirement to remain at the school was proper. Arbitrators have also found school boards could require teachers who leave the school building during their duty-free lunch period to use a sign-out sheet. It should also be noted that the right to a free lunch period has been held to extend to special education teachers in addition to classroom teachers.

For case-in-point, see Addendum V-22.

3. Teacher Evaluations: Due Process

Due process requirements in teacher evaluations parallel those discussed earlier in this chapter for public workers in general. Factors considered by arbitrators in determining whether the evaluation procedures utilized by school administrators comports with due process include:

a. Whether the teacher received a notice of the alleged inadequacies and a chance to correct his or her performance.

b. Whether the teacher has an opportunity to respond to the administrator as part of an investigatory process of the school.

c. Whether there is any evidence of discrimination.

d. Whether the requisite procedures have been followed. (For example, if a written report was required following observation of the teachers, then a mere summary is often considered inadequate.)

e. Whether the teacher received inconsistent evaluations without being informed of the relative weight of each.

f. Whether assistance and guidance were given to the teacher for improving competency.

g. Whether so-called complaints against the teacher's classroom performance are direct (e.g., pupils and visiting administrators) or just hearsay (e.g., parental).

For cases-in-point, see Addenda V-23 and V-24.

4. Assignment of Cocurricular Duties

Cocurricular duties are generally considered to be those above and beyond the basic classroom teaching assignment, some of which include supplement compensation (e.g., coaching assignments).

Generally, removal of teachers from such assignments is left to the discretion of the school board or district and tenured employees may be terminated from such extra-duty assignments at any time. As a rule such assignments are noncontractual. There is no requirement that the district reappoint employees to such extra-duty positions because they have been held in prior years. Seniority provisions have been held to be inapplicable to cocurricular assignments. The arbitrator will consider the following factors in the case of an employee who is not reappointed:

   a. That the district action is not arbitrary.
   b. That notice is given of the reasons for removal.
   c. That the district is not acting in reprisal for participation in union activity.

The contractual deadline for notification to teachers of changes in the teacher's program or schedule for the ensuing school year is not deemed applicable to extracurricular assignments performed after the regular school day. But if a school district establishes procedures and deadline requirements for application for extra-curricular assignments, they are bound by their own established procedural rules.

However, a district that takes the position that extracurricular assignments are nonnegotiable and voluntary cannot reprimand employees who refuse to participate in these activities. Even if the pay rate for extra-duty assignments is in the contract, there is no requirement that the district fill the position. The only requirement is that if and when it fills it, because it deems it necessary to do so, the district must pay the contract rate.

In at least one case the arbitrator found there was no contract violation when a principal decided to evaluate teachers on the basis of their involvement in cocurricular activities. It was only one factor upon which work performance was judged, so it was not arbitrary or capricious. In this school it was communicated to teachers that they were expected to participate in cocurricular activities. Teachers had known of the practice of considering this factor in evaluation for nine years.

It should also be noted here that the just-cause standard has been held inapplicable to a discharge for extracurricular posts such as basketball coach.

For case-in-point, see Addendum V−25.

5. Teaching Assignments and Displacement

Although the question of whether a particular subject can be assigned to a teacher to teach often arises as a grievance issue, arbitrators have been explicit in reflecting the court's position that tenure for teaching is with a school district and classification only. That is, the tenure provisions do not carry an entitlement per se to a specific subject matter, teaching assignment, or grade level. However, most agreements with teacher unions carry provisions for a test of reasonableness to be applied to reassignments and transfers. It is under the ambit of reasonableness that most grievances in terms of assignments occur. In addition, school administrators are often respondents in grievances resulting from their decisions to displace or reassign teachers due to a falling pupil enrollment.

Generally speaking, arbitrators will take into consideration a teacher's credentials, previous assignments, and seniority in determining whether or not the school principal has acted reasonably. School administrators need to be alert to the very real requirement that an objective rationality be established for such displacements or assignments. In other words, often the argument used is that another teacher junior to the grievant has been retained to teach the subject or grade level. In this context, the question of professional competency arises and unless the agreement language or district rules are specific, an argument may be mounted that the grievant is more entitled to such an assignment. This is particularly true if the assignment in question involves retention at the school site.

In such cases, a school administrator, particularly the principal, is well-advised to insure that he or she has given consideration to several factors before displacing or reassigning a teacher. Arbitrators will require such an objective analysis before supporting administration's right to make the reassignment, even though there is no tenured entitlement on a teacher's part. School principals, therefore, should look at the following as a checklist before making the necessary move to displace a teacher from a subject or school location assignment.

    a. Credentials.
    b. Seniority.
    c. Academic major and minor fields.
    d. Degrees obtained.
    e. Recentness of experience.
    f. Skills or qualifications (e.g., bilingualism).

Although this list does not contain any reference to the very sensitive and controversial areas of age, sex, or ethnic origin, contemporary litigation or school district rules may require the school administrator to consider these factors. For example, if the district is under an order to integrate staff or to otherwise balance staff ethnically or by sex, these factors would play a part in any criteria established by administrators in the process of displacement or reassignment of staff. Generally, however, arbitrators will ignore this, unless a specific statutory foundation is laid. In essence, then, school administrators need to establish a firm response to the test of reasonableness when implementing reassignments or changes of teacher assignments, particularly for tenured permanent teachers.

For cases-in-point, turn to Addenda V−26, V−27 and V−28.

WORKING CONDITION ISSUES

The treatment of common grievance issues in public employment would not be complete without a consideration of those rights disputes the roots of which lie in today's employee benefits package and/or working conditions. Such grievances are usually generated by the employer's denial of a presumed entitlement.

1. Overtime and Extra-Duty Assignments

Although not as significant an issue as it is in private employment, the question of overtime is still one of the most frequent causes of grievances in public agencies. It usually involves employees who either *want* to work overtime and feel they have been discriminated against in the assignment of premium pay, or among employees who *do not* want to work overtime when required by management and feel they are being forced to perform extra work.

The same considerations apply to extra-duty assignments, voluntary or assigned, involving additional compensation, though not at the premium pay overtime rates. Failure to pay overtime rates, especially on holidays, can of course be a violation of state and federal laws. However, unless there is a clear contract prohibition, management has discretion to require overtime of reasonable duration by employees qualified to do the work, pursuant to its right to schedule work and direct the work force. Reasonable excuses such as bona fide religious observances and employee's transportation problems must be recognized. "Equalization" is the main complaint by employees who want to work overtime, and should also be applied when employees object to being assigned. Equalization of desired overtime over a reasonable period of time avoids grievances, but is still within management's discretion unless equalization is required by the contract. In these cases, arbitrators will generally consider such questions as:

a. Why was (not) the grievant asked to work overtime?

b. When was it determined he/she would (not) be asked?

c. What are the grievant's overtime hours in comparison to those of other employees in the classification on this shift?

d. If the grievant was (not) assigned because he/she was (not) qualified to perform the overtime work, what (dis)qualified the grievant?

e. How long would it have taken to train this employee to qualify?

f. Was the grievant told the reason for the decision? Is that the real reason? Is that the only reason?

Where the contract implies equalization, private-sector cases have given monetary awards for lost overtime. Public-sector arbitrations have a tendency to follow private-sector decisions in specifying equalization by future overtime offering to the aggrieved employee.

For cases-in-point, see Addenda V–29 and V–30.

2. *Vacations*

Most authorities regard vacations as an economic benefit in the form of deferred compensation (a part of the wage package that attracts the employee to the job or induces the employee to stay) and as necessary relaxation from the job which will benefit both the employee and the employer (making the employee more efficient).[1]

As an economic benefit, grievances and arbitrations arise over the question of when the accrued vacation benefits have been earned or become "vested" (as in the case of an employee terminated before taking the vacation). Contracts, statutes, and civil service regulations are usually sufficiently clear concerning how long the

1. Elkouri and Elkouri, *How Arbitration Works*, 3d Edition, Bureau of National Affairs, Washington, D.C. pp. 681–687.

employee must work before vacation rights are vested, and how many vacation days have accrued during the time the employee has worked. Thus, these rights can be determined simply from computations based upon the employee's work record.

Disputes more often arise concerning the employee's own choice of vacation dates versus management's need to determine when the employee will take the vacation. Arbitrators sustain management's need to schedule (or limit the times the employee may choose for vacation) in order to maintain all business operations. However, they try to honor the employee's desires by inquiring whether management could have made other arrangements that would have kept the operation going (usually without requiring outside temporary help). Therefore, management should be sure it has considered all possibilities of maintaining its operations in order to give the employee the vacation dates he or she requests.

When employees in the same job request the same dates, seniority is usually the determining factor, unless the contract prescribes another method of choosing.

For case-in-point, see Addendum V−31.

3. Paid Holidays

Most contracts and agency regulations have now become quite specific concerning paid holidays, and arbitrators usually have to determine the applications of regulations or contract provisions to specific situations.

a. Entitlement.   There are usually specific provisions concerning how long the employee must have worked before becoming entitled to be paid for holidays, and whether the employee must work or be *authorized* leave the work days before and after the holiday in order to be paid for the holiday. However, if management has taken any actions that prevent or excuse the employee from qualifying for holiday pay (e.g., preventing him or her from accumulating the necessary time for entitlement or from working the day before or the day after *as compared to* similar employees), that employee should be entitled to be paid.

b. Holidays on nonwork days.   There is no inherent right to pay for holidays that fall on weekends or other regular nonwork days unless granted by the contract, regulations, or law.

c. Selection to work holidays.   Management can require certain employees to work on holidays when others do not work, in order to maintain necessary management operations. The consideration discussed under "Vacations" may apply in reverse since employees will not want to be selected to work holidays. Proper selection is also tested against the reasonableness, nondiscrimination, and "arbitrary and capricious" standards mentioned earlier. Employee excuses for not working are usually tested against the standards discussed under "Overtime." Where other employees are paid for the holiday, the one who works is entitled to premium or overtime pay unless the contract or regulations provide otherwise and provide a method of selecting which employees will work which holidays.

For cases-in-point, see Addenda V−32, V−33 and V−34.

4. Leaves of Absence

Leaves of absence, except for emergencies making it impossible for the employee to come to work, are not an inherent right, but are subject to the strict provisions of the contract, statute, or regulation which provide for such leaves.

To the extent that leave time has accrued, the employees are entitled to be paid for proper leave time. The employees' interest in complying with leave regulations is to be paid (if they have accrued benefits), to protect themselves from the possibility of termination or replacement, and to preserve their seniority and entitlement to other accruing benefits during leave. Since management's interest is in keeping the employee at work, it must define by contract or regulation both (1) the circumstances under which the employee may take leave, and (2) the length of time (regardless of the cause of the leave) before the employee can be terminated and replaced. The rights of temporary replacement employees must also be clearly defined in civil service employment.

These considerations apply equally to extended periods of leave and to the current practice of allowing employees to use portions of their accrued sick leave or vacation an hour or a day at a time.

a. "First Amendment" leave. The right to leave for religious holidays not common to all employees has been recognized by statutes and court decisions. Section 701(j) of Title VII, U.S. Code, requires reasonable accommodation (both work schedules and leave) of the employee's religious belief *unless* the employer *demonstrates* that he or she is *unable* to accommodate this without *undue* hardship to the business.

The right to leave for various union or employee organization activities is recognized, defined, and limited by various federal and state statutes, which usually provide that denial of proper union business leave is also an unfair labor practice with additional sanctions against management. These laws usually leave management free to define, or management and the labor organization free to contract what type of leave is granted and how much notice and proof can be required by management before it must grant the leave. Management's right to require prior notice and proof is otherwise limited only by the standards of "reasonableness under the circumstances" and nondiscrimination.

Arbitrators will generally be alert to any failure on management's part to insist on strict compliance with notice and proof requirements. Such a failure develops precedents or "past practices" which erode the leave regulations, and generally work to the advantage of any grievant.

b. Sick leave. Leave for job-related illnesses and injuries is defined by state statute, which usually carries additional sanctions against management for discrimination found to be due to job-related illness or injury.

Other sick leave is subject only to the regulations or contract. Where these do not specifically state the requirements for prior notice and proof, management's demand for the earliest notice and best proof of illness will generally be sustained as long as these demands are reasonable under the particular set of circumstances.

c. Maternity leave. The current decisions of arbitrators and courts in maternity leave cases are sufficiently conflicting that the situation should be resolved by contract provisions, regulations, or legal counsel. In their absence, "past practices" could limit management's right to grant or deny leave, or to terminate or not, from case to case. Management's regulations should be adopted so that they are uniform in application, require the employee to state her intentions regarding the return to work, and state that they intend to abolish past practice. Where no contract or regulation has been adopted, management should resolve the grievance by determining what its past practices have been and by asserting its discretion only within the limits of this past practice.

    d. Bereavement, personal business, personal necessity and other negotiated types of leave. There is no right to such leave, and no requirement concerning the type of leave that may be granted, in the absence of contract or state law. Contract provisions and laws vary considerably. The particular provision (including its requirements of notice and proof) should be strictly enforced.
    For case-in-point, see Addendum V−35.

5. Emergency Conditions

Management and employees both encounter situations where they cannot comply with the established procedures. The same standards should apply to both sides, whether management is calling for overtime (without proper notice or according to the established selection procedure) or denying leave due to an emergency, or whether an employee has failed to request leave or makes another demand without prior notice or usual proof. One arbitration case defined emergency as "an *unforeseen* combination of circumstances which calls for immediate action." (*Canadian Porcelain Co.*, 41 Labor Arbitration 407 [1963], quoted in Elkouri and Elkouri, *How Arbitration Works.*) The trend of arbitration decisions is to enforce the employee's obligation to come to work and carry out management's objectives unless the employee's situation is unforeseen and is of such severity that common sense would excuse the contractual obligation to work or to comply with notice and proof procedures.
    In deciding such an issue, management should also consider the impact on other employees from granting or disallowing a claimed emergency.
    Past practices and the conduct and habits of the other ordinarily conscientious workers should be looked at to determine (1) how this decision will affect or motivate other workers, and (2) whether this employee is attempting to abuse legitimate emergency exceptions (or even following a pattern of abusing emergencies).
    For case-in-point, see Addendum V−36.

6. Merit Pay and Incentives

Merit increases must be allowed by the contract or regulations, if only by providing a wage range for certain jobs. Even when they are allowed, it has been held all employees need not receive the same pay for the same work. There is no assumption that the mere passage of time makes the employee's work more valuable, unless seniority is the sole wage-increase criterion in the contract. In the absence of specific criteria, merit increases usually are solely within management's judgment. Arbitrators generally do not, and should not, substitute their judgment for that of the employee's supervisor unless the latter's action is shown to be unfair, arbitrary, or discriminatory.

"Incentive" awards are allowed if provided by civil service regulations, but are at management's discretion. Incentive or "piecework" pay (seldom applicable to public employees) must be based on, and in accordance with, the contract or regulations and preferably should be based upon the most objective standards possible.

7. Promotions

"Transfers" can be "promotions" without increase in pay if they involve better working conditions, and require greater or different skills from the previous job.

The usual issue in promotion grievances is the ability of the person promoted versus the seniority of the grievant. Seniority clauses or regulations often limit management's right to exercise its judgment regarding the abilities of the respective applicants or candidates for promotion. Where the contract or regulations give seniority preference only among competitors "of equal ability," arbitrators usually sustain management's judgment that abilities were not equal, unless bias in that decision can be shown. Before effecting a promotion, management should consider the following questions:

a. What factors qualified the junior employee and disqualified the senior employee?

b. If the junior employee's previous on-the-job experience is the basis of the award, what dates was the junior employee on the job? How did the junior employee obtain the experience?

c. Could the senior employee have received this training if he or she had been interested in it?

d. In determining the junior employee's qualifications for promotion, did management consider anything other than previous experience, such as attitude, attendance records, or ability to work well with other employees?

e. What records actually apply to the job being bid for?

f. How long did it take the junior employee to learn the job to the extent of being able to perform it as well as an average qualified employee?

g. What help and training were given to the junior employee?

h. How long would it have taken the potential grievant employee denied the promotion to become qualified for the job?

Answering these questions will show whether the most qualified employee was in fact selected and will show whether there is any basis for a claim of discrimination against the grievant. Both of these are factors critical to management's case in any grievance.

For case-in-point, see Addendum V–37.

8. Nondisciplinary Demotions and Reductions

There is a broad area of potential disputes when reductions in force, demotions, and layoffs occur.

Such grievances result from reduced requirements for a particular employee's or work unit's skills or functions, whether temporarily or permanently, and from budget or staffing reduction such as pupil enrollment decline in the schools. There is much less flexibility and management discretion in public employment than in private. Civil service rules usually are quite specific as to employee protections and privileges and their duration. Contract provisions may also be applicable. They incorporate the concept that (1) management must reduce the work force to meet budget limitations, (2) seniority is a compelling factor as to who is laid off, reassigned, or demoted, (3) "bumping" laterally or downward is based on seniority, but (4) is limited within certain organizational parameters, and (5) is limited by job classifications, job descriptions, and the employee's present abilities and former jobs. "Permanent status" of some sort as a civil servant is required before these employee privileges accrue. The timing of such reductions or layoffs may be related to the adoption of annual budgets.

To avoid a successful grievance, the civil service regulations and procedures must be carefully understood and explicitly followed before the action is taken. Teacher tenure is an example of such strict procedural requirement in the public service. The entire class of employees susceptible to demotion, layoff, and so on, and the groups susceptible to "bumping," must be considered and treated equally. Procedural requirements usually include (1) prior notice to affected employees, (2) the right to some type of impartial hearing, and (3) appellate review of the decision.

The employee's remedy for substantive or procedural errors or omissions by management is reinstatement with back pay, regardless of whether there is a budget provision for such money.

Compared to private industry, and except during any probationary periods in new jobs, demotion to a less desirable position is not a usual privilege where an employee is no longer qualified to perform his or her job. Regulations again should be carefully consulted, but job disqualifications such as loss of job-required licenses, physical or mental incapacity, or simply nonperformance of a job previously done adequately usually do not accrue seniority or bumping privileges — except where work-related injuries have caused the disqualification. Procedures for removal of the employee, under regulations regarding nonperformance in one's job, should be carefully followed. Often such procedural requirements are comparable to disciplinary terminations. Termination may indeed be the objective; the alternative of offering an available job compatible with the employee's present skill is at the discretion of management. However, long and adequate performance of prior service or eligibility for retirement or pension benefits in the near future will greatly influence an arbitrator in the employee's favor and impose on management a greater burden of proof to show the necessity of the action.

Physical or mental disability and advanced age can result in layoff, compulsory leave of absence, termination for inability to perform the job (including situations where employees are a hazard to themselves or others), or forced retirement. Before invoking any required or permissible termination for age alone, management must give detailed scrutiny to the contemporary statutes or regulations. Mandatory retirement ages are rapidly disappearing or being extended in the public sector. Pension, retirement benefits, or disability benefits will also be involved where the employee's benefits have already been vested due to length of service, or where the physical or mental disability is job-related. Alcoholism, drug addiction, and personality disorders might appropriately appear in this category or under disciplinary terminations.

Since the employee wants to continue to work, this kind of grievance usually requires the procedural safeguards of due process notice, causes, and hearing discussed earlier in this chapter. Often these result in a full court review of the decision of the employer, board, or arbitrator. Management must be able to show and to carry the burden of proving that the employee is unable to perform the job.

Objective job descriptions or requirements should be the substantiation of the physical or mental ability required in the job, and documented performance observations and medical examinations are necessary to prove that the employee cannot perform. Where (1) the disability is job-related, (2) there is a claim of discrimination (for instance, discrimination due to age, sex, or disability), or (3) provided by regulations or contract, then management may also have to show there is no other available job for which the employee is qualified or which can be secured by exercise of seniority rights.

For cases-in-point, see Addenda V−38 and V−39.

9. Other Working Conditions

Working conditions, or "terms and conditions of employment," is an omnibus term that can include almost any subject, depending upon the particular location, organization, regulations, negotiated agreement, previous negotiations, and current and past practices.

Management should be sensitive to grievances regarding working conditions because grievances frequently bring to light possible changes that will benefit both management and the employee, or situations that are decreasing the employee's efficiency. Grievances can indicate procedures that should be handled in other ways, even if the situation is not a proper subject of a formal grievance. Consultation with the employee organization (but with a clear reservation against establishing a precedent), past practice, scope of bargaining, or concession of grievability, may be appropriate or beneficial even if the subject is not within the scope of negotiations.

The master agreement grievance clause should be reviewed to determine whether it permits grievances on all subjects about which management and the employee organization could legally bargain, or if it is restrictive as to the proper subjects of a grievance. Generally, once the parties have bargained on a subject and included it in their agreement, the application of the agreement to a particular instance or fact situation becomes subject to interpretation or clarification by grievance procedure.

In private industry, the subjects discussed below traditionally have been bargainable and grievable. In public employment many of these subjects are traditionally prerogatives of management, reserved by management rights, statutes or court decisions.

A narrow definition of working conditions would include health and safety matters, rest period, preparations and clean-up time, the environment of the work station, increases in the amount of work assigned to the employee (sometimes including teacher's class size), extra assignments not constituting "overtime" work, the amount and duration of duties assigned to an employee outside of the job description or classification, emergency exceptions to rules or practices, work or "plant" rules, employees' appearance, personal phone calls, personal use of the employer's property and work areas, and problems with supervisors and peers.

By way of contrast, the Alaska Supreme Court recently interpreted the Alaska teachers' collective bargaining statute and compiled a summary of subjects which were or were not negotiable. This decision is very restrictive of management rights compared to teachers' rights in other states and compared to employees' rights in many other public agencies. It found as negotiable: union recognition, negotiation procedures, salaries, automatic cost of living increases, extracurricular and extra duty, extended contract, additional educational employment, life, health and liability insurance, automobile allowance, tuition/in-service workshops, reimbursement for physical examinations, sabbatical leave, career development, administrative leave, personal leave, sick leave, bereavement leave, leave of half-time employee, unpaid leave of absence, maternity leave, political leave, duty-free lunch, teacher preparation periods, monthly planning time, in-service days, discretional materials, personnel files, teacher transfer and retention, job openings, reduction of staff, teacher contracts, union rights and privileges (including information, release time for meetings, use of school buildings and equipment, supplies, mail facilities, "nonjeopardy," exclusive rights, professional leave, dues, deduction/continuing membership, other deductions, conformity to law, school board agenda, and preliminary draft of budget, subcontracting or "contracting out"), agreement print-up and dissemination, and duration of contract.

It found as nonnegotiable: relief from nonprofessional chores, class size, teacher load, "ombudsman," evaluation of administrators, teacher aides, paraprofessionals, "PTR formula," specialists, and calendar.

The leading authors on the subject of working conditions stress the need for the person deciding the grievance to get complete technical knowledge of the work process at issue (including the employee's job), to seek technical experts' advice (including immediate supervisors and foremen), and to prepare this technical information so that it will be understandable to an arbitrator who may eventually hear the case. This includes prompt investigation and documentation of the situation at the time of the complaint.

For cases-in-point, see Addenda V–40, V–41, V–42, and V–43.

10. Work or "Plant" Rules

Work or plant rules may cover any subject necessary to accomplish a legitimate management objective, unless management's right to make the particular rule has been preempted by statute or by the contract. Otherwise, establishing rules is a management prerogative unless the rule was or is applied in a manner which is discriminatory, arbitrary or capricious, clearly unreasonable, or in violation of the agreement or of a fundamental employee right (such as First Amendment rights).

Thus the burden is on the employee in a grievance to show that the rule, its application, or the adoption of a new rule is improper. The adoption of a new rule could, however, violate a past practice that has been affirmed or permitted by the bargaining agreement. In that case the change must be negotiated.

Rules should be published, posted, or affirmatively made known to employees (especially where their violation becomes the basis for disciplinary action).

Rules should be applied and enforced with consistency throughout the organization.

An employee is never on firm ground when violating a rule to test its validity. Arbitrators will invariably hold that the employee should have obeyed the rule and challenge it, if permissible, by the grievance procedure. This is based on the tried-and-true private sector principle of "obey now, grieve later."

For case-in-point, see Addendum V−44.

CONCLUSION

Although by no means all inclusive, the issues discussed in this chapter are those most frequently found as the basis for grievance complaints in the public sector. Although the nature of these major issues has of course varied, there is a prevailing theme that most public-sector supervisors would do well to recognize. Most arbitrators in these major issues require that management sustain its case as respondent by meeting the test of reasonableness and due process requirements. Inherent in this is the caution to public administrators that objectivity and due deliberation before acting is the key to subsequent success before the arbitrator. The specifics of due process requirements have been discussed, but as always, the paramount and critical importance of sound supervision, particularly at the first level, cannot be overemphasized.

MANAGEMENT CONSIDERATIONS
IN GRIEVANCE POLICY
(Literal Contact Approach)

1. A grievance to be defined as an actual misapplication or violation of the agency rules or master agreement only.
2. No delay in implementation of administrative decisions by the filing of a grievance — "work now, grieve later" concept.
3. Immediate initiation of grievance by employee after the alleged violation.
4. No binding arbitration. Advisory, if at all.
5. Strict adherence to filing on proper forms and documentation by all parties.
6. No limitation on informal discussion between the aggrieved employee and any member of the administration.
7. Numerous steps including conferences, within and "through channels."
8. Extended time limits for response by administration between steps.
9. Costs at least shared.
10. Actual processing to be after the working day.
11. Final decision by the Head of the Agency (e.g., County Administrator) or at the most by the policy-making body (e.g., Board of Supervisors).
12. Maximum effort to reach informal and equitable solution at the lowest possible level — first step.
13. No representation at first step of procedure.
14. Strict adherence to time limits by the grievant with forfeiture as penalty.
15. Preservation of administration prerogatives.
16. Grievance decisions not to be applicable Agency-wide.
17. No disclosure of the complaint prior to final decision — confidentiality.
18. Only individual employee grievances to be considered.
19. Any claim regarding the validity or applicability of the complaint to be resolved before proceeding to the next step.
20. Any third-party decision to be submitted in writing within thirty (30) working days following the close of the final hearing.

Case-in-Point: DISCIPLINE

Monroe County and *Civil Service Employees Association, Local 828*

The Employer properly suspended the grievant for five days for inappropriate and unprofessional behavior. The grievant, a Nurse, was charged with using overtones of cynicism and/or sarcasm in conversations with employees and patients. A number of patients and employees testified to improper remarks made by the grievant. The Union argued that the grievant had a good record and that her pattern of indiscreet language was not sufficient to justify the discipline imposed. The grievant had received verbal and written disciplines for identical conduct. The Arbitrator credited the testimony of the witnesses, finding that the grievant had made the remarks attributed to her. She held that the suspension was the proper progressive discipline to be imposed in light of the grievant's failure to respond to earlier disciplines. Therefore, the grievance was denied.

Reference: Case #829049, "Public Sector Arbitration Awards," Vol. 9, 1982, Labor Relations Press, Fort Washington, Pa.

Case-in-Point: DISCIPLINARY ACTION

Guilford, Town of, and *International Brotherhood of Police Officers, Local 343*

The Employer properly disciplined the grievant for rules violations regarding the handling of prisoners and filing of reports. The grievant, a Police Officer, was Shift Supervisor and Desk Officer on the night when the events leading to his discipline occurred. Following the arrest of two teenagers on a shoplifting charge, the only other officer on duty was occupied with one of the suspects and his father. The grievant allowed the other suspect's older brother, a custodial employee of the Police Department, to go to the prisoner's cell unaccompanied. An altercation ensued during which the prisoner's brother struck the prisoner, injuring him. The grievant's report for the shift did not contain reference to the altercation, reference to the injury, or reference to the fact that the grievant had allowed the prisoner's brother in the cell area unaccompanied. The Employer subsequently suspended the grievant for 30 days and placed him on a one-year probationary period. The Union argued that the grievant had exercised the discretion allowed him as Shift Supervisor when he allowed the prisoner's brother in the cell area unaccompanied, expecting that the brother would calm the prisoner who was very distraught. The Arbitrator found that the grievant's testimony was an admission of rules violations. He held that while the grievant was entitled to the exercise of discretion as a Shift Supervisor, it was subject to review and possible penalty. As the grievant's actions were in direct contravention of established rules and procedure, the Arbitrator denied the grievance. In a dissenting opinion, the Labor Member of the Board asserted that the penalty constituted double jeopardy and the grievant's exercise of discretion was proper.

Reference: Case #829019, "Public Sector Arbitration Awards," Vol. 9, 1982, Labor Relations Press, Fort Washington, Pa.

Case-in-Point: ABSENTEEISM

Sterling Heights, City of, and *Teamsters, Local 214*

The Employer violated the Agreement when it imposed a three-day suspension for excessive tardiness and absenteeism upon the Grievant.

The grievant had a poor disciplinary record of several warnings and suspensions. From the date of his last suspension for absenteeism, the grievant did not exceed contractual allowances for sick days or personal days. From the last discipline for tardiness, a warning, the grievant had not been tardy. The Employer suspended the grievant for three days for excessive tardiness and absenteeism following a determination that the grievant's record reflected excessive abuses.

The Union argued that the discipline was not for just cause. It asserted that the Employer never exercised its contractual right to require medical verification, and in the absence of any evidence, all evidence must have been considered as legitimate.

The Employer contended that the grievant was excessively absent and tardy, and thus was properly disciplined. It noted a pattern of Friday or Monday absences.

Arbitrator John B. Coyle found the suspension to be improper. He noted that, while the pattern of the grievant's absences could create suspicions as to whether or not the absences were meant to provide a long weekend, there had been no evidence that the grievant actually misused sick days. Further, he noted that the grievant had not exceeded his contractual allowance of sick days since his last discipline, nor had he been tardy since his previous discipline for tardiness. Thus, he held that the grievance possessed merit, and so sustained the grievance. The Employer was to reimburse the grievant for all wages lost as a result of the improper suspension.

Reference: Case #818061, "Public Sector Arbitration Awards," Vol. 8, 1981, Labor Relations Press, Fort Washington, Pa.

Case-in-Point: ABSENTEEISM

Southern California Rapid Transit District and *Brotherhood of Railway, Airline & Steamship Clerks, Freight Handlers, Express and Station Employees.*

The Employer did not violate the agreement when it discharged the grievant for excessive absenteeism.

The Union and the Employer are parties to an Agreement that provides for "justification for removal." There is a policy that provides for progressive discipline.

The grievant had been counseled for his excessive absenteeism, and had also received two suspensions totaling 15 days following further attendance problems. He was terminated after being absent on eight occasions subsequent to his last suspension.

The Employer contended that the grievant's discharge was for just cause.

The Union argued that the grievant was confused by an attendance policy change, and was unaware of the number of days he could be absent.

Arbitrator William S. Rule found that the discharge of the grievant was for just cause. He held that the grievant's argument of alleged confusion over policy was not sufficient in light of the progressive disciplines meted out to the grievant for his past attendance policy infractions. Thus, he denied the grievance.

Reference: Case # 818003, "Public Sector Arbitration Awards," Vol. 8, 1981, Labor Relations Press, Fort Washington, Pa.

Case-in-Point: ABSENTEEISM

Metropolitan Atlanta Rapid Transit Authority and *Amalgamated Transit Union, Division 732*

The Employer properly terminated the grievant for absenteeism, unsatisfactory job performance and submitting an invalid physician's statement; however, the basis of discharge was to be altered to a voluntary quit. The grievant, a Benefits Clerk, had received progressive discipline for repeated errors resulting in nonrecoverable losses to the Employer. Her final error resulted in overpayments of $11,000. Additionally, the grievant was absent 42 percent of her work days in the four-month period prior to termination. The Arbitrator found no evidence to support the charge of submitting an invalid physician's statement. He held that the grievant's absenteeism, while perhaps for valid reasons, had a negative impact upon her work, as the nature of her duties required continuous contact with employees and the grievant assumed sole responsibility for such duties, making her replacement difficult. The Arbitrator held that the Employer's proof of repeated overpayments made by the grievant established that she was incapable of performing the work assigned. While upholding the grievant's termination, the Arbitrator ordered that the basis for discharge be altered to a voluntary quit, without discussion as to his reasoning for such a holding.

Reference: Case # 829039, "Public Sector Arbitration Awards," Vol. 9, 1982, Labor Relations Press, Fort Washington, Pa.

Case-in-Point: INSUBORDINATION

Huntington Beach, City of, and *Huntington Beach Management Employees' Association*

The Arbitrator recommended that the demotion of the grievant for insubordination and improper conduct be rescinded and the grievant be placed in a position one grade below his former position. The grievant, a Division Chief-Operations, was demoted to the position of Fire Captain. The position of Battalion Chief was the only position between the two jobs previously mentioned. The Fire Chief had issued a "Special Notice" discontinuing a special program entitled "Employee Support Program" (ESP) developed by the grievant. One of the coordinators of that program was the grievant's wife. The program was discontinued due to the appearance of a "serious conflict of interest." Subsequently, the grievant issued a "Special Notice" stating that ESP was no longer in existence, but the services were still available for use at the employees' option. The grievant was demoted on a variety of charges stemming from the issuance of that "Special Notice" and revolving around alleged insubordination in "countermanding" the order of the Fire Chief to abolish the program, and the disruptive effect of his action. The Arbitrator found that the "Special Notice" clearly acknowledged that ESP was no longer in existence. He held that the grievant did not countermand the Fire Chief's order, but rather had erred in failing to perceive the possible impact of his "Special Notice" on the Fire Chief, and therefore violated certain of the specified rules. Thus, the Arbitrator recommended that the grievant be returned to the Battalion Chief level and made whole. The grievant was not returned to his previous level due to the broad discretion regarding trust and confidence which the Chief had in determining his Division Chief level staffing needs.

Reference: Case # 829034, "Public Sector Arbitration Awards," Vol. 9, 1982, Labor Relations Press, Fort Washington, Pa.

Case-in-Point: INSUBORDINATION

Greenburg, City of, and *International Brotherhood of Teamsters, Local 30*

A suspension of one week for two unreported accidents was found to be proper; however, termination for an insubordinate attitude was found to be too severe. The grievant, a Garbage Truck Driver, was suspended for one week for having one accident that he denied and later admitted, as well as for his failure to report a second accident. The grievant argued that he was not aware he struck anything in either incident. The grievant was subsequently terminated for insubordination. Details of the charge were sketchy. Apparently, the grievant was berating his supervisor to another employee. When the supervisor entered the conversation, the grievant walked away, refusing to answer questions. The Union argued that the grievant did not disobey an order, and asserted that the grievant walked away to avoid an escalation of the situation. The Arbitrator found the five-day suspension for failure to report an accident to be proper, based upon the credibility of the witnesses. He held that the penalty of discharge for insubordination was too severe. The Arbitrator found that the grievant was deserving of a one-month suspension based upon the testimony presented concerning the charge of insubordination, noting that while the grievant was abrasive, he was not insubordinate in the dictionary sense, but rather disrespectful. Therefore the grievance was granted to the extent that the grievant was to be reinstated and made whole for a period outside a five-week suspension.

Reference: Case # 829036, "Public Sector Arbitration Awards," Vol. 9, 1982, Labor Relations Press, Fort Washington, Pa.

Case-in-Point: UNION RIGHTS

Bristol School Committee and *Bristol Education Association*

A 1981 Rhode Island case involved the denial by the School Committee of a teacher Association representative request to attend a hearing before the Commissioner of Education on behalf of a teacher whose contract was not renewed. The employer argued that such Association activities were not defined in the agreement and therefore the contract provision requiring a day's work for day's pay was sufficient basis for denial. The Arbitrator found that the Superintendent had three times approved paid leaves for teachers in the past to attend such hearings, and this constituted a past practice. In view of the past practice the Arbitrator ruled for the grievant and directed the Committee to permit Association representatives to attend nonrenewal hearings to the same extent as had been previously granted.

Reference: "Arbitration in the Schools," 1981, American Arbitration Association, New York, N.Y.

Case-in-Point: UNION RIGHTS

Passaic Valley Board of Education and *Passaic Valley Education Association*

A New Jersey case involved a union president who called a meeting of teachers at 8:00 a.m. on a school day. The reason for the meeting was to discuss a teacher evaluation system instituted by the district. However, the meeting was called during school time without the advance permission of the principal. When the principal became aware of the meeting, he instructed the president to cancel it. When the president refused, he was given a reprimand. The arbitrator upheld the principal on the basis that the order was just and reasonable since the teachers had other duties to perform at 8:00 a.m.

Reference: "Arbitration in the Schools," 1978, American Arbitration Association, New York, N.Y.

Case-in-Point: INCOMPETENCY

Holly, Village of, and *Michigan Police Officers' Association*

The Employer did not violate the Agreement when it terminated the grievant for incompetency.

The Union and the Employer are parties to an Agreement that provides for just cause discipline. The Contract also establishes a probationary period of one year.

The grievant, a probationary dispatcher, was terminated for incompetence following her failure to respond to a report of a fire, and her failure to ascertain the fire's location once she was told to respond. On previous occasions, the grievant had sent police and fire units out of their jurisdiction, mishandled emergency reports, and failed to follow dispatch procedure. The grievant had received the standard training program and had also received additional training.

The Union argued that the grievant's termination was improper, as progressive discipline was not imposed. Further, it asserted a lack of sufficient training.

The Employer contended that the grievant was not living up to expectations, and that the decision to discharge her during probationary period was proper.

Arbitrator George T. Roumell, Jr., found the Employer properly discharged the grievant. He held that judgment on the Employer's decision to terminate the grievant during her probationary period was to be determined by whether or not the Employer's action was arbitrary, capricious, discriminatory. The Arbitrator found the decision was soundly based upon a determination that the grievant could not properly perform her duties despite additional training. Therefore, the grievance was denied.

Reference: Case #818132, ''Public Sector Arbitration Awards,'' Vol. 8, 1981, Labor Relations Press, Fort Washington, Pa.

Case-in-Point: OFF-DUTY MISCONDUCT

Pendleton, City of, and *International Association of Fire Fighters, Local 2296*

The Arbitrator found a 24-hour suspension for off-duty misconduct to be improper. The grievant had been arrested for driving while under the influence of intoxicants. During his arrest the grievant was uncooperative and disruptive, and injured a police officer. The Arbitrator found that the grievant's off-duty misconduct was not proper grounds for discipline in the absence of proof that the off-duty conduct injured the Employer. Citing the testimony of the police officers involved, who stated that their working relationship with the grievant was not adversely affected, the Arbitrator held that the Employer failed to prove that it was harmed by the grievant's actions. The Arbitrator also found that Civil Service Regulations forbidding drunkenness, discourteous treatment of a fellow employee, and disgraceful conduct were inapplicable to the instant case, as they were not specifically incorporated in the Agreement. The grievance was sustained, and the grievant was to be made whole for his losses.

Reference: Case #829001, "Public Sector Arbitration Awards," Vol. 9, 1982, Labor Relations Press, Fort Washington, Pa.

Case-in-Point: DRESS AND GROOMING

Cincinnati, City of, and *AFSCME Council 8, Local 223*

The Employer did not violate the Agreement by denying the right to wear beards to its Meter Enforcement Officers and Meter Enforcement Officer Inspectors.

The Union and the Employer are parties to an Agreement which provides that the Employer has the right to determine the methods and means by which operations are carried out. The Employer is required to negotiate with the Union prior to change in working conditions. The Agreement states that all provisions are subject to the laws of the United States.

The Employer issued a memorandum that forbade the growing of beards by certain personnel, giving rise to a class action grievance.

The Employer contended that it had the right to establish grooming standards for employees in the public eye. It further asserted that the institution of grooming standards did not involve wages, hours, and conditions of employment, and thus it was not required to negotiate grooming standards.

The Union argued that the Employer failed to consult or negotiate prior to the establishment of grooming standards; it noted that other employees in the agency were allowed to grow beards.

Arbitrator Daniel M. Seifer found that the grooming standards set by the Employer were reasonable. He cited the Supreme Court ruling in *Kelly* v. *Johnson,* 1976, 425 U.S. 238, 47L, Ed 2d 708, 96 S.CT 1440, in which the Court held that grooming standards could be established for county police. He held that Meter Enforcement Officers were, "for all intents and purposes" law officers, and could therefore be subjected to the grooming provisions found legal by the Court. He ruled that the methods and means of operations included the appearance of officers. Further, he opined that grooming standards were outside the realm of working conditions, and therefore did not require negotiation. Thus, the grievance was denied.

Reference: Case #818060, "Public Sector Arbitration Awards," Vol. 8, 1981, Labor Relations Press, Fort Washington, Pa.

Case-in-Point: DRESS AND GROOMING

East Hartford, Town of, and *International Brotherhood of Police Officers, Local 386*

The Employer did not violate the Agreement by prohibiting the wearing of beards by police officers.

The Union and the Employer are parties to an Agreement which provides that "hair shall be neat, clean and trimmed." It further provides that "officers shall be subject to, and must comply with, the ... appearance standards prescribed by the Chief of Police." The Agreement also stipulated that all prior rules and regulations were superseded by the current rules and regulations.

During his vacation period, the grievant grew a beard. Upon his return to duty, he was informed that the beard had to be shaved, pursuant to a policy directive issued in 1970. The grievant shaved, and filed the instant grievance.

The Union argued that the only reference to hair in the grooming standards was to cranial hair, and not facial hair. Further, it asserted that the Employer's reliance on the 1970 directive was improper, as that policy had been contractually superseded.

The Employer contended that the Chief of Police was within his authority in establishing specific grooming standards in accordance with the Agreement, regardless of whether or not the 1970 directive was superseded.

Arbitrator A.D. Joseph Emerzian found the rule prohibiting the wearing of beards to be proper. He held that the Chief of Police possessed authority to establish appropriate grooming standards, and that the grooming standard prohibiting beards had been in effect and consistently administered for approximatley 10 years. In the absence of a conflict between the prohibition of wearing beards and the language referring to hair, the Arbitrator denied the grievance.

Reference: Case #818075, "Public Sector Arbitration Awards," Vol. 8, 1981, Labor Relations Press, Fort Washington, Pa.

Case-in-Point: PROCEDURAL CONCERNS

Toledo, City of, and *Toledo Police Command Officers' Association*

The Arbitrator found the issue of parity between two similar positions in the Police and Fire Departments to be inarbitrable.

The Union and the Employer are parties to an Agreement which provides that "arbitration shall be limited to matters concerning the interpretation or application of the provisions of the Title of the Code. However, by mutual agreement, the grievance procedures set forth may be used in other matters."

The parties had negotiated a wage for the position of Police-Secretary. Subsequently, the Employer and the Union representing Fire personnel negotiated an Agreement in which a rate different from the Policy-Secretary wage was obtained for the position of Fire-Secretary. The Union grieved, asserting that a 12-year practice of parity between the two positions had been violated.

The Union argued that the issue should be heard on its merits, as parity between the positions had become binding past practice, and as such was arbitrable.

The Employer contended that the issue was improper subject matter, as parity was not mentioned in the Agreement or the Title of the Code. It noted that it was paying the negotiated wage for the position.

Arbitrator Thomas Coyne found the issue was not arbitrable. He held that since the issue of wage parity existed in neither the Agreement nor in the Title of the Code, and since the parties clearly had not agreed to submit the matter to arbitration, the grievance was not arbitrable.

Reference: Case #818172, "Public Sector Arbitration Awards," Vol. 8, 1981, Labor Relations Press, Fort Washington, Pa.

Case-in-Point: PROCEDURAL CONCERNS

Memphis and Shelby County Hospital Authority and *Tennessee Nurses' Association*

The grievances of two nurses were found to be timely. The grievants, Registered Nurses, grieved an alleged denial of experience pay benefits from 1978 and 1980, respectively. Those grievances were denied as not having been filed in time, and therefore, nonarbitrable. The agreement requires the filing of a grievance within 10 days of the time when the facts become known to the employees. The Employer's position was that it was inconceivable that the grievants were not aware of an alleged denial of pay for a two-year period. The grievants had made several inquiries concerning their pay, but were told by Employer representatives that they were receiving their proper pay. Subsequently, they inspected their personnel files, and learned they were not receiving experience pay, whereupon they filed the instant grievance. The Arbitrator found the grievances to be timely. He noted that there was no pay stub in evidence which would suggest that such pay was denoted as experience pay. He held that the Employer's assertions that the correct payment was being made indicated that the grievants had no prior knowledge of the denial until they inspected their records. Further, the Arbitrator found that since the violation was continuing in nature, the grievances were arbitrable.

Reference: Case #829026, "Public Sector Arbitration Awards," Vol. 9, 1982, Labor Relations Press, Fort Washington, Pa.

Case-in-Point: RECRIMINATION CHARGES

Escambia School Board and *Escambia Education Association*

A Florida case involved an association officer who was also a curriculum coordinator. After the grievant filed a grievance against the principal and supported a candidate for the school board against the advice of the principal, he was returned to the classroom. The principal claimed that the grievant's militancy undermined his authority since he was trying to resolve problems harmoniously.

The Board defended itself on the grounds that the association activities distracted the coordinator from his duties; however, the arbitrator found that the principal had evaluated the coordinator satisfactorily. The arbitrator held for the district.

Reference: "Arbitration in the Schools," 1981, American Arbitration Association, New York, N.Y.

Case-in-Point: RECRIMINATION CHARGES

Vermont, State of, Department of Correction and *Vermont State Employees' Association*

The Employer violated the Agreement by including materials relating to past grievances in the personnel file of the grievant.

The Union and the Employer are parties to an Agreement which provides that "every employee may institute ... grievances without threats, reprisal, or harassment by the Employer." It further provides for affirmative action to prevent future discrimination, and does not allow discrimination for membership in the Union.

The grievant, while checking his file for papers relating to a sought-after transfer, discovered a number of documents relating to prior grievances he had processed through the grievance procedure. He objected to the inclusion of those documents, giving rise to the instant dispute.

The Employer contended that such material was properly included in the grievant's personnel file, as no restriction was placed on the inclusion of such material.

The Union argued that the inclusion of such material could label the grievant as a troublemaker, and lead to future discrimination.

Arbitrator Kimberly B. Cheney found that the inclusion of such material constituted potential for discrimination in that the grievant could be perceived as "continually questioning Management's actions" and could therefore be denied a new position.

Reference: Case #818047, "Public Sector Arbitration Awards," Vol. 8, 1981, Labor Relations Press, Fort Washington, Pa.

Case-in-Point: PERFORMANCE EVALUATION

Montana, State of, Department of Social and Rehabilitation Services and *Montana Public Employees' Association*

The Employer properly discharged the grievant for unsatisfactory performance.

The Union and the Employer are parties to an Agreement which provides for just cause discharge.

The grievant, an Eligibility Technician, was slack in the proper completion of forms, kept clients waiting while socializing with co-workers, and in general performed his duties in a negligent manner. The grievant and the Employer entered into a Memorandum of Agreement tantamount to a last-chance Agreement. Further violations of this Agreement and work rules occurred during the term of the Agreement, and the grievant was discharged.

The Union argued that just cause for discharge did not exist. It cited a failure to inform the grievant of his performance and inaccuracies in the charges.

The Employer contended that the discharge was for just cause.

Arbitrator Edwin R. Render found the grievant's evaluation clearly indicated several deficient areas. He noted that the Memorandum of Agreement did not specifically state that it was a last-chance Agreement. However, he further noted that two Employer witnesses testified that it was, in fact, a last-chance Agreement, and the grievant had been warned that his job performance was unsatisfactory. He held that the grievant did not properly complete his case work, and kept clients waiting unnecessarily.

In light of the incidents, the Arbitrator found that the Employer met its burden of proof, and so denied the grievance.

Reference: Case #818024, "Public Sector Arbitration Awards," Vol. 8, 1981, Labor Relations Press, Fort Washington, Pa.

Case-in-Point: UTILIZATION OF PREPARATION PERIOD

Manatee County, School Board of, and *Manatee Education Association*

The Employer acted improperly when it directed the grievant, a teacher, to forego her preparation time to supervise a class when another teacher became ill.

The Union and the Employer are parties to an Agreement which provides that teachers are allowed one period per day for planning and preparation.

The grievant lost 35 minutes of her preparation time due to the directive, in front of a class, of the Assistant Principal to "go cover for" another teacher during her preparation period.

The Employer contended that an emergency situation arose when the teacher became ill, and therefore it had the right to require the grievant to forego her preparation time. Further, it asserted that the Assistant Principal had requested, not ordered, the grievant, and that she complied willingly.

The Union argued that the Agreement was unambiguous as to the amount of preparation time to be given each teacher. It asserted that the grievant perceived the directive as an order, and did not wish to appear insubordinate to a Supervisor in front of a full classroom.

Arbitrator Douglas C.E. Naehring found that an emergency that would infringe upon contractual rights did not exist, since situations such as the instant one had occurred repeatedly in the past and could be expected in the future. He further noted that the Employer could plan to guard against such occurrences. He held that the manner in which the Assistant Principal approached the grievant did not convey the Employer's alleged intent. Thus, he sustained the grievance, ordering that the grievant be compensated for 35 minutes at her regular rate of pay.

Reference: Case #818033, "Public Sector Arbitration Awards," Vol. 8, 1981, Labor Relations Press, Fort Washington, Pa.

Case-in-Point: UTILIZATION OF PREPARATION PERIOD

Lacey Township Board of Education and *Lacey Township Education Association*

The Employer did not violate the Agreement when it scheduled a post-observation conference and an in-grade conference during the grievant's preparation period in the same week.

The Union and the Employer are parties to an Agreement that provides for four preparation periods per week, during which teachers may not be assigned other "duty," excepting one period for in-grade conferences. Nontenured teachers are to be evaluated and assisted at least four times per year.

The grievant, a nontenured teacher, was given a post-observation conference and was involved in an in-grade conference during another of her preparation periods during the same week.

The Union argued that by assigning the duty of a post-observation conference during the same week as an in-grade conference, the Employer denied the grievant her contractual right to preparation time.

The Employer contended that it had the right to utilize the grievant's preparation time as had been done.

Arbitrator Lawrence I. Hammer found no violation of the Agreement. He opined that the evaluation of a nontenured teacher was a negotiated benefit for the teacher, as opposed to an assigned duty, and, therefore, not violative of the Agreement. Thus, the grievance was denied.

Reference: Case #818178, "Public Sector Arbitration Awards," Vol. 8, 1981, Labor Relations Press, Fort Washington, Pa.

Case-in-Point: DUTY-FREE LUNCH TIME

Rockaway Township Board of Education and *Rockaway Township Educational Association*

A New Jersey case involved a principal who assigned teachers to a rotating lunch period rather than giving all teachers a lunch break at the same time. The district argued that work and break assignments were not arbitrable since they were management rights and/or not negotiable. The arbitrator found that such time was negotiable, but that the scheduling, absent a provision in the contract, was a management right. Since the contract only required a duty-free lunch, which the teachers received, there was no violation.

Reference: "Arbitration in the Schools," 1976, American Arbitration Association, New York, N.Y.

Case-in-Point: TEACHER EVALUATIONS

School District No. 1, Denver, Colorado and *Denver Classroom Teachers' Association*

The Grievant, a beginning teacher of fourth, fifth and sixth grade, filed a grievance requesting that she be provided with a planned program, in writing, of steps to follow to improve her performance; she also requested that there be removed from her personnel file all references to teaching controversial subject matter, parent actions, and her clothing. The grievant began teaching on February 1, 1976. Her first evaluation, on May 10, resulted in a rating of "very deficient" in classroom control and management and instructional methods and techniques. Under the contractually required "Planned Program for Improvement" the Principal identified the personnel who would assist the grievant in correcting her deficiencies in selection of material, management and control, and instructional methods. The grievant was also given a lengthy narration of the events and meetings over the preceding weeks.

The Association argued that the grievant had not received the required written improvement plan with which she could improve her performance in the areas where she was deemed deficient.

The District argued that the assignment of personnel to assist the grievant met the requirement.

The Arbitrator concluded that: the plan for improvement had been required by the contract since 1971; the Principal was competent and sincerely wanted to help the grievant; the assistants showed great expertise; there had been many good suggestions for improvement made to the grievant during classroom visits; the "Planned Program" furnished to the grievant delineated the areas in which specified helpers would work with the grievant but did not give the grievant a planned program that she could follow herself to improve her performance; specific suggestions had been made orally but not in writing; the contractually required Program of Improvement was not met by the Principal or his assistants; the Arbitrator had no authority to order the deletion of the paragraphs in the personnel file regarding the complaint about controversial subject matter and the grievant's attire; the grievant's only remedy was to file an answer to those paragraphs. The Arbitrator ruled that the grievant was entitled to a written planned program of steps to follow to help her improve her teaching. He denied the request that certain references in the personnel file be deleted.

Reference: Case #77421, "Public Sector Arbitration Awards," Vol. 4, 1977, Labor Relations Press, Fort Washington, Pa.

Case-in-Point: TEACHER EVALUATION

Palm Beach County School Board and *Palm Beach County Classroom Teachers'
Association*

The Employer followed the evaluation procedures properly in the case of the
grievant. The grievant, a Teacher, was to receive two evaluations in her first year.
Her first evaluation listed several deficiencies. She was informed at her second
evaluation that insufficient information upon which to base an evaluation existed,
due to her absence during a maternity leave. Following her evaluation in the second
year, the grievant was informed that she would not have her Contract renewed. The
Union argued that the nonrenewal was improper. It raised three major points: first,
that she was renewed after her first year; second, that she was not notified in writing
that deficiencies existed which could lead to nonrenewal; and third, that there was
insufficient assistance provided to overcome the deficiencies of the grievant. The
Arbitrator found that while the grievant was renewed after her first year, the renewal
was recommended due to insufficient time to evaluate the grievant properly because
of her leave of absence; and that this problem was specifically discussed with her.
He held that while the grievant was not notified in writing of all her deficiencies, the
Employer substantively met that requirement by verbal communications. Noted was
the fact that the deficiencies listed in the grievant's first written evaluation were not
corrected. Finally, the Arbitrator held that while more assistance was possible, there
was no showing that it would have altered the situation, and the assistance offered
was sufficient. Thus, the grievance was denied.

Reference: Case #829068, "Public Sector Arbitration Awards," Vol. 9, 1982, Labor
Relations Press, Fort Washington, Pa.

Case-in-Point: ASSIGNMENT OF COCURRICULAR DUTIES

Jefferson County Board of Education and *Jefferson County Teachers' Association*

The Employer did not violate the Agreement when it required Special Education Teachers to audit the official records of their students. Pursuant to a directive from the State Bureau of Education ordering it to comply with state law concerning students' folders, the Employer directed Special Education Teachers to inventory and update student folders. The Union grieved, contending that such duties could not be so assigned. Public law provided that "Each teacher or other persons...shall make reports and inventories..." The Arbitrator found the assignment of the disputed duties to be proper. He held that the applicable state law allowed such an assignment, and noted that to rule otherwise would usurp the authority of the Employer. He opined that his decision was compatible with contractual language, which recognized that noninstructional duties existed for the teachers. Thus, the grievance was denied.

Reference: Case #829057, "Public Sector Arbitration Awards," Vol. 9, 1982, Labor Relations Press, Fort Washington, Pa.

Case-in-Point: TEACHING ASSIGNMENTS OR DISPLACEMENTS

Denver School District Number 1 and *Denver Classroom Teachers' Association*

In an Advisory Opinion and Award, the Arbitrator found the Employer had acted properly in transferring the grievant, a Physical Education Instructor, due to a reduction in force, notwithstanding the fact that the grievant had a higher relative qualification score than a nonreduced employee.

The Union and the Employer are parties to an Agreement that provides the teachers may not be discriminated against on the basis of sex. The parties had agreed on a numerical relative qualification score to determine which employee would be transferred, the lowest score employee being the one to transfer.

Due to the opening of a new school, a reduction in force was necessitated. In transferring physical education instructors, the Employer chose to retain one male and one female teacher, giving rise to the instant dispute. The parties agreed that the grievant had a higher score than did the female instructor.

The Employer contended that it would be improper to retain the grievant, a male, as an instructor in physical education for females.

The Union argued that the grievant was being discriminated against on the basis of sex. It asserted that a female teacher or female aide could be used for supervision in the locker room, under the supervision and direction of the grievant.

Arbitrator Charles F. Ipavec found that the instructor must be available to supervise and instruct the students during the entire class period. He held that the grievant was not competent, by virtue of his sex, to fill the assignment duties of a physical education teacher for female students. He questioned the ability of the Employer to assign female teachers to locker room supervision without infringing upon their contractual rights to preparation time and free periods. Finding no obligation on the part of the Employer to schedule two teachers simultaneously to perform the duties of one position, the Arbitrator recommended that the grievance should be denied.

Reference: Case #818046, "Public Sector Arbitration Awards," Vol. 8, 1981, Labor Relations Press, Fort Washington, Pa.

Case-in-Point: TEACHER DISPLACEMENT

Los Angeles County Board of Education and *Los Angeles County Education Association*

The Employer did not violate the Agreement when it did not award the grievant's transfer request.

The Union and the Employer are parties to an Agreement which provides that transfer requests are to be considered in priority of (a) certification and other qualifications, (b) the convenience and desire of the unit member, and (c) seniority. The Employer is directed to exercise the right to utilize staff in a "rational and lawful manner."

The grievant, a Teacher, requested a transfer to another school. That transfer request was denied. The grievant was senior to three of the selectees.

The Union argued that the grievant's "other qualifications" were equal to those of the selectees, and that her seniority should govern.

The Employer contended that the "other qualifications" considered (recency of experience, type of experience, educational background, training, past performance, and sex and ethnic balances) were properly applied, and the grievant was not deemed to be as qualified as the selectees. It asserted that, following mandated priority, the grievant's seniority did not come into play.

Arbitrator Joseph F. Gentile found no violation of the Agreement. He held that the considerations were valid, and were rational and lawful within the meaning of the Agreement. Finding the other qualifications to have been properly considered and applied, the Arbitrator recommended that the grievance be denied.

Reference: Case #818169, "Public Sector Arbitration Awards," Vol. 8, 1981, Labor Relations Press, Fort Washington, Pa.

Case-in-Point: TEACHER DISPLACEMENT

Cincinnati Board of Education and *Cincinnati Federation of Teachers*

The Employer did not violate the Agreement when it assigned the grievant to a high school against his preference.

The Union and the Employer are parties to an Agreement which provides that when surplus teachers are transferred, they may fill out a preference form. If a choice between two teachers must be made, and their "training, experience, and individual qualification" are substantially equal, seniority is controlling.

The grievant was surplus due to decreased enrollment. He was assigned to a school where he would not be required to coach, although that school was not his verbal preference. He had not completed a preference form. Two junior teachers who were willing to coach were assigned to the school the grievant preferred.

The Union argued that the grievant was not afforded his seniority rights because the Employer improperly considered the grievant's refusal to accept a coaching position as an "individual qualification."

The Employer contended that it had historically considered willingness to accept extracurricular assignments as an aspect of "individual qualification," and that this position was made clear to the Union in negotiations. Further, it asserted that the assignment was proper because the grievant did not complete a preference form.

Arbitrator George W. Van Pelt found no violation of the Agreement. He held that by failing to file a preference form, the grievant could not claim that his preference was not honored. Further, the Arbitrator held that past practice supported the Employer position that willingness to accept extracurricular assignments was encompassed in the term "individual qualifications," and that the Union had attempted and failed to change the individual qualification language. The Arbitrator, therefore, recommended that the grievance be denied.

Reference: Case #818179, "Public Sector Arbitration Awards," Vol. 8, 1981, Labor Relations Press, Fort Washington, Pa.

Case-in-Point: OVERTIME

Akron, City of, and *Akron Firefighters' Association*

The Employer failed to pay the grievant or provide the equivalent compensatory time off for hours worked in excess of 40 per week, thereby violating the Agreement.

The Union and the Employer are parties to an Agreement which provides that overtime shall be paid for hours in excess of the workweek, at either one and one-half times the regular rate, or by granting compensatory time off at one and one-half times the hours worked as overtime. Employees assigned to the Fire Prevention Bureau were to work a 40-hour week, while others were assigned to a 52-hour workweek.

The grievant had been working at Fire Station Number 7 unit. He was transferred to the Fire Prevention Bureau, the transfer list being dated June 8. In his old position, he had worked a 52-hour week; in the new position, he worked a 40-hour week. On June 9, the grievant went to Fire Station Number 7 to pick up his dress uniform before reporting to the Fire Prevention Bureau. He was told that the station was short of officers, and that he should remain there for eight hours. Subsequently, he was told to stay for the entire 24-hour shift. He did, and was given 16 hours of compensatory time equivalent to two Fire Prevention Bureau shifts. A grievance was filed, alleging that the grievant was entitled to an additional eight hours of compensatory time off. The grievant had logged in as a substitute from the Fire Prevention Bureau.

The Union argued that the grievant had been transferred effective as of June 8, and that the grievant was assigned a 40-hour week, thereby becoming eligible for overtime compensation.

The Employer contended that the grievant had been working a 52-hour week at the time, and that his transfer was not effective when he was assigned the 24-hour duty.

Arbitrator Roland Strasshofer, Jr. found the Employer was liable for the additional overtime compensation. He held that the effective date of transfer was June 8, based on the date of the transfer list and the log entry. From that finding of fact, the Arbitrator found the grievant had worked in excess of the 40-hour week provided for in his new job classification, and had been improperly compensated. Thus, the grievance was sustained, and the Employer was ordered to compensate the grievant for an additional eight hours.

Reference: Case #818065, "Public Sector Arbitration Awards," Vol. 8, 1981, Labor Relations Press, Fort Washington, Pa.

Case-in-Point: OVERTIME

Los Angeles County Fire Department and *Service Employees International Union Local 660*

The Employer violated a Memorandum of Understanding in failing to pay overtime to Fire Control Aides when they were required to spend a night in a camp, unless they were required to fight a fire.

The Union and the Employer are parties to an Agreement that provides, in a Memorandum of Understanding (MOU), that overtime shall be paid for hours in excess of 40 per week. Overtime is defined in the Fair Labor Standards Act (FLSA) by reference, requiring time spent in the performance of work ordered and approved by a department head in excess of the regular workweek.

Fire Aides were assigned to a 40-hour week. One or two nights per week, they were required to remain in camp overnight, in excess of their normal workweek. They were given food and lodging, but received no pay. At the time of their hire, Aides were told of that practice, which had been in effect prior to the MOU, and almost two years after the MOU was negotiated. The practice had not been previously challenged.

The Union argued that the Aides were working in excess of 40 hours per week when they were assigned to overnight camp duty, and therefore were entitled to overtime pay.

The Employer contended that the Aides were not working when at the camp overnight, and were paid overtime when they were required to work. It asserted that the issue of "restricted freedom" was not applicable to public employees. Further, it asserted that a past practice existed whereby food and lodging served as a quid pro quo for camp standby.

Reference: Case #818062, "Public Sector Arbitration Awards," Vol. 8, 1981, Labor Relations Press, Fort Washington, Pa.

Case-in-Point: VACATIONS

Birmingham–Jefferson County Transit Authority and *Amalgamated Transit Union, Division 725*

The Employer improperly denied prorated vacation pay for the portion of the year worked prior to layoff.

The Union and the Employer are parties to an Agreement that provides for vacation entitlement. Section three of the disputed provision states that employees will not be eligible for vacation until "completion of not less than twelve months of continuous and active service." Section nine of the same provision allows "furloughed" employees to receive a prorated vacation.

The ten grievants herein were furloughed. They requested and were denied prorated vacation pay for the time they worked. None of the grievants had completed one full year of service.

The Union argued that pursuant to Section nine, the grievants were entitled to vacation pay, prorated to the period of their employment.

The Employer contended that pursuant to Section three, the grievants were not entitled to any vacation benefits, as they had not been employed for one full year.

Arbitrator James J. Odom, Jr., found Section three to be ambiguous. He held that Section nine was controlling, as Section three set up the general vacation procedure, and Section nine dealt with a specific situation (i.e., vacation pay for employees placed on layoff status). Finding that Section nine best expressed the parties' intent, the Arbitrator granted the grievance. The Employer was directed to pay the proper vacation allowance to each of the grievants.

Reference: Case #818122, "Public Sector Arbitration Awards," Vol. 8, 1981, Labor Relations Press, Fort Washington, Pa.

Case-in-Point: PAID HOLIDAYS

Montclair Board of Education and *Montclair Education Association*

The Employer did not violate the Agreement when it declined to allow personal days with pay to be taken on the second day of Rosh Hashanah.

The Union and the Employer are parties to an Agreement which provides that the first day of Rosh Hashanah is a paid holiday.

New language in the Agreement disallowed the taking of a personal day following a holiday. The number of holidays had been reduced in exchange for a greater number of personal days. The prohibition against the use of a personal day following a holiday had in the past been invoked to apply to All Saints' Day, but was found to be improper due to a state statute not applicable in the present case.

The Union argued that the instant case was similar to the All Saints' Day situation, and amounted to religious discrimination. It denied any intent to negotiate away the second day of Rosh Hashanah as a paid holiday.

The Employer contended that its actions were nondiscriminatory. It noted that the All Saints' Day situation was not analogous to the instant case, since the former situation was governed by a state statute that was inapplicable to the present situation.

Arbitrator Ruth Russell Gray found the Employer had not violated the Agreement. She held that the Union should have been aware that the exclusions to personal days would apply to the second day of Rosh Hashanah as it had been applied to All Saints' Day. No evidence of discrimination was found, since there was no showing that the provisions of the Agreement were not uniformly applied to all employees. Noted was the fact that the grievants who wished to have the second day off received the day off, but without pay. The grievance was denied.

Reference: Case #818161, "Public Sector Arbitration Awards," Vol. 8, 1981, Labor Relations Press, Fort Washington, Pa.

Case-in-Point: PAID HOLIDAYS

Springfield, City of, Utilities and *Amalgamated Transit Union, Division 691*

The Employer violated the Agreement in the manner in which it calculated holiday pay when the bus system was shutdown for July fourth.

The Agreement called for the payment of overtime in addition to the holiday rate for employees who work on days celebrated as holidays. It further provided that if a holiday fell on a Saturday, as in the instant case, it would be observed on the Friday immediately preceding the holiday.

Group B, who would have worked on Saturday had the transportation system not been shutdown, received pay for 32 hours at the straight time rate and eight hours' pay at the holiday rate. Group A received pay for 40 hours at the straight time rate, eight hours of overtime, and eight hours at the holiday rate, since they observed the holiday on Friday, and did not normally work Saturdays.

The employer contended that the employees in Group B were not eligible for holiday pay, since they would have worked on Saturday had the system not been shutdown; therefore, they would have observed the holiday on Saturday rather than Friday. Noting that the Contract language was obscure, the Arbitrator found no reason why the Saturday holiday should not be observed on Friday by all employees, rather than just those who would not normally work on Saturdays. Therefore, he sustained the grievance and ordered that all Bus Drivers who worked on Friday, July 3, 1981 receive pay at the overtime rate for working on a holiday, in addition to holiday pay.

Reference: Case #829043, "Public Sector Arbitration Awards," Vol. 9, 1982, Labor Relations Press, Fort Washington, Pa.

Case-in-Point: HOLIDAY PAY

Washington State Ferry System and *Inland Boatmen's Union of the Pacific*

The Employer did not violate the Agreement when it paid eight hours of holiday pay to employees whose normal shift exceeded eight hours, when the holiday was not worked. The Employer was not entitled to recoupment of overpayments made in error.

The employees worked shifts of varying hours which totaled 80 hours every two weeks. Employees not working a holiday were entitled to "one extra day's pay." The Agreement stated that "for all practical purposes, eight consecutive hours shall constitute one work day."

A nonmanagement payroll agent paid employees holiday pay in accordance with the length of their particular shift. Following the discovery of the payroll agent's method of payment for holidays not worked, the Employer began paying only eight hours of holiday pay for time not worked, giving rise to the instant grievance.

The Union contended that a practice had been established whereby holiday pay for a holiday not worked was to equal the employees' normal daily working hours. The Employer argued that the language was clear, and that an error by the payroll agent, who did not have the authority to make such a decision, did not create a practice.

The Arbitrator found that, absent a specific provision concerning day length on nonworked holidays, the "for all practical purposes" language was controlling. She opined that the error by the payroll agent could not be considered a practice, as his decision was made without authorization and the Employer did not have knowledge of the alleged practice. Therefore, she held that the Employer properly determined that eight hours of pay for holidays not worked was correct. However, she found the Employer was not entitled to recoup monies paid in error, since its lack of training and policing of its payroll agent caused the overpayment.

Reference: Case #829050, "Public Sector Arbitration Awards," Vol. 9, 1982, Labor Relations Press, Fort Washington, Pa.

Case-in-Point: LEAVES OF ABSENCE

Broward County School Board and *Federation of Public Employees*

The Employer acted within its authority to rescind personal leave for 128 employees, although it improperly denied such leave to two employees who had given sufficient notice of intent to take personal leave.

The Union and the Employer are parties to an Agreement which provides that personal leave is available to employees "...as provided other School Board employees, on the terms and conditions as directed by the School Board..."

Two employees had requested personal leave in honor of Martin Luther King's birthday. Three days prior to that date, 128 transportation employees signed notices of intent to take personal leave, and on the day in question, a total of 149 transportation and food service employees were absent for personal reasons, and an additional 84 employees called in sick.

The Union argued that all absent employees were entitled to payment for the day in question.

The Employer contended that it had the right to rescind the personal leaves.

Arbitrator Paul W. Hardy found the evidence clearly demonstrated a combined effort to engage in a work stoppage. Opining that public interest and the parties' intent demanded that the Agreement not be construed to allow an illegal work stoppage, the Arbitrator found the Board properly rescinded personal leave on the day in question, excepting the two requests that were submitted on time. No mention of those who called in sick was made by the Arbitrator.

Reference: Case #818166, "Public Sector Arbitration Awards," Vol. 8, 1981, Labor Relations Press, Fort Washington, Pa.

Case-in-Point: EMERGENCY CONDITIONS

Tinker Air Force Base and *American Federation of Government Employees, Local 916*

The Employer violated Air Force Regulations when it posted the grievant AWOL without considering his leave request.

Air Force Regulations provide that "Arbitrary decisions to deny leave are not made."

At issue was whether or not a violation of Air Force Regulations had occurred. The grievant had previously discussed with his supervisor a personal problem that might cause an absence. On the day giving rise to the instant grievance, such a problem arose, requiring the grievant to respond to an emergency in his daughter's household. The grievant did not call prior to the start of his shift, but called as soon as possible. The supervisor informed him that he was AWOL, and refused to discuss the grievant's leave request for that day.

The Union argued that the action of the supervisor was arbitrary, and therefore improper.

The Employer contended that since the grievant did not call in until after the start of the workday, he had placed himself in the position of being AWOL.

Arbitrator Harold H. Leeper found the Employer's decision was arbitrary, in violation of Air Force Regulations. He cited the refusal of the supervisor to discuss the reason behind the grievant's request as the basis for his decision. In sustaining the grievance, he ordered that the Employer delete the AWOL charge from the grievant's record, charging the time to annual leave instead, and to pay the grievant accordingly.

Reference: Case #818056, "Public Sector Arbitration Awards," Vol. 8, 1981, Labor Relations Press, Fort Washington, Pa.

Case-in-Point: PROMOTIONS

Key West, City of, Utility Board, and *International Brotherhood of Electrical Workers, Local 1990*

The Employer did not violate the Agreement when it selected a junior employee for promotion to Maintenance Foreman. The job had been posted for bid and none of the applicants met the year-of-service requirement. The Employer selected a junior applicant, pursuant to its "right to fill the job from any available source" should the bidders fail to meet qualifications. It cited the selectee's supervisory experience in a prior position as the basis for its decision. The grievants, both senior applicants for the promotion, were found to be unqualified due to a lack of responsibility, as evidenced by several prior warnings in one case and a lack of supervisory experience in the other case. The Arbitrator found the selection of the junior employee to be proper. He found that the selection was properly based upon a fair review of qualifications and within the Employer's right to promote from "any available source" as no bidder met the service requirements. The grievance was denied.

Reference: Case #829045, "Public Sector Arbitration Awards," Vol. 9, 1982, Labor Relations Press, Fort Washington, Pa.

Case-in-Point: DEMOTIONS

Alaska, State of, and *Alaska Public Employees' Association*

The Employer violated the Agreement when it made retroactive a two-year freeze period on wages for employees voluntarily downgraded.

The Union and the Employer are parties to an Agreement which provides that downgraded employees' wages are to be frozen at their old rate until promotion to a position in which the salary range encompasses the frozen salary. Newly negotiated language, in an Agreement with an effective date of January 1, 1980, imposed a two-year maximum time period for frozen wages, in the event that the employees' wage at the downgraded position did not encompass the frozen salary before that time period.

The grievant, an Administrative Assistant who was downgraded to a Clerk position voluntarily, received the frozen wage. Subsequent to the newly negotiated language mentioned above, the Employer "unfroze" her salary and reduced the grievant to the lower wage.

The Employer contended its action was proper in accordance with the newly negotiated language. It asserted that the two-year period began from the date of action.

The Union argued that the two-year period began at the effective date of the Agreement that contained the new language.

Arbitrator Paul D. Jackson found no intent was expressed to make the disputed language retroactive to the date of action rather than the effective date of the Agreement. He noted several instances in which other provisions of the Agreement specifically "grandfathered" those provisions. Absent the specific designation of a unique retroactive date for the instant provision, the Arbitrator sustained the grievance, ordering that January 1, 1980 was to be used as the commencement date. The grievant and any other employee adversely affected by the Employer's interpretation of the disputed provision were to be made whole.

Reference: Case #818031, "Public Sector Arbitration Awards," Vol. 8, 1981, Labor Relations Press, Fort Washington, Pa.

Case-in-Point: DEMOTIONS

Waterville, City of, and *International Brotherhood of Teamsters, Local 48*

The Employer did not violate the Agreement when it reduced the grievant in rank from Sergeant to Patrolman, due to budgetary constraints. The Union argued that language governing layoffs "in the event it becomes necessary" required the Employer to justify the necessity of its actions. It asserted that no additional savings were realized due to overtime costs of the remaining Sergeants, and thus the grievant's reduction in rank was improper. The Arbitrator found that the phrase relied upon by the Union did not require the Employer to justify economic need, even assuming that the Employer should have perceived that add-on costs would neutralize projected savings. Absent any finding of arbitrary or capricious action, the Arbitrator denied the grievance.

Reference: Case #829038, "Public Sector Arbitration Awards," Vol. 9, 1982, Labor Relations Press, Fort Washington, Pa.

Case-in-Point: OTHER WORKING CONDITIONS

Fairfield Board of Education and *Ohio Association of Public School Employees, Chapters 205 and 568*

The Employer did not violate the Agreement when it required bus drivers to select a package of bus and route assignments in accordance with their seniority, rather than select the bus they wanted, and then the routes they desired. The grievance was found to be arbitrable.

The Union and the Employer are parties to an Agreement which provides that "all policies and procedures in effect at the date of the signing of the Agreement for transportation employees shall remain in effect until June 30, 1980." The Agreement further provides the parties' intent to encourage as informal an atmosphere as possible in the resolution of grievances. Grievances are to be initiated within 20 days of the date of occurrence. Arbitration is to be advisory.

Bus drivers had previously been allowed to select both the particular buses they wanted, and the route(s) they desired, in accordance with seniority, although those options were not contractually provided. The Employer instituted a new policy, effective July 1, 1980, whereby buses would be assigned particular routes, so that newer, more dependable buses would be used on rural routes. Drivers could select the bus they desired, but in choosing the bus, they were automatically assigned the route to which that bus was assigned. The drivers made their choices, as to buses and bus routes, under written protest at the time that they made their selections. A formal grievance was filed 23 days after the route assignments were made.

The Union argued that the new policy violated past practice, and a contractual provision relating to position or job vacancies.

The Employer contended that the grievance was not timely, by virtue of the filing of the grievance 23 days after the route assignments were made. On the merits, the Employer argued that no contractual violation occurred.

Arbitrator Langdon D. Bell held that the expressed intent of the parties was to promote an informal atmosphere. Further, he noted the fact that grievances did not have to take any specific form. The grievance was found to be timely, as the drivers had protested the assignments at the time the assignments were chosen. On the merits, the Arbitrator found that the contractual language cited by the Union did not fall within the context of the issue. He opined that it was improper to apply the principle of past practice for the purpose of bestowing rights and obligations not otherwise contractually conferred. Finally, the Arbitrator found that the express language of the Agreement terminated all policies and procedures as of a date prior to the implementation of the newly formulated procedure for the assignment of routes and buses. Thus, the grievance was denied.

Reference: Case #818078, "Public Sector Arbitration Awards," Vol. 8, 1981, Labor Relations Press, Fort Washington, Pa.

Case-in-Point: OTHER WORKING CONDITIONS

Stillwater, City of, and *International Association of Fire Fighters, Local 2095*

In deciding three grievances, the Arbitrator found the Employer acted improperly in discontinuing a practice whereby a firefighter would take time prior to the lunch period to prepare a meal for other on-duty employees; that firefighters were entitled to a test to determine the appropriateness of beards; and that the Employer properly issued restrictions concerning the scheduling of vacations.

The Union and the Employer are parties to an Agreement which provides that all rights, privileges, and working conditions would remain in effect, unchanged and unaffected. Statutes of the State of Oklahoma also provided for a continuation of practices except as modified by the terms of any Agreement. The Employer had a policy including a test to determine the appropriateness of facial hair. The Agreement also contained a Management Rights clause allowing the Employer to determine employees' schedules.

In the first grievance, the Fire Chief issued instructions that staff members would be barred from the kitchen or lounge areas except at specific times, including a 10:00 a.m. break, a 3:00 p.m. break, and a 12:00 noon to 1:00 p.m. lunch break. A practice had been to allow one or more employees to plan a menu, shop for the necessary food and prepare the daily lunch for the employees on duty. In the second grievance, a firefighter reported for work with a beard, and was instructed to shave before working. He did, and filed the instant grievance as a result of that directive. In the final grievance, the Fire Chief revised the policy regarding the scheduling of vacations as follows: (1) requiring the completion of a vacation request slip; (2) allowing three men to be on vacation providing requests were submitted two working shifts in advance; and (3) providing that short-term vacations, 24 hours or less, would be granted at the discretion of the Assistant Chief, with guidelines that: (a) such leave would not interfere with working schedules, operations, or training schedules; (b) less than two scheduled employees were off; and (c) that such would not require the call-in of employees on an overtime basis. The Assistant Chiefs were also directed to record the number of short-term vacation days taken during the workweek, and to limit such days to five per year.

The Union argued that the Employer violated the prevailing practice provision and Oklahoma Statute by unilaterally forbidding meal preparation and by unilaterally establishing the vacation policy. It asserted that the Employer violated the Agreement when it mandated that the grievant in the second issue shave his beard without first conducting a test to determine whether or not a mask would seal over the grievant's beard.

The Employer contended that it had the right to schedule employees; hence, both the vacation policy and the lunch policy were proper. Concerning the second grievance, the Employer argued that it had been reliably proven that the type of mask used could not be properly sealed on a bearded man. It noted that subsequent to the filing of the grievance, the policy concerning beards was modified due to the potential safety hazards.

Arbitrator Preston J. Moore found, with respect to the first grievance, that the Employer improperly denied time to prepare lunch to unit members. He held that the Employer failed to show that allowing employees to cook a noon meal interfered with the mission or efficiency of the Fire Department. He noted that the directive had been amended to allow one employee off duty at 10:00 a.m. to prepare the meal, prior to the arbitration hearing. In the absence of evidence that such time was not sufficient, the Arbitrator found such a policy to be reasonable, but noted that if more time was necessary when more employees were on duty, extra time should be granted. In sustaining the grievance the Arbitrator ordered that an additional 30 minutes should be allowed, if needed, when extra employees were on duty. In regard to the second grievance, the Arbitrator held that the Employer violated the Agreement in not providing the test used for determining the appropriateness of facial hair. He noted that the grievant suffered no loss as a result of the Employer's actions, and thus ordered no compensation for the grievant. In the final grievance, Arbitrator Moore held that the Employer would not be in violation of the Agreement by enforcing the instructions issued concerning vacation time. He cited the necessity of the Employer to schedule vacations to meet the operating requirements of the Fire Department, and the fact that past practice supported such a right. Noting that a modification of the practice for any reason except the operating needs of the City would be a change in the practice and, thus, a violation of the Prevailing Rights clause, the Arbitrator denied the grievance.

Reference: Case #818072, "Public Sector Arbitration Awards," Vol. 8, 1981, Labor Relations Press, Fort Washington, Pa.

Case-in-Point: OTHER WORKING CONDITIONS

UCLA Hospital and Clinics, Center for Health Sciences, and *Service Employees' International Union*

The Employer did not violate the Agreement when it allowed one half-hour lunch break and three 15-minute breaks during a 12-hour shift.

The Union and the Employer are parties to a Staff Personnel Policy which provides ''Rest periods not to exceed 15 minutes, once during each work period of three hours or more, may be granted to employees.''

A grievance was filed protesting the implementation at the San Francisco facility of the half-hour lunch and three 15-minute break periods, asserting that there should be four 15-minute breaks in addition to the lunch period. In a ''meet and confer'' session, the Employer formally acknowledged the one-hour-and-fifteen-minute total break period. Hearsay testimony indicated that other branches of the University hospitals allowed a half-hour lunch and four 15-minute breaks.

The Union argued that the policy was not uniformly applied, and that practice allowed a total of one-and-one-half hours of break time.

The Employer contended that no past practice existed, and that the granting of any break period was permissive under the disputed language.

Arbitrator Joseph F. Gentile found the break periods allowed by the Employer to be proper. He noted that the dispute turned on whether there could be a disparate application of the system-wide policy, if in fact there was a disparate application. He noted the hearsay nature of the testimony concerning the alleged practice at the other facility. He opined that there was no doubt that, as of the ''meet and confer'' session, the policy at the instant facility was formally acknowledged to allow one-and-one-half hours of lunches and breaks during a twelve-hour shift. Further, he found that the policy was sufficiently broad in scope to allow particularized adaptation at each individual facility. Thus, he held that the disparity was not unreasonable given the scope of the disputed language. Therefore, the grievance was denied.

Reference: Case #818144, ''Public Sector Arbitration Awards,'' Vol. 8, 1981, Labor Relations Press, Fort Washington, Pa.

Case-in-Point: OTHER WORKING CONDITIONS

St. Clair Shores, City of, and *St. Clair Shores Police Officers' Association*

The Employer violated the Agreement when it unilaterally issued a memorandum that disallowed a practice of overdrawing accumulated time, sick leave, vacation time, or personal-leave time.

The Union and the Employer are parties to an Agreement that provides for the maintenance of conditions in effect at the time of the signing of the Agreement. The Agreement does not prohibit the "borrowing" of any unearned leave time.

From the first negotiated agreement between the parties, police officers had been allowed to "borrow" unearned time, such as sick leave, when their leave was exhausted. This borrowing continued, and the officers were allowed to later make up the time they had "overdrawn" without limitation, until the issuance of a memorandum by the Police Chief in 1974, which required a repayment of overdrawn sick time twice yearly. Repayment could be made by any one, or combination of, the following: (1) accumulated time; (2) vacation time, or (3) deduction from pay at the applicable rate. In 1980, a new memorandum was issued, at the direction of the City Manager, which disallowed the use of any overdrawn time.

The Union argued that a binding past practice existed, allowing the continuation of the use of overdrawn time. It disputed the Employer's claim of a lack of knowledge of the practice, producing evidence of the City Manager's awareness of the practice through direct knowledge of some instances, and through a report by the City Accountant concerning an audit of accumulated time in the police department. Therefore, it asserted that there was a mutual acceptance of the past practice of allowing overdraws. It further argued that the policy could not be unilaterally altered.

The Employer contended that the clear language of the Agreement should be followed. It denied knowledge of the policy, written by the Police Chief, by those in higher authority, and, therefore, asserted a lack of mutuality in the alleged past practice.

Arbitrator Barry C. Brown found the 1980 memorandum was in violation of the Agreement and established past practice. Citing a prior arbitration award, he noted that a policy promulgated by the Police Chief, as an Employer agent, could arguably be considered as binding. He also found that mutual acceptance may be tacit. The Arbitrator held that the Employer should have been put on notice by the report made by the City Accountant. He therefore found that a binding past practice existed. Finding nothing in the Agreement which was contracted by the established past practice, the Arbitrator sustained the grievance. The parties were ordered to revert to the terms of the 1974 policy regarding the overdraw of sick leave pay.

Reference: Case #818077, "Public Sector Arbitration Awards," Vol. 8, 1981, Labor Relations Press, Fort Washington, Pa.

ADDENDUM V–43

Case-in-Point: WORK OR PLANT RULES

Minneapolis, City of and *Police Officers Federation of Minneapolis*

The Employer did not violate the Agreement when it required Police Officers to wear name tags. The Employer promulgated a rule requiring officers to wear name tags while on duty. The Union argued that doing so was not reasonable and therefore improper, that it subjected officers to increased stress and danger from the criminal element, and that the Employer did not properly notify the Union of the new rule before putting it into effect. The Employer contended that the name tags promoted personal accountability and improved public relations. The Arbitrator found that the Union had sufficient notice of the proposed change, citing the fact that the change was discussed in a Union newsletter prior to implementation. He held that the expert testimony presented by the Union did not establish an increased risk to the affected officers, noting that the testimony indicated that while stress may be increased, problems arising from the use of name tags were minimal. He also held that the rule requiring the wearing of name tags was a reasonable exercise of managerial rights. Therefore, the grievance was denied.

Reference: Case #829055, "Public Sector Arbitration Awards," Vol. 9, 1982, Labor Relations Press, Fort Washington, Pa.

Chapter **VI**

The Arbitration Hearing

PREPARATIONS PRIOR TO THE HEARING

Even though he or she may not be assigned as the advocate representing management in the arbitration hearing, the first-line and other supervisors can be of invaluable assistance in preparing management's case for arbitration, and during the hearing itself. As we have noted, in these proceedings the responding administrator often feels more like the defendant than merely the implementor of management policies. For this reason, it is in the immediate supervisor's best interests to be as helpful as possible in the preparation and prosecution of management's case. In order to be of maximum assistance, the administrator concerned should understand some basic facets of arbitration proceedings.

First, it is always useful if the supervisor can help the advocate separate argument from evidence for the purposes of the hearing. Argument is basically an oral presentation spelling out management's position in response to the grievance. There can be wide latitude in argument and the immediate administrator most familiar with the work situation can suggest points that may be persuasive because they are based upon logic, reasonableness, and just plain common sense. These points could relate, for example, to the practicality of day-to-day operations with which management's advocate might not be familiar.

The other major area in which the supervisor can be helpful is the selection of evidence. Evidence represents a presentation of the facts of the matter at hand, either by written documentation or in testimony of witnesses. Evidence is, of course, the critical ingredient of management's case and that to which the arbitrator will give the most weight. However, there are degrees of evidence and the supervisor can be helpful by suggesting the most credible or substantive information available. The best evidence is direct evidence, either by an eyewitness or a document that verifies or establishes the facts of the matter. With respect to selection of witnesses, the supervisor can be particularly helpful because he or she knows the personnel involved, their relationship to the work site, and their personalities. The specifics of selection and preparation of witnesses are discussed later in this chapter. It will suffice us here to say that the administrator can be most helpful by sorting out the hearsay witnesses—those who will testify about what somebody else told them—from the direct eyewitness testimony.

The immediate supervisor should prepare a list of witnesses for interview in order of importance, going from direct testimony to hearsay. A similar list of documents that would be potential exhibits at a hearing can also be prepared. The list of documents should also be arranged in priority order, covering the most significant items—direct communications between the supervisor and the grievant, rules, and so on—to the less significant items—notations of verbal conversations, and so on.

During this period preceding the hearing itself, the first-line supervisor can also assist the management representative with case preparation by:

1. Carefully examining the actual grievance letter or form requesting the arbitration (see Addendum VI–1) to identify which facts are in dispute. This review should include a consideration of any applicable master agreement clauses, agency rules or procedures.
2. Reviewing the past practice in his/her particular unit or operation as it bears on the grievance itself.
3. Arranging for a visit by management's counsel to the work site or preparing a blueprint or drawing of the site for the counsel's use. A visit to the actual scene of events can be a critical factor in management's case.
4. Selecting and recommending witnesses and questions for management counsel's consideration.
5. Assessing key points which the supervisor feels strengthens management's case in this particular grievance and which would be helpful in crystallizing arguments.
6. Playing the "devil's advocate" by analyzing the union's major points and anticipating weaknesses in management's case which could be exploited.
7. Communicating with other members of the management team, both superiors and subordinates, for their advice and experience with similar grievance issues. This provides a cross-section of management practice and perspective on the issues and can be very helpful, particularly if the management representative is not an employee of the agency.
8. Reviewing similar grievances brought against management in the department or agency, and the awards rendered. This is valuable material for preparing both argument and briefs in an attempt to persuade the arbitrator of the soundness and consistency of the management position.

Still other contributions which the administrator concerned can make toward preparation of management's case are illustrated in the checklist shown in Addendum VI–2.

SELECTION AND PREPARATION OF WITNESSES

As noted above, the immediate administrator can be of inestimable value to management's counsel in the selection of key witnesses. The testimony of witnesses constitutes the most direct evidence, and therefore the most weighty, in the hearing. Obviously, such selection is crucial to management's case, and the immediate administrator is in the best position to know which employees can make the greatest contribution as witnesses for the management position. Conversely, of course, it is the first-line supervisor who also knows more about most of the grievant's witnesses, in terms of their credibility, past performance on the job, and other circumstances that would bear upon the validity of their expected testimony.

In selecting the witnesses to recommend for management's case, first-line and other supervisors should keep some general rules in mind as they make their choices. The most desirable witnesses for the management case are those who can contribute direct eyewitness testimony based upon their own personal observations, or at least experience. This qualification at least reduces, if not eliminates, the charge of hearsay. Having determined who has the most direct testimony to offer, management should then proceed to select witnesses on the following basis:

1. Those best qualified to testify on the major point(s) in dispute. In this regard, it is probably better to select a few good witnesses, rather than a large number of those less qualified.
2. Those who will not withhold any information from the representative, even though they may consider it detrimental.
3. Those who are truthful, and have a reputation for veracity and integrity.
4. Those who enjoy credibility and respect with their peers.
5. Those who are employed in similar, or like, positions as the grievant.

After selecting witnesses carefully, it is necessary to prepare them for giving truthful testimony. Perhaps it should be emphasized here that not only is there nothing illegal or unethical about proper preparation of witnesses, but it is an expectation and requirement upon which arbitrators insist. In fact, arbitrators will often scold opposing representatives for what is an obvious failure to prepare their own witnesses for testimony. The thorough and forthright preparation of witnesses should include some fundamental points with which the first-line and other supervisors can assist management's counsel.

First, witnesses should be oriented with respect to the hearing process itself. This is generally done by the management representative handling the case, as the latter is more familiar with the mechanics and sequence of hearing agenda. In any event, the administrator concerned should see that the witnesses he/she is recommending are well-versed in what to expect at the hearing itself, particularly if this is their first testimony in such proceedings. Following an orientation, witnesses should be asked to recount in their own words what events they witnessed surrounding the essential points of the grievance. After this, management's representative will generally prepare a list of questions for each witness and go over with the individual what responses the witness would make. This will set the intended witness at ease in terms of what to expect in a hearing and what questions to anticipate from management's counsel. With regard to cross-examination questions from the union's representative, those which can be anticipated should be brought to the attention of the witness.

It is often helpful, particularly if there has been a long interval between the event giving rise to the grievance and the date of the hearing itself, for a witness to refer to notes that he or she has prepared at the time of the event. There is nothing wrong with the witness having such written documentation if it is a recitation of facts. It should, of course, be an event of which the witness has firsthand knowledge at the time. Such notations could have been prepared either by the witness at the time the facts or events occurred, or by a third party if the witness examined the notes at the time. Such notation falls into the category of past recollection recording and can be extremely helpful to a witness whose memory has diminished over the passage of time. However, it should be emphasized that such notations must have been at least generated by the witnesses themselves at the time of occurrence.

With respect to their direct testimony, the witnesses may be assured of the questions to anticipate as noted above. However, they should also understand that their own representatives may wish to amplify by asking the witnesses further questions, either to jog the memory or expand on some point that the counsel feels the arbitrator may have missed. Therefore, the witnesses should be aware that their direct examination will not necessarily be restricted to the questions listed in advance. With regard to cross-examination, management's witnesses should be instructed not to hesitate to say, "I don't know" rather than try to "wing it" by saying "I think ..." or "it might be ..." Also, it is a good technique to advise management witnesses beforehand to allow a reasonable period of time before answering under cross-examination in order to give the management representative an opportunity to raise an objection to the question if appropriate.

There is an important, but less tangible, area of preparation with which immediate supervisors can assist. This is with respect to the dimension or overall image of a particular witness. Arbitrators will determine the credibility of a witness not only on the basis of the witness' perception, memory and communication skills, but on the overall image that the witness is able to project. The more positive attributes manifested by the witness, the more likely the arbitrator is to accept as fact what the witness says on the stand. Although these attributes appear minor and sometimes difficult to define, they are critical. For example, the witness' eye contact is important. The witness should maintain direct contact with the person who is questioning him or her. The witness should dress in normal work clothes at the time of the hearing, cleanly and neatly, and should maintain an upright posture on the stand, avoiding a slouching or lackadaisical appearance. Included here also should be advice on minor, but potentially harmful personal habits, such as chewing gum or smoking on the witness stand.

Additional specific items that may be discussed with potential witnesses relative to their testimony are illustrated in Addendum VI−3. In essence, a witness who is prepared to answer questions truthfully and succinctly on the basis of information with which he or she is familiar will present the positive kind of imagery essential to the case and will be management's best contribution to a fair and just resolution of the case.

DOCUMENTARY EVIDENCE

Another factor essential to winning a grievance proceeding is in the category of documentation or written evidence. In this regard, the immediate administrator can review such items as the master agreement itself, any memorandum of understanding, agency rules or policies, personnel and other data records which may be pertinent; the negotiating history (parol evidence) is also an essential item for review.

Generally, the immediate administrator can be most helpful by assembling any items that might be evidence for the arbitration hearing, and then allowing the representative to make a determination as to their value. In that regard, some general rules are worthy of note. Any correspondence that has been mailed by U.S. mail is always presumed to have been received by the intended recipient. In addition, any written statement of position by either management or union representatives is presumed to be authorized as policy. However, memoranda that constitute written entries of a subjective nature by management personnel are internal management communication, commonly called "work product." For example, if individual research were to be done as part of an investigation which contributed to a subjective analysis by management personnel, this would not be the kind of material that would *have* to be introduced into a hearing. However, it would be the kind which the immediate administrator should make the representative aware of in case he or she desires to use it. The best evidence is always that which establishes a finding of fact so the arbitrator will consider it substantive material.

HEARING TECHNIQUES

There are some basic guidelines which participants in grievance arbitration hearings would do well to note. These include the following suggestions:

1. During the course of the hearing, the immediate administrator, who will generally be the respondent, should be careful to communicate with the management counsel by notation. Verbal comments directed to the representative are distracting and prevent the latter from giving close concentration to the testimony being given.
2. Most opening statements in a hearing are predicated on an intention to show and to orient the arbitrator. They should generally be short.
3. Unless the material introduced by management makes a contribution to the arbitrator's knowledge, bears directly on the subject matter, and is more objective than subjective, it should probably not be introduced.
4. Any offers of settlement should not be introduced.
5. The summary closing usually includes arguments previously given by either side.
6. It is generally advisable for the immediate administrator to make notes as the hearing progresses for the benefit of his/her particular counsel to include in counsel's final closing argument.

GENERAL CONSIDERATIONS

There are some pitfalls that should be avoided on both sides of the table in grievance proceedings. These are common mistakes which only weaken the case for the party concerned. Management supervisors who may be involved in grievance hearings should be alert to some of these errors so they may contribute to avoiding their commission. Some of the tactics to be avoided include the following:

1. Any exaggeration of the management position in response to the allegations.
2. Either concealment of fundamental facts or a distortion of them.
3. Frustrating and delaying the proceedings with various legal technicalities.
4. Manifesting an uncooperative attitude toward the arbitrator.

In addition to the above, there is an area of ethical conduct which is of paramount importance to the facilitation of the hearing, its proper resolution, and the comfort of all concerned. Certain kinds of errors and mistakes not only hurt the case for the party concerned, but make the hearing process unpleasant for all participants. These include such negative conduct as the following:

1. Disregarding the ordinary rules of courtesy and polite social behavior.
2. Becoming embroiled argumentatively in verbal exchanges with the other side.
3. Failing to concentrate efforts on convincing the arbitrator, rather than the opposing party.
4. Communicating with the arbitrator directly when the other party is not present.

All of the above are considered a breach of good conduct and courtesy and serve only to exacerbate differences of opinion and traumatize the hearing process.

It should be noted that when the arbitrator does make his or her award, regardless of whether one party or the other thinks it justified or not, the proceedings normally cannot be reopened. In some cases, there may be need for a mutual agreement to reopen the proceedings, but this is rare and depends, for the most part, on technical error. Absenting some master agreement language to the contrary, the parties must live with the decision of the arbitrator as it stands. In some states, there is a provision for requesting a clarification or modification of an award, but there are no appeals absenting a technical infraction.

As noted at the beginning of this chapter, the more familiar the supervisor is with the specifics of the hearing, the more helpful he or she can be to the advocate representing management. For the supervisor who has never been an active partici-pant in a hearing, some orientation and anticipation of what to expect can be achieved by reviewing transcripts of actual hearings. Such a transcript based on an actual case may be found in Addendum VI–4.

CONCLUSION

The first-line supervisor or middle-management person involved in the grievance can make a valuable contribution to the preparation of management's case. However, this requires an understanding and appreciation of the procedures, including the sequence of events, inherent in the hearing process itself. Before the hearing begins, the administrator concerned can be most helpful by reviewing all of the appropriate documentation and references which may be needed, including an outline of the work location if appropriate. In the area of selecting and preparing witnesses, the immediate supervisor can be of critical importance. Witness orientation and preparation is crucial to management's success in an arbitration hearing and the immediate supervisor's credibility with the personnel concerned makes him or her invaluable in this regard.

The immediate administrator needs some familiarity with basic evidence and rules of procedures. Since conduct is also an important part of a productive arbitration hearing, supervisors need to be alert to the basic requirements of courtesy and decorum in order to adhere to them themselves, and to communicate these requirements to employees who may be testifying on management's side. In that regard, the emphasis should be at all times on convincing the arbitrator, not the grievant, of the justice and fairness of management's position. An immediate supervisor who makes himself or herself familiar with these details will be of inestimable value to management's representative in the arbitration process.

TYPICAL ARBITRATION REQUEST

CITY OF _____

Original — Personnel Department
Copy 2 — Return to Grievant
Copy 3 — Department Head
Step 2
Copy 4 — City Manager
Copy 4 — Grievant's File

GRIEVANCE FORM—STEP 3

Request for Arbitration — This section must be completed by the grievant. Copy #2 of completed Grievance Forms, Steps 1 and 2 must be attached.

I hereby request an Arbitration Panel be convened to consider the grievance outlined on the attachments. My representative is:

_____

_____   _____
       Date   Signature

Upon completion of this section, grievant shall present original; copies #2, 3 and 4; and all attachments to the Personnel Services Division. Copy #5 should be retained by grievant.

Report of Arbitration Panel   Signed copies of the report of the Committee of Review shall be attached. Original shall be presented to Personnel and copies #2, 3 and 4 forwarded to the Department Head who rendered decision at Step 2.

_____ Date of formation of Arbitration Panel

_____ Date of submission of this report

City Manager's Review: _____

_____

_____   _____
       Date   Signature

Upon completion of this section, the City Manager shall present the grievant with copy #2, and retain copy #3.

ADDENDUM VI–1

ADMINISTRATOR'S PREPARATION
CHECKLIST FOR ARBITRATION

I. Study the Case Objectively

_____ Verify that all the procedures have been followed.

_____ Identify the agency rule(s) or contract clause(s) which apply to each issue.

_____ Identify the facts that go with each issue.

_____ Identify effective witnesses who can support the facts.

_____ Look for other supportive evidence (e.g., documentary).

_____ Look for other arbitration decisions on the same issue.

_____ Evaluate the issue's importance to management:

    _____ What management purpose will be served by a favorable arbitrator's decision?

    _____ Will a favorable decision establish a needed guideline?

    _____ Will a decision settle a continuing dispute?

    _____ What will be the result of an unfavorable decision?

    _____ What will it cost to get a decision?

II. Help Your Representative to Prepare the Case

_____ Identify your main argument.

_____ Confer with each witness:

    _____ Determine what he or she knows about the case and understands about the relationship of the testimony to your argument.

    _____ Make a written summary of the important points of each witness' testimony.

    _____ Outline the questions you think will be asked.

_____ Try to talk to grievant's witnesses.

_____ Recommend the order in which to call the witnesses.

_____ Try to identify weak spots in Management's case and how to plug them.

_____ Organize the supportive evidence for the representative:

    _____ Consider graphs, charts, records, pictures, video tapes, moving pictures, and so on.

    _____ Suggest which witnesses will introduce evidence.

    _____ Make duplicate copies for arbitrator and grievant.

    _____ If other party has documents ask for them and, if refused, ask arbitrator to get them for you.

_____ Conduct a visit to the site of the grievance.

CHECKLIST FOR TESTIFYING AS A WITNESS

_____ Tell the truth. As a witness for either side you have no purpose to serve other than to give the facts as you know them.

_____ Give only information that you have readily in mind. If you do not know certain information, do not give it. If asked, state that you do not know.

_____ Do not answer any question unless you thoroughly understand it.

_____ Answer each question completely and to the best of your ability but do not volunteer more than is asked.

_____ Take your time in answering a question.

_____ Pause briefly before answering each question. Gather your thoughts carefully before answering and do not permit yourself to be hurried.

_____ If your representative begins to speak, stop whatever answer you may be giving and allow him or her to make a statement. If this is an objection to the question being asked of you, do not answer the question until the arbitrator advises you to go ahead and complete your answer.

_____ Never attempt to explain or justify your answer. You are there to give the facts as you know them. You are not supposed to apologize or attempt to justify those facts. Any attempts as such would make it appear that you doubt the accurateness or authenticity of your own testimony.

_____ Never state facts you don't know. Even if you feel you should know the answer, but do not, don't guess or estimate what the answer should be. This is a mistake. Even though you feel ignorant or evasive by stating you don't know, you should nevertheless do so. A guess or an estimate for an answer is almost always wrong, and one from which the opponent can show you don't know what you are talking about or imply you are deliberately misstating the truth.

_____ Do not memorize your testimony; instead tell the facts as you know them and in a manner intelligible to those who have no knowledge whatsoever of the case.

_____ Avoid demonstrations of anger, belligerence, sarcasm or discourtesy.

_____ Do not let the opposing representative get you angry or excited.

_____ Your initial testimony will be similar to what follows:
a. You will be called by name and should come forward.
b. You will swear to give honest answers.
c. The counsel who has summoned you will probably ask:
  (1) your name
  (2) your occupation
  (3) your place of work
  (4) how long you have been at your place of current employment

(5) the title of your job

(6) the qualifications for the job you perform

(7) the type of work you perform

(8) your acquaintance with respondent and grievant

(9) what occurred at a specific time and place

(10) any other pertinent questions

d. Following the above, opposing counsel will ask you questions.

ARBITRATION CASE STUDY

Swampside Mosquito Abatement District

A. Transcript of Arbitration
B. Exhibits of Hearing
C. Brief of Employer
D. Brief of Association
E. Decision of Arbitrator

Acknowledgment: The authors are grateful to Arbitrator Joseph Gentile for his help in preparing a sample arbitration record.

This case provides typical examples of the good and bad points we try to illustrate throughout this book. It also illustrates how what appears to be a "locked" case can fall apart.

1	In the Matter of the Arbitration)
	Between:)
2	Swampside Mosquito Abatement District,)
	)
3	Employer,)
	)
4	and)
	)
5	Swampside Employees Association)
	)
6	Union.)
7	
8	JOSEPH GENTILE, ARBITRATOR
	11620 Wilshire Boulevard
9	Suite 550
	Los Angeles, California 90024
10	
11	
12	
13	
14	
15	
16	
17	
18	
19	
20	
21	
22	
23	
24	
25	

ADDENDUM VI−4

1
2
3
4
5
6
7
8
9
10
11
12
13
14
15
16
17
18
19
20
21
22
23
24
25

<u>INDEX</u>

AGENCY WITNESSES	DIRECT	CROSS
TERRY DUFFY	11	17
SUSAN CONWAY	21	
(Recalled)	35	
KEVIN LENT	29	33

ASSOCIATION WITNESSES		
WILL GRIPE	37	42

REBUTTAL WITNESSES		
TERRY DUFFY	45	47

1   E X H I B I T S

2

3

JOINT EXHIBITS

4

5   1   Document - Collective
              Bargaining Agreement

6

7

8

AGENCY EXHIBITS

9

10   1   Document - Copy of Grievance
              Report

11

    2   Document - Copy of Disciplinary
12   Action Form dated 6-27-79

13   3   Document - Copy of letter on
              Employer's stationery dated
14   7-5-79

15   4   Document - Copy of letter on
              Union's stationery dated
16   8-9-79

17   5   Document - Copy of Employer's
              work rules and regulations

18

    6   Document - Investigation Report
19   of Looking Glass Investigations

20   7   Document - Driver's Daily Tally
              for 6-22-79

21

    8   Document - Copy of Disciplinary
22   Action Form dated 3-2-79

23   9   Document - Copy of Disciplinary
              Action Form dated 11-20-78

24

10   Document - Copy of Personnel
25   Action Form dated 3-31-77

1

E X H I B I T S   (CONTINUED)

2

3

11   Document - Copy of Personnel
4   Action Form dated 8-16-76

5   12   Document - Notes on Surveillance

6

7

8

9

10

11

12   ASSOCIATION EXHIBITS

13   1   Document - Letter dated
             3-16-79 to Will Gripe
14   from George Sharp

15

16

17

18

19

20

21

22

23

24

25

LOS ANGELES, CALIFORNIA

January, 1980   10:15 A.M.

(Whereupon, Joint Exhibit No. 1 was
marked for identification by the
Arbitrator and received into evidence.)

THE ARBITRATOR: This is the time to commence the arbitration in the matter of the Swampside Employee's Association.
Would counsel for the employer please identify
himself for the record.

MR. RITE: B. Rite, of Rite and Rong, for the District.

THE ARBITRATOR: Counsel for the Association.

MR. DANCE: Dance and Dodge by Ken Dance.

THE ARBITRATOR: Prior to going on the record, the
parties supplied to the Arbitrator copies of the applicable
Collective Bargaining Agreement Sections under which this
matter is being brought. They have been marked and received
as Joint Exhibit 1.

Parties also indicated that they were able to
agree on the specific issue they wished the Arbitrator to
address and determine in this proceeding.

Either counsel please state it for the record.

MR. RITE: Yes.

The issue is: Was the termination of Will Gripe

1   proper under the terms and conditions of the Collective

2   Bargaining Agreement between the Agency and the employee?

3   If not, what should the remedy be?

4   THE ARBITRATOR: Do you stipulate to that Counsel?

5   MR. DANCE: So stipulated.

6   THE ARBITRATOR: Do you stipulate the matters are

7   properly before me, gentlemen?

8   MR. DANCE: I think that is contained in the addition-

9   al stipulations prepared by counsel.

10   THE ARBITRATOR: We will just hold off on that.

11   I guess if there are no other preliminary matters,

12 why don't you tell me about the stipulation that you were

13 able to agree to prior to going on the record, gentlemen?

14   MR. RITE: The agreement is timely. The grievance has

15 been processed in accordance with the terms and conditions

16 of Article I of the Collective Bargaining Agreement. All

17 the procedural requisites for bringing this matter to arbi-

18 tration have been satisfied and the Arbitrator is vested

19 with the authority to settle the dispute under the termina-

20 tion subject only to the limitation contained in the agree-

21 ment; namely, the Arbitrator has no right to change, alter,

22 or amend any provisions of the Agreement in making an

23 award with respect to this agreement.

24   MR. DANCE: So stipulated.

25   THE ARBITRATOR: Thank you very much.

1   Is there anything further of a preliminary

2 nature?

3   MR. DANCE: Yes. I would like to make a motion to

4 sequester all witnesses.

5   THE ARBITRATOR: Will you make comment on that, Counsel?

6   MR. DANCE: I am delegating Egar Tusu as the Employ-

7 ee Association Representative. I believe he has the right

8 to be here. The grievant, Will Gripe, has a right to be

9 here, and Mrs. Gripe is here because it beats soap operas

10 on television.

11   MR. RITE: I have no objection to the motion.

12   THE ARBITRATOR: The motion is granted.

13   Counsel, why don't we go off the record.

14   (A discussion was held off the record.)

15   (Whereupon, Agency Exhibits 1 through 4, inclu-

16   sive, were marked for identification by the

17   Arbitrator.)

18   THE ARBITRATOR: During the off-the-record four docu-

19 ments were marked as Agency Exhibits in this proceeding.

20   Agency Exhibit 1 is a copy of the grievance re-

21 port which apparently gave rise to the instant arbitration.

22   Agency Exhibit 2 is a copy of the disciplinary

23 action form, which apparently was used by the Agency, which

24 has a date of June 27, 1979.

25   Agency Exhibit 3 is a letter on the stationery

1 of the employer in this matter, dated July 5, 1979.

2   Agency Exhibit 4 is a letter dated August 9,
3 1979, on the stationery of the Swampside Employees' Asso-
4 ciation.

5   Agency Exhibit 5 is a copy of the employer's
6 work rules and regulations.

7   (Whereupon Agency Exhibit 5 was marked for
8   identification by the Arbitrator.)

9 THE ARBITRATOR: Agency Exhibit 6 --

10 MR. DANCE: There is going to be a strenuous objec-
11 tion to Agency Exhibit 6.

12 THE ARBITRATOR: I am receiving it simply for identi-
13 fication.

14   Agency Exhibit 6 is a copy of an investigation
15 report on the stationery, apparently, of Looking Glass
16 Investigation.

17   (Whereupon, Agency Exhibit 6 was marked for
18   identification by the Arbitrator.)

19 THE ARBITRATOR: Agency Exhibit 7 is a copy of the
20 driver's daily tally for June 22, 1979.

21   (Whereupon, Agency Exhibit 7 was marked for
22   identification by the Arbitrator.)

23 THE ARBITRATOR: Agency Exhibit 8 is a copy of a dis-
24 ciplinary action form dated March 2, 1979.

25   (Whereupon, Agency Exhibit 8 was marked for

1   identification by the Arbitrator.

2   THE ARBITRATOR: Agency Exhibit 9 is another disci-

3   plinary action form dated November 20, 1978.

4   (Whereupon, Agency Exhibit 9 was marked for

5   identification by the Arbitrator.)

6   THE ARBITRATOR: Agency Exhibit 10 is a Personnel

7   Action Form dated March 31, 1977.

8   (Whereupon, Agency Exhibit 10 was marked for

9   identification by the Arbitrator.)

10   THE ARBITRATOR: Agency Exhibit 11 is another Person-

11   nel Action Form which appears to have the date of August

12   16th, 1976.

13   (Whereupon Agency Exhibit 11 was marked for

14   identification by the Arbitrator.)

15   THE ARBITRATOR: All those documents are at this

16   point simply marked for identification.

17   Any more, Counsel?

18   MR. RITE: No. That does it.

19   MR. DANCE: Can you give me just a moment to review

20   some of them?

21   THE ARBITRATOR: Surely.

22   Off the record, please.

23   (A discussion was held off the record.)

24   THE ARBITRATOR: Counsel, do you want to make an

25   opening statement?

1 MR. RITE: Yes.

2

3 OPENING STATEMENT

4 BY MR. RITE:

5 Mr. Arbitrator, the case is really one involving

6 rather simple facts. The grievant was terminated for

7 violating the Agency Rules and the specific rule is a major

8 offense. I believe you will find it on Page 4 of Agency

9 Exhibit 5. The offense is drinking alcoholic beverages

10 while working. The rules are well known to the grievant.

11 He was involved in discipline in the past as various Agency

12 Exhibits do show.

13 The evidence that will come out will show that

14 it is the Agency's procedure during the initial interview-

15 ing process to hand to the new employee, prospective employ-

16 ee, the rules. As those rules are acknowledged, they are

17 posted on the employee bulletin board and subsequently

18 reviewed with the employee each time that discipline may

19 be warranted.

20 In this case discipline had been handed out to

21 the grievant on several occasions. On about May of 1979

22 the Agency, in addition to experiencing a substantial

23 amount of theft presumably off the truck, had also exper-

24 ienced or it had noted that the trucks that normally get

25 7 - 12 miles a gallon were getting one mile a gallon. The

1 trucks run on unleaded gas, so it was at least possible

2 that the trucks were leaving the Agency's premises and the

3 tanks were being siphoned off by employees or possibly non-

4 employees.

5   Because of what the Agency had observed, at

6 least in the records, they obtained the services of Looking

7 Glass Investigations and had Looking Glass tail various

8 trucks as they left the yard, basically to find out whether

9 it was the drivers who were involved in siphoning and pos-

10 sibly diverting the Agency's material on the way to delivery

11 or whether, in fact, the gasoline was siphoned off and

12 products were taken off of trucks before the driver ever

13 got possession.

14   On the 22nd of June, Will Gripe was asked to take

15 a truck, Truck No. 4, on a delivery. Mr. Gripe signed an

16 acknowledgement of taking the truck. I believe that is

17 Agency Exhibit No. 7. He left the yard. Mr. Gripe was

18 picked up on routine surveillance by Officer Bob Magee, who

19 was employed at the time by Looking Glass.

20   On the way to one of the deliveries the officer

21 noted that the grievant had stopped off at a liquor store,

22 purchased a half-pint bottle of Black Velvet Whiskey and

23 on the way to the first delivery proceeded to drink that

24 bottle of whiskey and threw the bottle out of the truck.

25 The investigator followed Mr. Gripe to the delivery where

1   the delivery was, in fact, made properly, and then fol-
2   lowed Mr. Gripe on the way back to the yard.
3   On the way back to the yard Mr. Gripe stopped
4   off at a liquor store at the corner of Main and 23rd.
5   He went into the liquor store and purchased a quart bottle
6   of Colt 45 Malt Liquor and drank the liquor on the way
7   back to the plant while he was operating the truck. Once
8   he got back to the plant the surveillance broke off, the
9   officer returned to Looking Glass offices and immediately
10 made a report. It is on that report that was made to the
11 Agency several days later that the discipline occurred.
12   THE ARBITRATOR: Would you like to make a responsive
13 opening statement or would you like to reserve it?
14   MR. DANCE: I prefer to reserve it.
15   THE ARBITRATOR: Call your first witness, sir.
16   MR. RITE: The first witness will be Terry Duffy.
17   THE ARBITRATOR: Why don't you come up here, please.
18   Off the record
19   (Whereupon Agency Exhibits 2, 3, 4, 5, 7, 8, 9
20   and 10 were received into evidence.)
21   THE ARBITRATOR: Let the record indicate that the
22 Agency exhibits which were previously identified and marked
23 2 - 11 have been received into evidence, except for Agency
24 Exhibits 6 and 11. They are still to be treated as marked
25 for identification only.

1

2   TERRY DUFFY,

3   Called as a witness by and on behalf

4   of the Agency, having been first duly

5   sworn, was examined and testified as

6   follows:

7

8   THE ARBITRATOR: Let the record indicate that the

9   witness has been sworn.

10   Would you state your full name for the court

11 reporter please?

12   THE WINTESS: Terrance Duffy

13   THE ARBITRATOR: Counsel, your witness

14

15   DIRECT EXAMINATION

16 BY MR. RITE:

17   Q: What is your position with the Agency?

18   A: I am The Assistant Director in Charge of Spraying.

19   Q: How long have you been in that position?

20   A: Nine years.

21   Q: What are your responsibilities?

22   A: I am responsible for the spraying of pesticides

23 and for Agency kill quotas. I make all body counts.

24   Q: Could you describe the Agency's operations just

25 very briefly?

1   A: Yes.

2   We are an autonomous government agency formed

3 under the State Constitution.   Our duty is to destroy all

4 mosquitoes in the Swampside area.

5   Q: How many employees do you have?

6   A: It varies from 160 to 225.

7   Q: Where is the yard located?

8   A: 100 Boggy Boulevard, Swampside.

9   Q: Can you describe just very briefly the hiring

10 procedure that you utilize?

11   A: Yes.

12   They are brought in, interviewed and they go to

13 the nurse first, fill out a form and she interviews them

14 as far as their health is concerned.

15   Q: "Them" meaning prospective employees?

16   A: Right.

17   And it is turned over to me, we interview them,

18 see what their backgrounds are, and look over their appli-

19 cation and determine what department they would fit into

20 best or what job they should apply for.   They are given a

21 copy of the Agency safety rules, a copy of the Agency rules,

22 per se.   They sign for them on the slip that they have

23 received them and do have them.   These rules were okayed

24 by the Swampside Employees' Association and when they were

25 okayed by the SEA, a copy was given to every employee when

THE ARBITRATION HEARING **163**

the new set of rules came out.

Q: When you refer to the rules, are you talking about Agency Exhibit No. 5?

A: Yes. I am talking about Swampside's Work Rules and Regulations.

Q: Thank you.

A: And they are also signed to say that they are citizens of the United States or are here legally. That is about it.

Q: Are the Agency rules also posted from time to time?

A: Yes.

As some of them become violated several times, we will take that section of it out and post them, stating to the people that they are beginning to get a little lax in this area, and they are posted and the full rules have been posted several times.

Q: Has the Agency had problems with thefts in the past?

A: Yes, we have.

Q: Could you describe the problem just very briefly?

A: Yes.

We have had problems with theft of pesticides, spray nozzles and hoses, to the extent that from time to time over the past six years I have had to hire Looking Glass to come in and investigate to see what they can find

1   out, plus a problem with narcotics, which was investigated

2   also.

3   Q: In approximately May of 1979, did you review

4   any records pertaining to gasoline consumption?

5   A: Yes, we did, because at the time I received a

6   notice from the oil companies that my allotment of gasoline

7   was being cut to 80 percent and we had to start cutting

8   back and checking up to see whether we were lax in our fuel

9   consumption because we could not get by with the percentage.

10   I had the accounting department go through the gasoline

11   log, so that we kept showing the number of trucks, who

12   signed for them, the odometer reading on the truck at the

13   time, the number of the truck, and we noted that over the

14   past prior two weeks some of the trucks that had been get-

15   ting from 7 - 10 miles per gallon suddenly dropped to 1

16   and 2.

17   Q: What, if anything, did you do in response to

18   that finding?

19   A: We called Looking Glass and told them that we

20   had no way of proving whether it was being taken at the

21   plant overnight or whether the drivers were taking it or

22   where it was going or what the problem was.

23   Q: Did you instruct them to do anything?

24   A: We gave them the list of all the truck license

25   numbers because some of our drivers have the same type of

trucks, so we identified our trucks by number and license

plates and told them to pick up different trucks each day

and tail them and give us a report on what they found.

Q: How did you get Looking Glass's name?

A: We got that from the Sheriff's Department approximately six years ago as a reputable organization.

Q: Did you receive a copy of the investigator's report that is dated June 25, 1979, that and certain other reports which are attached as Company Exhibit No. 6?

MR. DANCE: Excuse me, Mr. Arbitrator. I am going to object to the Arbitrator even considering that document until there is a foundation laid with respect to its authenticity and how it was prepared.

MR. RITE: Mr. Arbitrator, that will be done in due course.

THE ARBITRATOR: Fine.

He is not offering it at this point.

MR. DANCE: All right. Go right ahead.

BY MR. RITE:

Q: Mr. Duffy, did you receive a copy of that document?

A: Yes, I did. I received it the following week.

Q: Do you recall what date you received that?

A: It was on a Tuesday because it had not arrived in the mail when they notified me by phone what had happened.

1   Q: Who is "they"?

2   A: Looking Glass.

3   And I didn't receive it until Tuesday.

4   Q: When you did receive this report, what if any-

5   thing did you do?

6   A: I called my yard manager, Kevin Lent, and told

7   him to investigate it, find out what the problem was,

8   and if there was any truth to it, find out the other side

9   of it, hold a meeting and act on it.

10   Q: Do you know what Mr. Lent did?

11   A: Yes. He informed me that he had terminated

12   Mr. Gripe.

13   Q: After Mr. Gripe was terminated, were there any

14   meetings held between the Agency and the Employees' Asso-

15   ciation concerning Mr. Gripe?

16   A: There were several meetings with the Association

17   representatives.

18   Q: Were you present at some of those meetings?

19   A: Yes, I was.

20   Q: At one of those meetings did Mr. Gripe indicate

21   his lack of desire or interest ever to come back to the

22   Agency?

23   A: Yes. He inferred to Mr. Mayer that regardless

24   of how it came out he would not report to this Agency any

25   longer.

1   Q: Were you present at that time?

2   A: Yes, I was.

3   MR. RITE: No further questions.

4   THE ARBITRATOR: Your witness, Counsel.

5   MR. DANCE: One second.

6   (Recess)

7   MR. RITE: I do have just one or two more questions.

8   MR. DANCE: Sure.

9   BY MR. RITE:

10   Q: Mr. Duffy, have you received Mr. Gripe's per-

11   sonnel file?

12   A: Yes, I have.

13   Q: And has there been prior disciplinary action taken?

14   A: Yes, there has.

15   Q: Could you take a look at Agency's Exhibit No. 11?

16   Do you recognize that document?

17   A: I have seen the document. I do not know what it

18   is about. I did not sign this one.

19   Q: Is that document contained in Mr. Gripe's file?

20   A: Yes, it is.

21   MR. RITE: Mr. Arbitrator, I move that Agency Exhibit

22   No. 11 be introduced into evidence.

23   MR. ARBITRATOR: Any objection, Counsel?

24   MR. DANCE: Yes.

25   MR. ARBITRATOR: Why don't you state it for the record?

1   MR. DANCE: Objection: lacks foundation. This wit-

2   ness has no personal knowledge of any of the contents con-

3   tained therein and there is no evidence that the document

4   was given to the grievant.

5   THE ARBITRATOR: Was this being offered for the truth

6   of the contents contained therein or simply that it is a

7   part of the personnel file?

8   MR. RITE: Simply that it is part of the personnel

9   file and because discipline was taken.

10   THE ARBITRATOR: I will receive it under that basis.

11   (Whereupon, Agency Exhibit No. 11 was

12   received into evidence.)

13   MR. RITE: Your witness.

14

15   CROSS-EXAMINATION

16   BY MR. DANCE TO MR. DUFFY:

17   Q: I gather there was a grievance meeting that was

18   held with respect to the grievance that was filed?

19   A: Yes.

20   Q: Do you recall when that meeting took place?

21   A: It was approximately two weeks after it was taken.

22   Q: Do you know whether it was two weeks or three

23   weeks?

24   A: I do not know. Two or three weeks. I did not

25   write the date down.

1 Q: Who was in attendance?

2 A: George Sharp and myself and Will Gripe and an

3 Association Representative. Darn. His name escapes me.

4 MR. TUSU: Ronald Reynolds.

5 THE WITNESS: Ronald Reynolds, I'm sorry.

6 MR. DANCE: Mr. Arbitrator, will you caution those

7 that are in attendance --

8 THE ARBITRATOR: I already have with the move of my

9 hand.

10 BY MR. DANCE:

11 Q: At the conclusion of the meeting, did Mr. Gripe

12 tell you that he would see you in court or see you in

13 Arbitration?

14 A: Yes.

15 Q: He did not indicate to you that he had any inten-

16 tion of withdrawing his grievance?

17 A: He gave me no indication of such.

18 Q: Did Mr. Gripe advise you that he was unjustly

19 accused and that there was no basis for his discharge?

20 A: I don't recall his making a statement like that,

21 no.

22 A: Did you review the grievance that was filed?

23 A: Yes.

24 Q: When did you review the grievance?

25 A: Several weeks ago. Not lately.

1   Q: Would you review Agency Exhibit 1 to see if that

2   indicates to you whether or not Mr. Gripe was advising you

3   that he was unjustly accused, that the charges were false?

4   A: This is the grievance, yes.

5   Q: And at the grievance meeting did Mr. Gripe explain

6   to you or articulate to you that he was unjustly accused?

7   A: Yes, he did.

8   Q: Are you familiar with the disciplinary action form

9   that is in evidence as Agency Exhibit 8?

10   A: Yes, I am.

11   Q: Are you familiar with the facts and circumstances

12   with respect to the disciplinary action that was taken and

13   the disposition thereof?

14   A: Yes, I am.

15   Q: Am I correct in stating that on or about March

16   22, 1979 the grievant was terminated?

17   A: That is right.

18   Q: And as a result of the disposition of this griev-

19   ance, Mr. Gripe was brought back to work?

20   A: Yes, that's correct.

21   Q: And what date do you recall Mr. Gripe reported

22   back to work?

23   A: I don't recall the date. It was shortly after

24   this meeting.

25   Q: And it was indicated that the termination was

1 converted to a three-day disciplinary layoff; is that

2 correct?

3   A: That is correct.

4   Q: Am I correct in stating that with respect to the

5 other days between the date of discharge and the date of

6 his recall that Mr. Gripe was paid back pay for those days?

7   A: Not to my knowledge.

8   Q: You have no knowledge of that?

9   A: No.

10   Q: Or you just do not recall?

11   A: I have no knowledge of it.

12   Q: You mentioned the name George Sharp. Who is

13 Mr. Sharp?

14   A: He is also an Assistant Director.

15   Q: Are you familiar with the signature of Mr. Sharp?

16   A: Yes, sir.

17   Q: Let me show you a letter dated March 16, 1979.

18 It is addressed to Will Gripe and it appears to be signed

19 by a George Sharp. I ask you if you recognize the signature.

20   THE ARBITRATOR: Show it to Counsel first.

21   THE WITNESS: Yes, sir: it is his signature.

22 BY MR. DANCE:

23   Q: That is his signature?

24   A: Yes, sir.

25   MR. DANCE: I would like to have that introduced into

1   evidence as Association Exhibit 1.

2   THE ARBITRATOR: Any objection, Counsel?

3   MR. RITE: No objection.

4   THE ARBITRATOR: It will be received.

5   (Whereupon, Association Exhibit No. 1 was

6   marked for identification by the Arbitrator and

7   received into evidence.)

8   (Witness Excused.)

9

10   SUE CONWAY,

11   called as a witness by and on behalf of

12   the Agency, having been first duly sworn,

13   was examined and testified as follows:

14   THE ARBITRATOR: Please state your name for the court

15   reporter.

16   THE WITNESS: Susan Conway, C-O-N-W-A-Y.

17   THE ARBITRATOR: Counsel, your witness on direct.

18

19   DIRECT EXAMINATION

20   BY MR. RITE:

21   Q: Miss Conway, by whom are you employed?

22   A: Looking Glass Investigations. I am the office

23   manager and I am part owner of the company. One-third.

24   Q: What type of business is Looking Glass engaged in?

25   A: Investigations and polygraphing.

1   Q: And in order to engage in that type of business,

2 is it your understanding that there is a requirement for

3 licensing?

4   A: That's right. We are licensed under the state.

5   Q: What are requirements, if any, to become licensed

6 by the State?

7   A: We go through the Department of Consumer Affairs.

8 First, whoever the license is taken out under, their name,

9 that person has to have two years of investigative experience

10 and then take a test. Once you have passed your test you

11 apply and you are fingerprinted and when all of the umpteen

12 pages of paper work are done, you apply to the Department

13 and become licensed.

14   Q: What are your responsibilities with Looking Glass?

15   A: I keep the books, I do the scheduling. I hire

16 investigators, I fire investigators, I work on investiga-

17 tions myself.

18   I am also a polygrapher and I do polygraphs.

19 I take reports when they are called in or brought in, see

20 that they get typed up and sent out.

21   Q: Do you have any supervisory duties over the

22 office staff?

23   A. Yes. Completely, over everybody.

24   Q: What about over the investigative staff?

25   A: Same thing.

1   Q: In approximately May of 1979, did you receive a
2   request from Swampside?

3   A: Yes, we did.

4   Q: What was that request?

5   A: Mr. Duffy called and we had worked for him in the
6   past, I believe 1977 was the first time that we went to work
7   for him, and he called us up on the phone and asked us if
8   we could come to the office, that he had some more work
9   that he would like us to do. So that first meeting, I
10 believe, I went with Mr. Sills, who is also a partner, and
11 we went over and talked to Mr. Duffy. At that time he
12 told us he was having problems with the gasoline specifically,
13 on the trucks. The mileage was not tallying up with - -

14 MR. DANCE: Let me just impose an objection.

15   Not to cut her off, but I think the evidence is
16 already clear on the record as to the reason Looking Glass
17 was brought in and this is not really any more for the
18 record. If you want to entertain it, fine.

19 THE ARBITRATOR: I think the record is sufficient as
20 to why they were brought in.

21 THE WITNESS: Okay.

22 BY MR. RITE:

23 Q: In response to Swampside's request, what, if
24 anything, did you do?

25 A: They wanted us to get started on it right away

1 so my first thing was to talk to several investigators who

2 worked for us and set up a schedule trying to alternate

3 what vehicles they would use and make them aware of where

4 they should go, what time to start the surveillance and get

5 it set up.

6   Q: Was an individual named Magee employed by your

7 company?

8   A: Yes.

9   Q: What is his first name?

10   A: Bob.

11   Q: And was Bob Magee involved in the investigation

12 with regard to Swampside?

13   A: Yes.

14   Q: And when was Mr. Magee involved in that investi-

15 gation?

16   A: I probably called him that first day. Barry

17 Black was another one, and I asked him if he would work

18 on it and he said yes and I told him I would get back to

19 him.

20   Q: What experience had Mr. Magee had in investigat-

21 ing?

22   MR. DANCE: Objection: no foundation.

23 BY MR. RITE:

24   Q: Do you have any personal knowledge of Mr. Magee's

25 experience in investigating?

1   A: Yes.

2   Q: And what experience is that?

3   MR. DANCE: Excuse me.

4   How would she get that personal knowledge unless

5   she followed him around on all of his assignments?

6   That is the only way I can imagine she would

7   have personal knowledge.

8   THE ARBITRATOR: Did you hire Mr. Magee?

9   THE WITNESS: Along with my partner, yes.

10   THE ARBITRATOR: All right. Satisfied.

11   BY MR. RITE:

12   Q: What was Mr. Magee's experience?

13   A: He worked for us on our surveillances, investi-

14   gations, whatever that entailed, and he also worked under-

15   cover for us.

16   Q: For how long did Mr. Magee work for Looking Glass?

17   A: A little over a year.

18   A: How long had he worked for Looking Glass up to

19   June of 1979?

20   A: Say about 10 months, something like that.

21   Q: Did Mr. Magee make reports to you concerning

22   what he observed during the surveillance?

23   A: Yes.

24   Q: And is it his obligation to report to you or to

25   some other supervisor?

A: If I wasn't there, it would have been my partners, Todd Binder and Paul Sills.

Q: Do you recall a report being made by Officer Magee on June 22, 1979?

A: Yes, I do.

A: And do you recall when that report was made?

A: It was shortly after lunch when he came in and he just finished following a truck from Swampside and he related to us what had occurred and I think he was still there in the office, as a matter of fact, when Todd suggested that we call Mr. Duffy to make him aware. Even though we type up the reports and get them out, if there is anything that we think is of special interest we call verbally first, and I think it was Todd who made the call to Mr. Duffy.

Q: Did you supervise the preparation of the report?

A: Yes, I did.

Q: And what, if anything, did you do or did the company do, to your knowledge, after the report was prepared?

A: I do not think I know what you mean other than the fact that the report was typed up and mailed out and the phone call made to Mr. Duffy.

Q: Is the document that has been marked Agency Exhibit 6 the report to which you are referring?

A: Yes, which we have a copy of in our files from the home company. All the reports from all the work that

1   we have done for Swampside are in the file.

2   Q: The documents that are cumulatively referred to

3   as Agency Exhibit 6, have you had an opportunity to review

4   those documents before the hearing today?

5   A: Yes.

6   Q: Are those the copies of the documents that are

7   contained in your file and which you transmitted to Swamp-

8   side?

9   A: Yes, they are.

10   MR. RITE: Mr. Arbitrator, I move that Agency Exhibit

11   6 be admitted.

12   MR. DANCE: Objection. It's all hearsay. She did not

13   make the preliminary observations that are reflected in this

14   report. I am not even sure that she is the one who typed

15   up the report. There are no notes with respect to the

16   preparation of this report. It goes to the central issue

17   in this case and clearly would prevent the grievant from

18   his right of confrontation and cross-examination of his

19   accusers.

20   MR. RITE: In response to that, Mr. Arbitrator, the

21   Evidence Code permits the introduction of this document

22   into evidence as a business record.

23   THE ARBITRATOR: I will receive it.

24   MR. DANCE: I would like to further remind the Arbi-

25   trator that if he is receiving it into evidence that --

1   THE ARBITRATOR: I will weigh it accordingly.

2   MR. DANCE: -- no material facts can be drawn from it

3   if it is just hearsay by itself.

4   THE ARBITRATOR: I understand. I know what I am

5   supposed to do with it and not do with it.

6   (Whereupon, Agency Exhibit 6 was

7   received into evidence.)

8   BY MR. RITE:

9   Q: After the report was made and transmitted to

10   Swampside --

11   MR. DANCE: Excuse me. One other thing.

12   I gather that the report is not being admitted

13   for the truth of the matter contained therein but merely

14   that is a copy of a report that was made; is that correct?

15   THE ARBITRATOR: At this point.

16   MR. DANCE: Thank you. I want that clear on the record.

17   THE ARBITRATOR: At this point.

18   MR. RITE: I would like a clarification on just what

19   that was.

20   THE ARBITRATOR: What he said, as I understand it,

21   and let me articulate it. The document has been received

22   as a record that appears in the files of Looking Glass and

23   as a record that was, in fact, transmitted to Swampside.

24   MR. RITE: All right.

25   THE ARBITRATOR: -- but the contents contained in this --

1   what he is saying, as I understand his statement, - are

2   not being received for the truth of the matter asserted

3   therein. He is also saying that these documents are

4   certainly in fact, a business record and have been trans-

5   mitted as such.

6   MR. RITE: Mr. Arbitrator, the document as well as

7   the contents of the document are initially under the

8   Evidence Code.

9   THE ARBITRATOR: I received it and I said I would

10   weigh it accordingly.

11   MR. RITE: All right.

12   Q: Miss Conway, since the termination of surveillance

13   by Looking Glass over the operations of Swampside, has

14   Officer Magee remained an employee of Looking Glass?

15   A: He worked on another case for us after that with

16   a large company undercover, which resulted in about five

17   people being involved with drugs, four on thefts. It was

18   necessary in this particular case that we had to use him

19   and expose him. Since that time Mr. Magee has left the area.

20   I made repeated efforts. I talked to his wife

21   several times and she said that he had gone to Nevada and

22   as far as she knew he was still hiding and had changed his

23   name.

24   Q: I have no further questions.

25   THE ARBITRATOR: Your witness, Counsel.

ADDENDUM VI—4

1   BY MR. DANCE:

2   I have no further questions.

3   DIRECT EXAMINATION

4

5   BY MR. RITE:

6   Q: Mr. Lent, what is your position with the Agency?

7   A: Spraying Supervisor.

8   Q: What are your responsibilities?

9   A: I have 110 employees and am in charge of the

10   mosquito spraying operations.

11   Q: Prior to Mr. Gripe's termination, were you aware

12   of his prior disciplinary record?

13   A: Yes, I was.

14   Q: In reaching your decision to terminate Mr. Gripe,

15   what part, if any, did Mr. Gripe's prior disciplinary

16   record play?

17   A: I studied the complete file very carefully and

18   I also studied the report that was made, and from his past

19   record and having this report in front of me I felt that

20   there was a strong possibility that this did occur.

21   Q: When you are talking about this report, are

22   you referring to Agency Exhibit 6?

23   A: Yes.

24   Q: On June 22, could you describe what occurred in

25   the morning?

1   A: Okay. We had a meeting in my office. Those

2 present were the shop steward, the department foreman,

3 Gripe and myself.

4   Q: Mr. Lent, there may be confusion. June 22 is

5 a Friday.

6   A: Okay. Okay.

7   MR. DANCE: May I inquire as to why the witness is

8 looking at Agency Exhibit 6?

9   MR. RITE: I feel that Agency Exhibit 6 may refresh

10 his memory.

11   MR. DANCE: Before we refresh his memory let us make

12 sure his memory is exhausted.

13   THE ARBITRATOR: I agree.

14   MR. DANCE: Will you remove the document please?

15   Thank you.

16 BY MR. RITE:

17   Q: Mr. Lent, do you have any recollection as to

18 what occurred on June 22, 1979?

19   A: Just from the report that was handed to me, the

20 discussion that I had with the Assistant Director.

21   Q: Do you recall what day June 22, 1979 was? What

22 day of the week?

23   A: Wednesday.

24 BY MR. RITE:

25   Q: The 22nd?

1   THE ARBITRATOR: What is the mystery? Let us get a
2 calendar. Do you have a calendar you can show the witness?
3   MR. RITE: No, I do not.
4   THE WITNESS: I think I have a calendar.
5   Can I have my glasses down there, please?
6   June 26th was a Friday.
7 BY MR. RITE:
8   Q: June 22.
9   A: June 22 was a Friday. And this is the date that
10 Gripe made a run to -- I forgot the truck number but he
11 was assigned to a vehicle No. 4 that day and he made a run.
12   Q: Was there anything unusual that occurred that day,
13 to your knowledge?
14   A: No.
15   Q: When did you first receive or review a copy of
16 Agency Exhibit 6?
17   A: It was the following Tuesday.
18   Q: What day of the month was that then? You can
19 take a look at your calendar.
20   A: I believe it was the morning of the 26th.
21   Q: What if anything did you do once you received a
22 copy of the report?
23   A: I looked it over, read it, and I asked for some
24 other reports, you know, that were made on other surveil-
25 lances, and I discussed it with the Assistant Director.

1 I said, "We have a person like this driving a
2 vehicle? We're in trouble."
3 Q: Was Mr. Gripe in the yard at the time that you
4 first reviewed Agency Exhibit 6?
5 A: No, he was out on a run.
6 Q: What if anything did you do at that point?
7 A: I took the surveillance report, I went to Per-
8 sonnel, pulled his file, and I went to my office, I studied
9 his file very carefully, I looked over the report very care-
10 fully, I reviewed some of the other reports that were made
11 and then I called the department foreman in.
12 Q: For what purpose?
13 A: To discuss this with him. And I requested that
14 Mr. Gripe not be sent out the following morning or assigned
15 a vehicle so that we can have a meeting and go over it.
16 Q: Did you subsequently have a meeting with Mr.
17 Gripe concerning this report?
18 A: On Wednesday when he wasn't sent out we got a
19 hold of the Association Steward. Whenever I have a meeting
20 with any of the employees I always make sure that the steward
21 is present.
22 Q: Where was this meeting held?
23 A: In my office.
24 Q: What time?
25 A: I believe it was around 10:00 o'clock in the

1   morning, if my memory serves me correctly. I am not sure.

2   Q: Who was present at that meeting?

3   A: Jose Gomez, the department foreman, J. Gomez

4   and I believe it was Mann, the shop steward, and Gripe and

5   myself.

6   Q: And what occurred at that meeting?

7   A: Okay, at this time I confronted the employee in

8   the presence of all that were at the meeting, I read the

9   report to him and asked him if he was involved in this

10   and he stated no. He got flushed in the face, he got a

11   little excited, and he was talking at the same time I was

12   talking so I stopped and I asked him to calm himself down

13   and pay strict attention to what was being said because

14   it could very well mean his livelihood and he calmed down

15   and then I started over again from the beginning and I be-

16   lieve I re-read the report again and I again asked him if

17   he had done what was in the report and he stated no.

18   Q: At that point what if anything did you do?

19   A: Okay. I then explained to him that people at

20   Looking Glass Investigations had made several surveillances

21   and that I had studied the reports and it was evident to me

22   that the investigator who had made this report had no axe

23   to grind, he was just calling the shots as he had seen

24   them, and I told him that he would be terminated and at

25   that time I handed him his paycheck and I believe he handed

1   me his badge.

2   I also told him that if he had -- if there was

3   anything that wasn't right in his paycheck to make sure

4   to report it, we would take care of it. I asked him to

5   check out his paycheck to make sure he got all the money

6   that was due him, I believe.

7   MR. RITE: I have no further questions.

8   THE ARBITRATOR: Your witness, Counsel.

9

10   CROSS-EXAMINATION

11   BY MR. DANCE:

12   Q: Did you base your entire judgment with respect

13   to whether or not disciplinary action would be imposed upon

14   the grievant based upon the report that is in evidence as

15   Agency Exhibit 6?

16   A: Well, it was his folder, our rules and regulations

17   and the report. I studied all three.

18   Q: Let me just stop you.

19   I am not asking you what you considered with re-

20   spect to the measure of discipline that should be imposed,

21   my question was did you determine that disciplinary action

22   should be taken solely based upon your review of the report

23   that is in evidence as Agency Exhibit 6?

24   A: I think all of the -- the folder and the report --

25   Q: Before you decided to take some disciplinary

1   action did you speak to anyone?

2   A: Yes. I spoke to the Assistant Director.

3   Q: And who is that?

4   A: Terry Duffy.

5   Q: Did you speak to anybody else?

6   A: No.

7   I discussed it with the department foreman and

8   I hadn't told him what action would be taken, I just gave

9   him what facts I had.

10   Q: What did you say to the department foreman?

11   A: I just reviewed with him what we had confronting

12 us and the fact that we have, you know, people out on the

13 street driving and the Agency is responsible. If we have

14 somebody out there drinking, we're in a lot of trouble,

15 we are going to have to do something about it.

16   Q: Did the department foreman say anything to you?

17   A: Not really.

18   Q: Did you inquire of the department foreman as to

19 whether he had made any observation of the grievant on that

20 day?

21   A: Yes, I did.

22   At the time Gripe came back on the 22nd, it was

23 after lunch sometime and the department foreman was in a

24 meeting with another Assistant Director going over schedul-

25 ing for the following two weeks, and so he wasn't in the

1   yard when Gripe came in.

2   MR. DANCE: I have no further questions.

3   MR. RITE: Agency rests.

4   THE ARBITRATOR: Thank you very much.

5   (Witness Excused.)

6   (Recess.)

7   MR. RITE: I have one more question --

8   THE ARBITRATOR: Counsel wants to reopen?

9   MR. RITE: Just very briefly.

10   THE ARBITRATOR: What is your pleasure, Counsel?

11   MR. RITE: Miss Conway.

12

13   SUSAN CONWAY,

14   recalled as a witness by and on behalf

15   of the Agency, having been previously

16   duly sworn, was further examined as follows:

17

18   DIRECT EXAMINATION

19   BY MR. RITE:

20   Q: Ms. Conway, during the recess, did you take a

21   look at your files?

22   A: Yes, I did, and in the file --

23   Q: No. Wait. There is no question pending.

24   In the file there is a copy of a document that

25   I have marked Agency Exhibit 12. Have you seen that document?

1   A: Yes, I have

2   MR. DANCE: May I see it?

3   MR. RITE: I am sorry. I thought I had given you one.

4   MR. DANCE: One second.

5 BY MR. RITE:

6   Q: Could you please identify Agency Exhibit 12?

7   A: Those are the notes on the surveillance that's

8 in question on the 22nd; that the typewritten report was

9 taken from.

10   Q: Do you know whose handwriting that is?

11   A: I am not sure. I believe it is my partner's,

12 Todd Binder's. Bobby's handwriting was atrocious. Since

13 he was on a bike that day there's no way he can write while

14 he's going along. I was there when he verbally did it

15 and it was Todd that wrote it down. It's not my handwriting.

16   Q: That was the only handwritten --

17   A: Handwritten.

18   Q: -- note, to your knowledge?

19   A: I have others on the other reports but not on

20 this one.

21   MR. RITE: I move for admission of Agency Exhibit 12.

22   MR. DANCE: Objection: no foundation. Lack of founda-

23 tion. She cannot identify whose document this is.

24   THE ARBITRATOR: I will receive it, weigh it according-

25 ly.

1   (Whereupon, Agency Exhibit No. 12

2   was marked for identification by the

3   Arbitrator and received into evidence.)

4   MR. RITE: Agency rests.

5   (Agency Rests.)

6

7   THE ARBITRATOR: Counsel, what is your pleasure?

8   MR. DANCE: I am not sure if you will entertain a

9   motion for a direct verdict, so to speak, on the basis

10 of the evidence on the record. Agency has not sustained

11 the burden of proof of establishing that it had just cause

12 to terminate the grievant, Will Gripe. The only evidence

13 that is in the record for you is a hearsay document that

14 has not been corroborated by any direct evidence in the

15 record from any percipient witness and I do not think that

16 the Agency has sustained its burden of proof of establish-

17 ing that it had just cause to terminate the grievant.

18 THE ARBITRATOR: I will reserve a ruling on your

19 motion.

20 MR. DANCE: Very well.

21

22 A S S O C I A T I O N

23 MR. DANCE: I would like to call the grievant.

24

25 WILL GRIPE

the grievant herein, called as a

witness by the Association in his own

behalf, having been first duly

sworn, was examined and testified

as follows:

THE ARBITRATOR: Give your name to the court
reporter, sir.

THE WITNESS: Will Gripe

DIRECT EXAMINATION

BY MR. DANCE:

Q: Will, did you work for the Agency on June 22, 1979?

A: Swampside?

Q: Yes.

A: Yes.

Q: And what was your job classification?

A: At the time when I was terminated I was a truck
driver.

Q: What were your duties as a truck driver?

A: I was to load my own truck, to put all the pesticides on it and go down the list as far as to the spraying
sites. I had certain pesticides that had to go on certain
positions on the side, so I had to load them on the truck
accordingly and I would do that, then I'd take them out

1   to the sites and I would drop them off.

2   Q: Did you drive a vehicle on Friday, June 22, 1979,

3   that was owned by Swampside?

4   A: Yes, I did.

5   Q: Could you describe that vehicle, please?

6   A: It was blue, I think, about a two-ton flat bed

7   truck. No. 4, to be exact.

8   Q: Was the truck loaded?

9   A: At the time?

10   Yes, it was.

11   Q: What time did you report to work on June 22nd?

12   A: At 7:00.

13   Q: And what did you do when you reported to work?

14   A: Proceeded to load my truck.

15   Q: And could you describe what you had on the truck?

16   A: Pesticides, spraying tanks, hoses and test equip-

17   ment.

18   Q: How high was the truck loaded?

19   A: How high?

20   Q: Yes.

21   A: As far as height?

22   Q: From the bed of the truck to its greatest height.

23   A: Probably about the highest point maybe 8 feet.

24   Q: Is there a window on the rear of the cab?

25   A: There was a window but there's a buck board

1   behind you, a wooden thing, in case something comes un-

2   tied it doesn't get through the window at you.

3   Q: Could you describe the size of the window?

4   A: You mean the hole that was in the buck board,

5   itself?

6   Q: Yes.

7   A: It was probably like maybe a foot high, a foot

8   wide, or two feet wide.

9   Q: After you loaded the vehicle, did you proceed

10   to use the vehicle to make deliveries?

11   A: Yeah. I went directly from Swampside to Cuca-

12   monga and unloaded the load.

13   Q: Where did you unload the truck?

14   A: On the end of Anophlos Avenue.

15   Q: At any time from the time you left Swampside to

16   the time you completed the unloading of the deliveries,

17   did you make any stops to purchase any alcoholic beverages?

18   A: No, I didn't.

19   Q: At any time from the time you left the yard to

20   the time you delivered the material that was on the truck,

21   did you consume any alcoholic beverage?

22   A: No, I didn't.

23   Q: After you completed your deliveries, what did

24   you do?

25   A: I returned directly to Swampside and proceeded

1   to load the truck for the next day, the same thing I

2   normally do.

3   Q: From the time you completed making your deliveries

4   to your return to Swampside, did you make any stops any-

5   where to purchase alcoholic beverage?

6   A: No, I didn't.

7   Q: Following the completion of your deliveries to

8   your return to Swampside, did you consume any alcoholic

9   beverage?

10   A: No.

11   Q: Approximately what time did you return to Swamp-

12 side on Friday, June 22?

13   A: Probably around 1:00 in the afternoon, something

14 like that. 12:30, 1:00.

15   Q: What did you do upon your return to the yard?

16   A: I started to load my truck for the next day.

17   Q: And what did you load your truck with?

18   A: The same as always, every day.

19   Q: How long did you spend following your return to

20 the yard loading your truck?

21   A: About four hours, approximately. I worked

22 until around 4:30.

23   Q: During the period from your return from making

24 deliveries to the time you clocked out Friday, June 22nd,

25 did any supervisor, foreman or any other individual come

1 up to you and question you about whether or not you had

2 consumed an alcoholic beverage?

3   A: No. No one did.

4   Q: Did anybody ever question you about the consump-

5 tion of an alcoholic beverage while you were still at

6 work prior to the time that you had a meeting with Mr.

7 Lent?

8   A: No. No one did.

9   Q: Did you report to work on Monday, the 25th of

10 June?

11   A: Yes, I did.

12   Q: And what did you do?

13   A: Loaded the truck and went out on the run the same

14 as normal.

15   Q: Did anybody have any conversation with you on

16 that date about your work on June 22nd?

17   A: No, huh-uh.

18   Q: On June 26th, Tuesday, did you report to work?

19   A: Yes. 7:00 as usual.

20   Q: Did you work all day?

21   A: Yes, I did. I believe I even worked overtime

22 because it was quite busy at the time.

23   Q: Did anybody engage you in any conversation

24 with respect to your performance on Friday, June 22nd?

25   A: No, sir, no one did.

1   Q: When was the first time somebody had a conver-

2   sation with you regarding your work performance on Friday,

3   June 22nd?

4   A: It was at the time Kevin Lent presented the

5   material to me, the Looking Glass investigation report.

6   Like you said, I left. Thought it was funny.

7   Q: You say you thought it was funny. In what

8   respect?

9   A: I thought it was a joke, to be honest.

10 Q: In what respect did you think it was a joke?

11 A: The fact that somebody was actually accusing me

12 of something I knew nothing about, something in that aspect,

13 anyways, and all.

14 Q: Have you ever been counseled or accused by your

15 employer in the past of consuming an alcoholic beverage

16 on the plant premises or during working hours?

17 A: No, sir, I haven't, not that I can remember.

18 MR. DANCE: I have no further questions.

19 THE ARBITRATOR: Your witness Counsel.

20 MR. DANCE: One other question.

21 Q: Did you ever make a statement to Mr. Duffy or to

22 anybody that you did not want to return to work?

23 A: No, 1 don't believe I did.

24 MR. DANCE: Thank you. I have no further questions.

25

1   CROSS-EXAMINATION

2 BY MR. RITE:

3   Q: Mr. Gripe --

4   A: Yes.

5   Q: -- on the 22nd when you were headed out to make

6 your delivery, did you make any stops at all?

7   A: No, I didn't. I went directly.

8   Q: Could you describe once again just what type of

9 items were on the truck that day?

10   A: It was pesticides, and spraying equipment.

11   Q: Any hoses?

12   A: Yeah, I believe there was.

13   Q: And then when you came back on that day, the 22nd,

14 you spent the remainder of the day loading your truck?

15   A: Yeah.

16   Q: Does the Agency operate on Saturdays?

17   A: Only when there's overtime.

18   Q: Did the Agency operate that Saturday?

19   A: Not to my knowledge.

20   Q: Did the Agency operate on that Sunday, the next

21 Sunday?

22   A: Not to my knowledge. I don't know.

23   Q: On Monday, the 25th, did you drive the same truck

24 that you drove on Friday?

25   A: Yes, I did. I always drove the same truck,

1 No. 4 from the day I started driving.

2   Q: You testified that on the 25th of June when you

3 got in in the morning that you loaded the truck; is that

4 correct?

5   A: Right, or finished up. I started to load it the

6 evening before, I believe.

7   Q: How long does it take to load a truck?

8   A: Depending on the load, approximately two, three

9 hours, depending.

10   Q: You testified that the items that were placed

11 on the back of the truck possibly went out to a height of

12 8 feet?

13   A: Above the bed of the truck, not from the ground.

14   Q: Was your view from the rear window obscured?

15   A: It always is. You can't see anything.

16   Q: Are you not able to see traffic in your rear

17 view window?

18   A: No, you can't.

19 MR. RITE: I have no further questions.

20 THE ARBITRATOR: Anything further?

21 MR. DANCE: Nothing further.

22   Association Rests.

23

24   (Association Rests.)

25

1   THE ARBITRATOR: Thank you very much.

2   (Witness Excused.)

3   THE ARBITRATOR: Is there anything further from the

4 employer?

5   MR. RITE: Let me just take a two-minute break.

6   THE ARBITRATOR: All right.

7   (Recess)

8   THE ARBITRATOR: Counsel, what is your pleasure?

9   MR. RITE: I would like to call one rebuttal witness.

10   THE ARBITRATOR: Fine

11

12   REBUTTAL

13

14   TERRY DUFFY,

15   called as a witness in rebuttal

16   having been previously duly sworn,

17   was further examined and testified,

18   as follows:

19

20   DIRECT EXAMINATION

21 BY MR. RITE:

22   Q: Mr. Duffy, are you out in the yard very often?

23   A: Yes.

24   Q: How often?

25   A: Oh, 10, 15 minutes a day.

1   Q: Have you seen trucks being loaded and unloaded?

2   A: Over periods of time in the last nine years,

3 yes, daily.

4   Q: How long does it take to load a one-ton truck?

5   A: Just the truck alone, an hour, two hours maximum.

6   Q: How long is a one-ton truck?

7   A: 12 foot, unless he's pulling a trailer.

8   Q: Would you take a look at this document and identify

9 it?

10   MR. DANCE: Any chance that I can get a look at it?

11   MR. RITE: Certainly.

12   Q: What is it?

13   A: This is a load Will took. His signature is on

14 it, showing he delivered it, and the man who signed for it

15 on the other end is on here.

16   Q: What day was that delivery for?

17   A: It is scheduled for the 22nd.

18   Q: Is it your testimony that that is the load or

19 the load order for the items that Mr. Gripe took?

20   A: That's correct.

21   Q: On the 22nd of June?

22   A: Yes. Yeah.

23   Q: Yes?

24   A: Yes.

25   Q: Are you familiar with the operations of Swamp-

1 side?

2   A: Yes, sir.

3   Q: Are there any hoses listed on that order?

4   A: No.

5   Q: Is there any spraying equipment that is listed

6 on that order?

7   A: No.

8   Q: What is the highest or the tallest item that is

9 listed on that order?

10   A: Five and a half feet high.

11   Q: Could you describe how the items are loaded

12 onto the truck?

13   A: By lots.

14   In other words, the various deliveries are load-

15 ed so that the last on is the first off.

16   Q: Are the items stacked one on top of the other?

17   A: Yes.

18   Q: Is the rear window obscured by the items that

19 are loaded on the truck?

20   A: No.

21   MR. RITE: No further questions.

22   THE ARBITRATOR: Your witness, Counsel.

23

24   CROSS-EXAMINATION

25 BY MR. DANCE:

1   Q: You indicated that to load the truck would take
2   one to two hours, correct?

3   A: Uh-huh.

4   Q: What if the truck had a trailer on it? How long
5   would it take?

6   A: Maximum of three hours, depending on the load.

7   Q: So it would not be uncommon to spend three hours
8   loading the truck and trailer?

9   A: Maximum of three hours, depending on the load.

10   Q: So it would not be uncommon to spend three hours
11   loading the truck and trailer?

12   A: Right.

13   MR. DANCE: I have no further questions.

14   THE ARBITRATOR: Anything further?

15   MR. RITE: Nothing further.

16   THE ARBITRATOR: Thank you very much. Any more
17   rebuttal?

18   MR. RITE: Nothing further.

19   THE ARBITRATOR: Counsel, any rebuttal?

20   MR. DANCE: No.

21   (Witness Excused)

22   THE ARBITRATOR: How do you want to handle argument?

23   MR. RITE: By written brief.

24   THE ARBITRATOR: All right.

25   Off the record.

1   (A discussion was held off the record.)

2   THE ARBITRATOR: Let the record indicate that closing

3 arguments will be presented to the Arbitrator in written

4 form. These written arguments should be submitted to the

5 Arbitrator in duplicate, two weeks after receipt of the

6 transcript as indicated in the letter of transmittal from

7 the court reporting firm.

8   Upon receipt of the written argument the Arbi-

9 trator will exchange it between the parties, at which time

10 the matter will stand fully submitted.

11   Anything further?

12 MR. RITE: Nothing further.

13 MR. DANCE: I do not believe so.

14 THE ARBITRATOR: Thank you very much.

15   The matter stands submitted pending receipt of

16 the written argument.

17   (Whereupon the proceedings were concluded.)

18

19

20

21

22

23

24

25

EXHIBITS

Joint Exhibit 1

Article XX *MANAGEMENT RIGHTS*

Except as specifically modified by the provisions of this Agreement, the Agency retains the exclusive right to manage the yard and daily operations thereof, and direct the working forces, to make and enforce reasonable shop rules.

Editor's note: Joint Exhibit 1 constituted the entire collective bargaining agreement between the parties. However, only the pertinent section of Article XX is reproduced here for the reader.

Agency Exhibit 1

G R I E V A N C E
R E P O R T
_____

This grievance report should be filled out only
after the dispute has been reported to your foreman
and your shop steward, without results.

REMARKS: I, Will Gripe, have been terminated from Swampside
based upon false accusations. These accusations were drinking alcoholic beverages while driving a company truck during
working hours. These accusations were presented to Swampside from Looking Glass Investigations. I would like to see
pictures or some kind of physical evidence or even witnesses
from the stores where I was said to have bought the liquor.

I also want these false charges dismissed from my work
records. Swampside will be responsible for all lost wages
from the date of termination to the day these requests are
granted.

_____ Clock _#_12_ Date _4/28/79_ Signature:

Will Gripe
Will Gripe

P. S. (I also would like action taken on the
grievance report filed on 6/11/79 by
myself. It seems to have been forgotten
about.) _This grievance was answered
on 6/13/79!_
Will G

Agency Exhibit 2

DISCIPLINARY ACTION FORM

SWAMPSIDE MOSQUITO ABATEMENT DISTRICT

Warning Notice _____   Termination Notice ___X___

NAME: _Will Gripe_

DEPARTMENT: _130_

SHIFT: _DAY_

EFFECTIVE DATE OF THIS ACTION: _6/27/79_

VIOLATION

Union Contract Clause _____ Warning _1_

COMPANY CODE OF CONDUCT: _MAJOR OFFENSES #5_

COMPANY SAFETY RULES: _____

DESCRIBE VIOLATION: _Drinking alcoholic beverages while driving a company truck during working hours._

(not in agreement)
EMPLOYEE SIGNATURE: _Will Gripe_

ACTION TAKEN: _Employee terminated._

Agency Exhibit 3

SWAMPSIDE MOSQUITO ABATEMENT DISTRICT

July 5, 1979

Mr. Ronald Reynolds
Bus. Rep. and Rec. Secy.
Swampside Employees' Association

SUBJECT: Grievance Report from Will Gripe received June 28, 1979

Mr. Reynolds:

On June 22, 1979 Mr. Will Gripe was assigned to deliver a
load in Cucamonga.

The load for Cucamonga was on truck No. 4, License 9999-01.
See attachments.

As the truck departed from the plant it was under surveillance.
Investigator Magee working for Looking Glass Investigations
did not know Will Gripe was assigned as the driver. Investigator Magee picked truck No. 4 at random and a surveillance
was made. See attachment.

Investigator Magee has no ax to grind, he was doing what he
was assigned to do, surveillance.

Investigator Magee is employed by the Looking Glass Investigations firm; they are specialists who devote themselves to
this kind of activity.

Had Will Gripe made his assigned trip without stopping for
alcoholic beverages, Investigator Magee's surveillance report
would have been the same as this report on June 20, 1979.
See attached report.

Grievance denied.

Kevin Lent

KEVIN LENT
Yard Manager

Agency Exhibit 4

SWAMPSIDE EMPLOYEES' ASSOCIATION

August 9, 1979

Mr. George Sharp
Assistant Director
Swampside Mosquito Abatement District

SUBJECT: Grievance -- Will Gripe, Termination

Dear George:

After repeated attempts at trying to resolve the above named
Grievance, I feel at this time that the only way we can effectively
resolve this matter is through formal arbitration.

I have brought this case to the attention of our attorney, whose
name and address is noted on this letter.

Please refer any and all correspondence to him.

Sincerely,

Sam Strip

Sam Strip
President

cc: Ken Dance
     Dance and Dodge

Agency Exhibit 5

SWAMPSIDE MOSQUITO ABATEMENT DISTRICT —
WORK RULES & REGULATIONS

Disciplinary Procedures:

To insure the wellbeing of all employees, violations of Agency regulations must result in disciplinary action appropriate to the nature of the offense. The severity of disciplinary action in response to a violation of Agency regulations will be determined by such considerations as the impact of the offense on Agency operations, the extent of damage caused, and the circumstances of the offense.

To assist you in meeting standards of conduct, the Agency makes a distinction between General Offenses and Major Offenses and has outlined a formal procedure for notifying employees of unacceptable conduct.

When it is reasonably established that you have committed an offense or violated an Agency regulation, a notice will be issued. The severity of the notice will be determined by the nature and frequency of the violation. Such notices are usually issued by your immediate supervisor and are intended to help you avoid further infractions.

You are required to acknowledge receipt of written notices of offenses by signing them. This does not constitute admission of guilt. If notices are felt to be without justification, you may seek assistance through supervisors or Employee Relations. If you refuse to sign such notices you may be suspended or eventually terminated. You may be suspended for a period not to exceed five working days to allow for a complete investigation of the facts concerning the offense when supervision or Employee Relations considers such suspension appropriate in potential discharge situations.

The offenses listed are not all-inclusive but are representative of unacceptable conduct for employees. In the absence of special circumstances, the following offenses are subject to the disciplinary action indicated.

* * *

(v) Introduction, possession or use of liquor or illegal drugs on Agency premises or reporting under the influence of same. The Agency reserves the right to request a chemical analysis or other tests of beverages, medicines, drugs, etc. brought on Agency premises. If appearing to be under the influence of intoxicating beverages or illegal drugs, you may be requested to submit to an impartial medical examination. You may elect to refuse to submit to the above, but if you do, the Agency may terminate your employment as a quit for personal reasons. A period of 12 months without any recorded warnings will clear the record.

ADDENDUM VI—4

Agency Exhibit 6

<u>LOOKING GLASS INVESTIGATIONS</u>

Surveillance Report

6/25/79

Surveillance report for the two days of 6/20/79 and 6/22/79 on subject truck

Wednesday, 6/20/79   Inv: Magee   Miles: 22   Hours: 5

6:50 AM	On Station
7:10 AM	Subject departed yard and went to Valley Blvd. Valley Blvd. to 6th St., to Don Julian to the other yard and unloaded truck, and then returned to yard.
12:00 PM	Returned to office.

Friday, 6/22/79   Inv: Magee   Miles: 86   Hours: 6

7:00 AM	On Station
7:05 AM	Subject departed yard. Went south on Vineland to Valley Blvd. Valley Blvd. to the 605 Fwy. 605 Fwy. north toward I10. Prior to getting on I10, subject stopped at a liquor store and bought a ½ pint of Black Velvet Whiskey. The subject then entered I10 Fwy., and went east to Anophlos Ave. He drank the ½ pint and threw out the bottle as he entered Anophlos and unloaded his whole load. He stayed there about 2½ to 3 hours. On his return, he stopped at Anophlos and Baseline at another store and bought a quart of Colt 45 Beer, and drank it on the way back to the yard. He went via Anophlos to I10 west, and exited at Baldwin Park Blvd, south to Amar, and then back to the plant arriving at about 1:00 PM.
1:10 PM	I returned to the office.

Agency Exhibit 7

DATE: *6/22/79*

DRIVER'S DAILY TALLY

#4   Lic. 9999-01

DRIVER'S NAME: *WILL GRIPE*

Customer or Destination	Gas Speedometer	OUT GP Speedometer	IN GP Speedometer	TIME Departed GP	TIME Arrived GP
CUCAMONGA					

Agency Exhibit 8

SWAMPSIDE MOSQUITO ABATEMENT DISTRICT

DISCIPLINARY ACTION FORM

☐ Warning Notice	☒ Termination Notice		
NAME *WILL GRIPE*	CLASSIFICATION *DRIVER*		DATE *3-2-79*
DEPARTMENT *191*	SHIFT *DAY*	EFFECTIVE DATE THIS ACTION *3-2-79*	

VIOLATION

Association Contract Clause: Warning Number:

Agency Code of Conduct: *MAJOR - 1*

Agency Safety Rules:

Describe Violation: *INSUBORDINATION, FAILURE OR REFUSAL TO PERFORM ASSIGNED WORK.*

EMPLOYEE FAILED TO COMPLETE SPECIAL SHIPPING ORDER AS INSTRUCTED BY FOREMAN AND IMPROPERLY FILLED OUT BILL OF LADING.

Employee Signature   *Will Gripe*

ACTION TAKEN: *TERMINATION*

3/19/79 - FOLLOWING DISCUSSIONS BETWEEN THE AGENCY, THE ASSOCIATION, AND THE EMPLOYEE, IT WAS DECIDED THAT THE TERMINATION WOULD BE CHANGED TO A 3-DAY DISCIPLINARY LAYOFF EFFECTIVE MARCH 5TH, 6TH AND 7TH

Agency Exhibit 9

SWAMPSIDE MOSQUITO ABATEMENT DISTRICT

DISCIPLINARY ACTION FORM

☐ Warning Notice	☐ Termination Notice	
NAME WILL GRIPE	CLASSIFICATION DRIVER	DATE 11-20-78
DEPARTMENT 191	SHIFT DAY	EFFECTIVE DATE THIS ACTION 11-20-78

VIOLATION

Association Contract Clause: Warning Number: ①

Agency Code of Conduct: G-15

Agency Safety Rules:

Describe Violation: FAILURE TO PUNCH OUT OR IN TIME CLOCK WHEN LEAVING AGENCY GROUNDS FOR LUNCH

LATE RETURNING FROM LUNCH THURSDAY 11-16-78

Employee Signature   *Will Gripe*

ACTION TAKEN: WRITTEN WARNING

Agency Exhibit 10

PERSONNEL ACTION FORM

DEPT.	SHIFT	NAME		CLOCK NO.	JOB TITLE	HIRING DATE
200	DAY	WILL GRIPE			RECEIVING	
HIRING RATE	PRESENT RATE	WAS EFFECTIVE	Effective Date of This Action	ATTENDANCE RECORD		PRESENT DATE
						3-31-77

STARTING NOTICE ☐   CHANGE OF STATUS ☐

	FROM:	TO:
DEPARTMENT		
JOB TITLE		
SHIFT		
PAY RATE	___ Hr. ___ Wk. ___ Mo.	___ Hr. ___ Wk. ___ Mo.

VACATION NOTICE ☐   LEAVE OF ABSENCE ☐

VACATION DUE: _____ Days.   FROM _____ THROUGH _____
LEAVE OF ABSENCE: _____ Days.   FROM _____ THROUGH _____
WITH PAY WEEK ENDING _____   DAYS LEFT _____   ☐ WITHOUT PAY

WARNING ☑   TERMINATION NOTICE ☐

☐ LAY OFF   ☐ RESIGNED WITH NOTICE   ☑ WARNING NOTICE
☐ DISCHARGE   ☐ RESIGNED—NO NOTICE   Last Day Worked _____
_____ Days Severance Pay   _____ Days Vacation Pay   Eligible for Rehire ☐ Yes No ☐

Remarks:

PESTICIDE SPILL

Will Gripe

DEPARTMENT HEAD	PLANT SUPER.	PERSONNEL MGR.	ACCOUNTING DEPT.	MANAGEMENT

Agency Exhibit 11

PERSONNEL ACTION FORM

DEPT.	SHIFT	NAME	CLOCK NO.	JOB TITLE	HIRING DATE
200	1	WILL GRIPE		HELPER	
HIRING RATE	PRESENT RATE	WAS EFFECTIVE	Effective Date of This Action 8-16-76	ATTENDANCE RECORD	PRESENT DATE 8-16-76

STARTING NOTICE ☐   CHANGE OF STATUS ☐

	FROM:	TO:
DEPARTMENT		
JOB TITLE		
SHIFT		
PAY RATE	_____ Hr. _____ Wk. _____ Mo.	_____ Hr. _____ Wk. _____ Mo.

VACATION NOTICE ☐   LEAVE OF ABSENCE ☐

VACATION DUE: _____ Days.   FROM _____ THROUGH _____

LEAVE OF ABSENCE: _____ Days.   FROM _____ THROUGH _____

WITH PAY WEEK ENDING _____   DAYS LEFT _____   ☐ WITHOUT PAY

WARNING ☑   TERMINATION NOTICE ☐

☐ LAY OFF	☐ RESIGNED WITH NOTICE	☐ WARNING NOTICE
☐ DISCHARGE	☐ RESIGNED—NO NOTICE	Last Day Worked _____
_____ Days Severance Pay	_____ Days Vacation Pay	Eligible for Rehire ☐ Yes No ☐

Remarks:

UNSATISFACTORY PERFORMANCE of
ASSIGNED DUTY!

DEPARTMENT HEAD	PLANT SUPER.	PERSONNEL MGR.	ACCOUNTING DEPT.	MANAGEMENT

Agency Exhibit 12

6/20/79   INV. Magee   MILES: 22   Hours: 5hrs

0650   DEPARTED PLANT AND WENT TO VALLEY.
Valley to 6th to the PLANT on DON JULIAN.
LEFT WHILE LOAD THERE, AND RETURNED
TO PLANT
1200   DEPARTED PLANT AND ENTERED OFFICE.

6/22/79   INV. Magee   MILES: 86   Hrs: 6hrs.

0700   FRIDAY - SUBJECT (LIC # 9999-01) DEPARTED
PLANT. WENT SOUTH ON VINELAND to VALLEY.
Valley to 605 FWY 605 No. TOWARD I10.
PRIOR to GETTING ON I10 Subject stopped
AT A LIQUOR STORE AND BOUGHT A ½ PINT
OF BLACK VELVET WHISKEY. SUBJECT THEN
ENTERED I10 FWY AND WENT EAST to
ANOPHLOS AVE. HE DRINKS THE ½ PINT AND
THREW THE BOTTLE AS HE ENTERED
ANOPHLOS AVE. HE THEN WENT NORTH to
THE END OF ANOPHLOS AND UNLOADED HIS
WHOLE LOAD. ON HIS RETURN to THE PLANT
HE STOPPED AT ANOPHLOS AND BASELINE
AT ANOTHER STORE AND BOUGHT A QUART
OF COLT 45 BEER, AND DRANK IT ON THE
WAY HOME (TO THE PLANT).

Association Exhibit 1

SWAMPSIDE MOSQUITO ABATEMENT DISTRICT

March 16, 1979

Mr. Will Gripe
251 East Terrace
Los Angeles, Ca. 90009

Dear Will:

Per verbal agreement of Don Rick, Swampside Employees'
Association, we are changing disciplinary action of March 2
to three-day layoff and requesting you to report to work
Monday, March 19, 1979 at 7:00 a.m. Back pay from noon,
March 2 through Friday, March 16, less a three-day
disciplinary layoff will be paid.

George Sharp
George Sharp
Vice President

GS/kg

BRIEF OF THE EMPLOYER

BEFORE AN IMPARTIAL ARBITRATOR

In the Matter of Arbitration) Between:)) SWAMPSIDE MOSQUITO ABATEMENT DISTRICT)) and)) SWAMPSIDE EMPLOYEES' ASSOCIATION)) WILL GRIPE: TERMINATION)))	BRIEF OF THE EMPLOYER

I.

STATEMENT OF THE CASE

This matter arises on a timely grievance filed by Will Gripe
(Agency Exhibit 1), protesting the company's termination of his
employment for drinking intoxicating beverages while working
(driving a company-owned vehicle). (Agency Exhibit 2) The
grievance was processed in accordance with the terms and provisions of Article XXI of the collective bargaining agreement
between the Agency and the Association. (Joint Exhibit 1)

On January 18, 1980, a hearing was held on this matter,
with Joseph Gentile presiding as the impartial arbitrator. At
the hearing, the parties stipulated that all of the procedural

prerequisites for bringing this matter to arbitration have been
satisfied and that the arbitrator is vested with jurisdiction to
resolve the dispute over Will Gripe's termination, subject only to
the limitation contained in the Agreement that the arbitrator has
no right to change, alter, or amend the terms and provisions of the
Agreement in rendering his award.

II.
STATEMENT OF THE FACTS

Swampside Mosquito Abatement District (hereinafter the
"Agency") is a State charted public agency whose mission is the
control and eradication of mosquitoes in the swampside area.

The Agency employs between 160 and 225 employees overall, with
approximately 110 workers employed at the yard. Notwithstanding
its collective bargaining agreement with the Association, the
Agency hires its employees only after they have filled out a job
application and completed an intricate interviewing process.

During the application/interview process, the interviewer
provides the job applicant with a pamphlet of materials, including
copies of the Agency's safety and yard rules. Thereafter, the
applicant, if hired, is required to sign a statement that he or she
has read and understands both the Safety Rules and Work Rules and
Regulations (Agency Exhibit 5).

Throughout their employment, employees have ample opportunity
to read and re-read the Agency rules. The full text, as well as

selected portions thereof, are posted from time to time on the employee bulletin board.

Over the last several years, the Agency has had an enormous problem with theft of its property, in addition to the possession, use and sale of narcotics by employees. The Agency loses through theft materials and supplies in the aggregate value of approximately $50,000.00 per year, extremely large number of readily marketable, small, portable tools, equipment and supplies such as sprayers, pesticides, and so on.

In approximately May of 1979, during the fuel shortage, Terry Duffy, the District's Assistant Director, received a notice that the Agency's oil and gasoline allotment was being cut by 20%. In response, Duffy ordered a check of the oil and gasoline records to see where consumption might be trimmed. The Agency's accounting department dug through and analyzed the records as requested, but when completed, the analysis revealed that the Agency's vehicles, which normally get from seven to ten miles per gallon, during the two weeks prior had managed to get only one to two miles per gallon.

Suspecting theft, Duffy contacted Looking Glass Investigations, a firm that the company had used for a number of years after its being recommended by the Sheriff's Department, to trace the source and reasons for the losses. Duffy gave to Looking Glass Investigation the license numbers for all of the company's vehicles and instructed Looking Glass to tail each vehicle and to report back on what the investigators observed.

On June 22, 1979, Will Gripe, the grievant, was assigned to deliver a load to Cucamonga. Contrary to Gripe's assertion, there were no hoses or spraying equipment loaded on the truck. Nor was the load on the truck eight feet high (off of the bed). Gripe signed for the load on Truck No. 4, California License No. 9999-01 (Agency Exhibit 7), and then departed. Unknown to Gripe, Looking Glass Investigator Magee followed Truck No. 4 on the routine, random surveillance ordered by Duffy.

On route to Cucamonga, Investigator Magee observed Gripe stop at a liquor store and buy a ½ pint bottle of Black Velvet whiskey. Gripe then got back in his truck, drove east on Interstate Highway 10, drinking the liquor as he drove, exited on the Anophlos Avenue off ramp, and threw the bottle out of the truck window as he turned north onto Anophlos. (Agency Exhibit 6) After making his delivery as scheduled, Gripe stopped off at a liquor store at the corner of Anophlos Avenue and Baseline Drive. While there, Gripe bought a quart bottle of Colt 45 Malt Liquor, which he drank on the way back to the plant. It should be noted that the truck that Gripe drove was not fully loaded, the rear window was not obscured, and the driver would have been visible to someone following the truck.

Once Gripe returned to the plant, Investigator Magee broke off his surveillance and returned to Looking Glass offices to make out his report. Gripe testified that he spent the remainder of the afternoon, approximately four hours, loading his truck for Monday's delivery, but that he was unable to finish the load until Monday morning. The truthfulness of Gripe's testimony, however, is highly questionable. At the most, it takes only one to two hours to load a truck such as Truck No. 4.

After the Swampside investigation wound down, Bobby Magee was assigned to work undercover at another company. As a result of his undercover work, five individuals employed by that company were charged with drug violations and for theft. Accordingly, Magee's identity was exposed and he immediately left the area. It is believed that Magee is now living in Nevada under an assumed name. Looking Glass has made considerable efforts to locate Magee, but to no avail. He has, quite literally, disappeared. (Agency Exhibit 6)

On Tuesday, June 26, 1979, Looking Glass delivered Magee's report to Terry Duffy. Upon reviewing the report, Duffy summoned Kevin Lent, the superintendent, and instructed Lent to take action on the matter.

Lent immediately reviewed both the report and Gripe's personnel file. Gripe's file reveals that he was no stranger to the company's disciplinary procedures during his tenure as an employee. In fact, Gripe was terminated from his employment on March 2, 1979 for insubordination and failure or refusal to perform assigned work, which termination was converted into a three-day disciplinary layoff without pay. (Agency Exhibit 8) Additionally, Gripe received three other written warnings for failure to punch in or out on the time clock and for returning late from lunch (Agency Exhibit 9), for carelessness resulting in a pesticide spill (Agency Exhibit 10),

and another for unsatisfactory performance of his assigned duties
(Agency Exhibit 11). Lent discussed the matter with Gripe's department foreman, Jose Gomez. Since Gripe had already left for
the day, Lent scheduled a meeting for early the next morning.

On Wednesday morning, June 27, 1979, Lent met with Gomez,
Gripe, and the Association shop steward, Chavez. When all were
present, Lent confronted Gripe with Magee's report and asked for
an explanation. Gripe immediately broke into nervous laughter and
denied the charge. Lent felt constrained, however, to believe the
report's truthfulness, since Magee obviously had no ax to grind,
was a professional, and would have reported that nothing unusual
or noteworthy had occurred if such had been the case. Accordingly,
Gripe was terminated.

III.

STATEMENT OF THE ISSUE

Was the termination of Will Gripe proper under the terms
and conditions of the collective bargaining agreement in effect
between the Agency and the Association?

If not, what should the remedy be?

IV.

ARGUMENT

A. Will Gripe Was Properly Discharged For
    Drinking Intoxicating Beverages While Driving

An Agency-Owned Vehicle.

The Agency Work Rules and Regulations (Agency Exhibit 5) is divided into three parts: the first describing General (minor) Offenses, the second listing Intermediate Offenses, and the third listing Major Offenses. It provides for, and the company follows, progressive discipline for General and Intermediate Offenses. Major Offenses, however, call for immediate discharge.

As noted, in May and June of 1979, the Agency engaged the services of Looking Glass Investigations to conduct a random surveillance of the company's trucks and drivers, in an effort to expose the source, or reasons for, the extensive losses of both fuel and materials. Since the Agency had used Looking Glass in the past, since Looking Glass was licensed by the State, and had come highly recommended by the Sheriff's Department, the Agency had every expectation that the investigation and surveillance would be carried out in a thorough and professional manner.

On June 22, 1979, Looking Glass Investigator Bobby Magee picked Truck No. 4 at random and followed the truck from the plant to the delivery destination. Will Gripe was driving Truck No. 4 on that day.

During the course of the surveillance, Magee observed Gripe stop at a liquor store and purchase a ½ pint bottle of Black Velvet whiskey. Magee also observed Gripe drink the whiskey while driving eastbound on Interstate Highway 10 and observed Gripe throw the empty bottle from the truck when he exited from the highway and

turned north on Anophlos Avenue. Magee further observed Gripe,
after making his scheduled delivery, stop at the liquor store
at the corner of Anophlos and Baseline, purchase a quart bottle
of Colt 45 Malt Liquor and drink the brew on route back to the
yard. Once Gripe arrived at the yard, Magee broke off the surveillance, returned to Looking Glass Offices and made out his report.

Several days later, the report was forwarded to Terry Duffy
and, based thereon, Gripe's employment was terminated for violation of Major Offense V (Agency Exhibit 5).

Notwithstanding the Agency's work rule absolutely prohibiting
the possession or use of intoxicants while working, and making
such possession or use an immediately dischargeable offense, arbitrators have long ruled that employees who drink alcoholic beverages
during the working day are properly discharged if they are caught
doing so. As Arbitrator Ben Nathanson stated in Specialty Paper
Box Company, 51 LA 120, 126 (Nathanson 1968), wherein he denied
the grievances of two former employees who were observed drinking
alcoholic beverages by an undercover agent:

> Drinking is of itself a major deterrent to
> efficiency, safety, employee morals, good
> working conditions and for a truck driver,
> good public relations. It is difficult to
> rule other than that discipline (i.e., discharge)
> must be imposed for such violations.

Here, Gripe was caught drinking while driving an Agency truck
on Agency time. Accordingly, his discharge was proper.

B. <u>The Investigator's Report Is Entitled</u>
<u>To Great Weight In Determining Whether</u>
<u>Gripe's Discharge Was Proper</u>.

At the hearing, the Agency introduced Investigator Magee's report, along with copies of other reports of the surveillance that Looking Glass conducted during May and June of 1979. The Association objected to the introduction of the reports on the ground that they constitute hearsay. While the report, indeed, is hearsay, it falls squarely within the business record exception to the hearsay rule, and thus is admissible to prove the truth of the matters stated therein (i.e., to prove that Gripe was guilty of drinking alcoholic beverages while working).

California Evidence Code Section 1271 provides:

Evidence of a writing made as a record of an act, condition, or event is not made inadmissible by the hearsay rule when offered to prove the act, condition, or event if:

(a) The writing was made in the regular course of a business;

(b) The writing was made at or near the time of the act, condition, or event;

(c) The custodian or other qualified witness testifies to its identity and the mode of its preparation; and

(d) The sources of information and method and time of preparation were such as to indicate its trustworthiness.

As the report itself shows, and as the testimony of Susan Conway establishes, the report was made in the regular course of business (an investigator's report made during the course of an investigation requested by the Agency) and was made at or near the time that Gripe was observed drinking the alcoholic beverages (the same day). Susan Conway also testified that she was present when the report was prepared and further testified as to the mode of its preparation. Moreover, the report was based on an eye-witness account by a trained and experienced independent investigator who obviously had nothing to gain by lying or inaccurately reporting the facts, and who was employed by a state-licensed private investigation company. Furthermore, a review of the reports submitted show that where nothing unusual occurred or was observed, that fact was also reported. In other words, if Gripe had not stopped off at either of the two liquor stores to purchase whiskey and malt liquor, and if Gripe had not drunk the beverages, the report submitted would have been clear, just as it was on the other dates for which reports were submitted. (See especially Agency Exhibit 6, report for 6/20/79: "Subject departed plant . . . unloaded truck, and then returned to yard.")

Thus, the report is admissible and is entitled to great weight under law. See Taylor v. Centennial Bowl, Inc., 65 Cal. 2d 114 (1966); Rousseau v. West Coast House Movers, 256 Cal. App.2d 878, 886 (1967). Moreover, the introduction of and reliance by the trier of fact on records that fall within the business records exception does not deny the person against whom the records are introduced a fair hearing (i.e., constitutional due process),

People v. Gambos, 5 Cal.App.3d 187, 194 (1970).

In an analogous case, Fox v. San Francisco Unified School
District, 111 Cal.App.2d 885 (1952), the Court of Appeal ruled
that teacher efficiency evaluation reports were admissible as
business records and properly supported the District's discharge
of a teacher. Thus, the discharge based on the reports was sustained, even though the supervisors who prepared the reports did
not testify at the administrative hearing at which the discharge
decision was made.

Moreover, arbitrators have long held that reports of investigators, "spotters," and "checkers" are admissible and are entitled
to great weight, even where the percipient witness does not appear
at the hearing to testify. In Los Angeles Transit Lines, 25 LA 740
(Hildebrand 1955), the employer relied on reports of professional
"spotters" in discharging a bus driver for violations of the company rules governing the collection of fares; however, the company
refused to produce such spotters at the arbitration hearing. Thus,
the spotters were not available for confrontation and cross-examination by the discharged employee and his attorney. The company
argued that the spotter system and disciplinary action based on
spotter's reports was necessary to ensure control over its employees
"for the safety of the public, as well as protection of the company
and efficiency of the company." The company also argued that the
spotters need not appear at the hearing to testify, since their
effectiveness would be destroyed if their identities were revealed.

In ruling that the reports were both admissible and controlling,

Arbitrator Hildebrand wrote:

(1) These reports are a record of specific
acts and events. Obviously they are relevant to
the issue being tried.

(2) The superintendent of detectives, Forkner,
was a qualified witness. He testified extensively
regarding the selection and training of the operatives, the nature of their work and assignments,
and the instructions that control the preparation
of their reports. (3) The reports were made in
the regular course of business, at or near the time of
the act and event. The basic assignment of the
operatives is to ride company vehicles as trained
observers and to report on adherence to or infractions of company rules. A regular reporting form
is used and the purpose and procedure governing
each report is uniform, though the factual content
may vary and though it may emerge either from a
casual spot-check or from a more intensive special
assignment. Thus the reports rest upon a well-
established routine and are similar in nature to the
efficiency reports at issue in <u>Fox vs. San Francisco
Unified School District</u>, 111 Cal.App.2d 885 (1952).

(4) The information was obtained by trained
observers, who are taught to be accurate and objective.
In selecting them, the company tries to obtain persons
capable of these qualities and who do not know any

company employees. The operatives are not supposed
to have personal contacts with the employees, and are
shielded from such contacts by various safeguards.
No reason was submitted to show that they had incentive to falsify the facts. The reports they rendered
are succinct, specific and dispassionate; and they
are uniform as to quality. They were prepared within
twenty-four hours after the acts were observed. They
were not prepared after the charge of NAP had been
made and the issue joined.

* * * *

Beyond the specific requirements of the business
records statute, two tests are decisive in an arbitration proceeding. (1) It must be shown that the reports
were prepared before the decision to discharge had been
taken and the issue joined between the parties. This
condition was satisfied here. (2) There must be no
tangible basis for believing that the company is biased
against the employee and has set out to get him. In
this case no serious charge of this sort has been made
and no factual evidence submitted even to raise the
question. Thus the spotters' reports pass these additional tests, which are decisive. Ibid. at 744-45.
(emphasis added)

Based on the reports, the arbitrator concluded that the company
had a reasonable basis for its decision to discharge the grievant.

Accordingly, the grievance was denied.

In this case, as noted, all of the prerequisites to the introduction of business records have been satisfied. Additionally, the concerns or requirements of Hildebrand's accepted test have been met: (1) the report was prepared on June 27, 1979 -- five days prior to Gripe's discharge -- and, in fact, was the evidentiary basis for the discharge; and (2) there is no tangible basis nor allegation that the Agency, in ordering the surveillance, was "out to get" Gripe. To the contrary, the surveillance ordered was random and the reports showed that no unusual or noteworthy activity was reported when none occurred. Coupled with Gripe's prior disciplinary work record, Magee's report should be credited.

Furthermore, the Agency did not deliberately absent Magee so that neither Gripe nor the Association's attorney would have an opportunity for confrontation and cross-examination. Both the Agency and Looking Glass made efforts to locate Magee, but such efforts were unsuccessful due to Magee's fully understandable decision to leave the area and to live under an assumed name. Since his undercover work resulted in numerous arrests and discharges at another large company and since his identity has been revealed, Magee is literally a "marked man" whose safety would be gravely endangered if it were learned that he had returned to the Southern California area, for whatever reason.

Also, in Shenango Valley Transportation Co., 23 LA 362 (Brecht 1954), the arbitrator ruled that the reports of checkers were controlling in regard to a discharged employee's guilt for violation of the company's Rules and Instructions. In so doing, the arbitrator reasoned:

> <u>Status of the Checker</u>-- It is a universal
> practice in a variety of industries where employees
> handle cash to use the services of a checker. . . .
>
> <u>The use of a professional checker has the obvious</u>
> <u>advantage of anonymity, specially developed skills, and</u>
> <u>strict objectivity</u>. <u>There is no question of, nor oppor-</u>
> <u>tunity for, personal bias or favoritism</u>. <u>It follows</u>
> <u>that his observation and report can be depended upon</u>
> <u>to be essentially correct</u>.
>
> Although he failed to appear in person at the
> arbitration hearing to support his charge against the
> grievant, the reasons for his nonappearance are quite
> apparent. It would destroy his future usefulness; and
> it is very doubtful whether all the cross-examination
> in the world would alter his findings in any major
> respect. Such a conclusion does smack of course of
> 'jumping the gun,' but <u>his unique qualities of impar-</u>
> <u>tiality, professional talent, and anonymity support the</u>
> <u>validity of his observations</u>. In ordinary circumstances
> due process of law would require the direct testimony
> of the checker, but <u>it is felt that the unique elements</u>
> <u>of his service justify his nonappearance in this case</u>.
> Ibid. at 365. (emphasis added)

See also, <u>Apollo Merchandisers Corp.</u>, 70 LA 614 (Roumell
1978) (customers' written complaints of rude service by an employee

admissible even where not all of the customers who complained
testified at the arbitration hearing); B.F. Goodrich Company,
69 LA 922 (Klein 1977) (sworn statement of clinical psychologist
who diagnosed an employee as "psychotic" when that employee
assaulted a co-employee; ruled admissible and given great weight
in determining the propriety of the employee's discharge, notwithstanding the company's contention that the deposition was "new
evidence" and that the company never had an opportunity to cross-
examine the psychologist concerning his findings and conclusions);
New York Telephone Company, 66 LA 1037 (Markowitz 1976) (the company properly relied on "grapevine" evidence that an employee was
intoxicated when it discharged him for unauthorized use of a company vehicle and for driving under the influence of alcohol);
United States Steel Corp., 58 LA 694 (Kreimer 1972) (written statements by employees who witnessed the grievant attack and stab
another employee were admissible, even though the employees were
not present and did not testify at the arbitration hearing, where
copies of the statements were given to the union prior to the
hearing); and South Haven Rubber Company, 54 LA 653 (Sembower
1970) (an affidavit of the company's attorney and chief negotiator
who died during the course of an arbitration hearing on a contract
interpretation dispute was held admissible, even though the affidavit bore directly on the issue to be decided by the arbitrator
and was based on the deceased attorney's perception and memory of
the negotiations on the issue).

Thus, it is submitted that Magee's report is both admissible and controlling evidence of Gripe's guilt of drinking alcoholic beverages while driving an Agency vehicle. The discharge, therefore, was fully warranted under the collective bargaining agreement, under the Agency rules, and under the traditional, well-established notions of the law of the shop. Accordingly, the grievance should be denied in its entirety.

C. <u>Although the Collective Bargaining Agreement Contains No Just-Cause Requirement, the Instant Discharge Is Clearly Supported by Just Cause.</u>

The collective bargaining agreement between the Agency and the Association contains no provision mandating that management's decisions to terminate employees be supported by "just cause." In fact, there is no specific clause delimiting management's rights, save the extremely broad Article XX Management Rights provisions, which states that:

> Except as specifically modified by the provisions of this Agreement, the Agency retains the exclusive right to manage the yard and daily operations thereof, and direct the working forces, <u>to make and enforce reasonable shop rules</u> . . . . (emphasis added)

The only contract provision that speaks at all to "just cause" is Article X: Seniority. Section three thereof simply provides that employment continuity shall be deemed broken, <u>inter alia</u>, if the employee is discharged for just cause. The remainder of the section speaks to the termination of employment continuity in the event of "layoff" or "voluntary quit." Presumably, if an employee is discharged for less than just cause, his employment continuity will terminate in accordance with the layoff provisions of Section three. Nowhere does Article X, or the Agreement as a whole, impose a mandate that discharges be supported by "just cause."

Where the language and the intent of the parties is clear, arbitrators are loathe to import just-cause concepts into the agreement. For example, Arbitrator Edgar Jones, who is not generally known for his sympathetic views towards management prerogatives, stated in Los Angeles Dodgers, Inc., 58 LA 489 (Jones 1972)*, the following:

> The most reasonable conclusion is that the bargainers here intended to reserve to the Employer that measure of control over discipline, including discharge, that makes unwarranted the implication of a just-cause limitation on managerial discretions in disciplinary matters. That being so, the Arbitrator has no contractual power to assess the propriety of Grievant's termination in terms of just, good or proper cause. Ibid., at 491.

Notwithstanding that no "just-cause" requirement may be properly imported into the parties' agreement, the Agency did

---

*Interestingly, the Association's counsel herein also represented the Association in Los Angeles Dodgers, Inc., supra. In that case, the contract contained no seniority clause per se and management was simply required to notify the union of its decision to terminate an employee by way of a "complete report."

indeed have cause to terminate. Will Gripe was observed drinking alcoholic beverages while driving an Agency-owned truck by a trained and impartial investigator. The Agency cannot and must not tolerate such irresponsible and dangerous behavior. Accordingly, the Agency's termination of Will Gripe's employment was necessary and proper under the terms of the agreement.

CONCLUSION

For the foregoing reasons, it is respectfully submitted that the instant grievance must be denied in its entirety.

DATED: February 12, 1980

BY: _B. Rite_____
            B. Rite

BRIEF OF THE ASSOCIATION

January 31, 1980

Mr. Joseph Gentile
Arbitrator
11620 Wilshire Boulevard
Los Angeles, California 90024

Re: In the Matter of the Arbitration between Swampside Mosquito Abatement
     District and Swampside Employees' Association (Will Gripe, Grievant)

Dear Mr. Gentile:

Please consider this letter as the post-hearing brief submitted on behalf
of SEA with respect to the above matter.

The Employer has attempted to establish that it had just cause to terminate
Will Gripe based upon the investigative report submitted by Bobby Magee
of Looking Glass Investigations.

Notwithstanding the introduction of the report of Mr. Magee, who did not
testify at the hearing, the matter contained in said report was refuted
by the direct testimony of the Grievant who denied that he consumed any
alcoholic beverages while he was working for the Agency on June 22, 1979.

Interestingly enough, when the Grievant returned to the yard after deliver-
ing the load, he proceeded to load the truck for the following day's
delivery, and at no time did any supervisor or other individual question
him about the consumption of an alcoholic beverage on that date.

If the report of Mr. Magee was to be accepted, it would be amazing for the
Grievant to still be standing on his feet after allegedly consuming a half
pint of whiskey and a quart of malt liquor within a period of approximately
4-5 hours. In addition, thereto, it is rather odd that no one at the yard
even questioned the Grievant with respect to his physical condition, considering the amount of alcoholic beverages he allegedly consumed. Further, it
would be rather preposterous for the Grievant to thereafter work approximately 3 more hours loading the truck in the alleged condition the Agency
asserts that he was in based upon the Magee report.

Therefore, it is respectfully submitted that the direct testimony of the
Grievant outweighs the reliability of the hearsay report of Magee, and
accordingly, in the absence of any further evidence, it is clear that the
Agency did not sustain its burden of establishing that it had just cause
to terminate the Grievant.

It is therefore respectfully submitted that the Grievant should be reinstated
and made whole for any wages and benefits lost as a result of the wrongful
termination.

Respectfully submitted,

Tim Dance

Dance & Dodge
A Professional Corporation

OPINION AND AWARD OF ARBITRATOR

```
In the Matter of Arbitration          )
                                       )
     - between -                       )
                                       )
Swampside Mosquito Abatement District  )
                                       )
     The Employer,                     )
                                       )        OPINION AND AWARD OF
                                       )            ARBITRATOR
                                       )
     - and -                           )
                                       )
Swampside Employees' Association       )
                                       )
     The Union and Grievant            )
                                       )
                                       )
Re:  Termination                       )
_____)
```

<u>BACKGROUND</u>

Pursuant to Article XXI of the applicable Collective Bargaining Agreement between Swampside Mosquito Abatement District (herein either "Employer" or "Agency") and Swampside Employees' Association (herein "Association"), the undersigned was mutually selected to serve as the impartial Arbitrator to hear and render a decision in the matter of Will Gripe's termination.

An evidentiary hearing was held on Friday, January 18, 1980, in the law offices of Dance and Dodge.

During the course of the hearing all parties were afforded a full and complete opportunity to be heard, present relevant evidence, cross-examine witnesses and develop arguments. An official transcript was made of the hearing by the court reporting firm of Hargroves Co. All witnesses appearing before the Arbitrator were duly sworn. Closing arguments were reserved to Post-Hearing Briefs; these were exchanged on February 18, 1980. The matter stood fully submitted as of that date.

Will Gripe (herein "Grievant") was fully and fairly represented by the Association. He attended the entire hearing and testified.

For the Association: For the Employer:

  Dance & Dodge by Ken Dance Esq.   Rite and Rong by B. Rite Esq.

ISSUES
and
PROCEDURAL CONSIDERATIONS

At the commencement of the proceeding, the parties framed and stipulated the following as the specific issue to be addressed and determined in this proceeding:

> ...was the termination of Will Gripe proper under the terms and conditions under the Collective Bargaining Agreement between the Agency and the... Association...? If not, what should the... (remedy)...be?[1]

The parties also stipulated that the matter was properly before the Arbitrator.[2]

The Association made a request to exclude witnesses until called to testify; this motion was granted.[3]

APPLICABLE CONTRACTUAL PROVISIONS

Two provisions of the Agreement were particularly relevant in the instant case: (1) Article X and (2) Article XX. Article X noted that "employment continuity shall be broken if...the employee is discharged for just cause..." Article XX grants to management the right to "...make and enforce reasonable shop rules...subject to the terms of this Agreement."

The Employer's "Agency Work Rules & Regulations" provided in pertinent part that the following offense was considered as a "major" offense and would subject an employee to discharge:

> (v)   Introduction, possession or use of alcoholic beverages or harmful drugs on Agency premises or reporting to work under the influence of same.

It should be noted parenthetically that the Association never argued that the above rule was unreasonable.

FACTUAL SUMMARY

The Grievant was employed by the Agency as a truck driver. On June 27, 1979, the Grievant was terminated for violating certain of the Agency's rules and regulations; specifically, the Grievant was charged by the Agency for having violated Rule (v) quoted above.

ADDENDUM VI-4

On the Grievant's terminination form, the following description was provided by the Employer:

> Drinking alcoholic beverages while driving an
> Agency truck during working hours.

The factual basis for the Employer's decision to terminate the Grievant was an Investigative Report dated June 25, 1979 (herein "Report"), and prepared by an investigator with Looking Glass Investigations. The investigator's name was Robert Magee. The circumstances surrounding the Agency's employment of Looking Glass need not be amplified herein; however, the evidence clearly demonstrated that a particular need existed for certain undercover investigations and that Looking Glass was hired to assist in this regard. The propriety of placing the Agency's vehicles under surveillance by personnel of Looking Glass was not directly related to the reason for the Grievant's termination.

The essential facts recorded by Magee in the Report were as follows: On June 22, 1979, the Grievant was observed in Truck No. 4 in route to Cucamonga with a load. Magee stated in his Report that he observed the Grievant stop at a liquor store and purchase a ½-pint bottle of Black Velvet Whiskey. The Grievant then got back into his truck, drove East on Interstate Highway 10, drinking the liquor as he drove. The Grievant exited on the Anophlos Avenue off ramp and threw the bottle out of the truck window as he turned north onto Anophlos. After making a delivery as scheduled, the Grievant stopped off at another liquor store at the corner of Anophlos Avenue and Baseline Drive. While there, the Grievant purchased a quart bottle of Colt 45 Malt Liquor, which he drank on the way back to the yard. Once the Grievant reached the yard, Magee broke off his surveillance and returned to Looking Glass's offices to make out his report.

On Tuesday, June 26, 1979, Looking Glass delivered Magee's Report to Mr. Duffy, a high-level Agency representative. Upon receipt of this Report, Duffy contacted Mr. Lent, the Plant Supervisor, and instructed him to take action on the matter.

Lent immediately reviewed both the Report and the Grievant's personnel file.[4] The matter of the Grievant's situation was also reviewed with the Grievant's foreman. At this time the Grievant had already left for the day. Lent scheduled a meeting for early the next morning.

On Wednesday morning, June 27, 1979, Lent met with the Grievant, his foreman, and the Association's Shop Steward. The Grievant denied the charges contained in Magee's Report. Management felt the Report was accurate and reliable; thus, the Grievant was terminated.

The Grievant disagreed with the Employer's action and filed a grievance on June 28, 1979, challenging the contractual propriety of the Agency's action. Thus, the factual basis for the instant arbitral proceeding.

Magee did not testify in this proceeding.[5] The Report was identified by an executive of Looking Glass and received into evidence over the strong objections of the Association.[6]

EMPLOYER'S POSITION

The Employer made the following arguments in support of its position that the Grievant's discharge should stand:

1. The Reason for the discharge more than supported the degree of discipline which was administered; under the established and published Agency rules and regulations, the conduct and acts of the Grievant were in clear violation of a "major offense" and therefore subjected him to termination.[7]

2. The Report of Magee should be accorded "great weight" in determining whether the Grievant's discharge was proper. In this regard, the Employer developed the following two contentions: (a) the Report was clearly within the business record exception to the hearsay rule[8] and (b) the contents of the Report should be entitled great weight under California law[9] and the rationale enunciated by various arbitrators in analogous factual situations.[10]

3. The Agreement contains no "just cause" requirement; however, the facts more than support the presence of "just cause" to substantiate the Employer's contention in this case.[11]

UNION'S POSITION

The thrust of the Union's position was essentially threefold: (1) the Grievant's testimony outweighs the reliability of the hearsay Report of Magee, (2) thus, in the absence of any further evidence, the Agency did not sustain its burden of establishing that it had "just cause" to effect the Grievant's termination, and (3) assuming arguendo that the Report is credited over the Grievant's direct denial, it is inconceivable that the Grievant, with the amount of alcoholic beverages he was supposed to have consumed, could have continued to work for three hours loading a truck.

Thus, the Grievant should be reinstated with full seniority and made whole for any wages and benefits lost as a result of the wrongful termination.

OPINION AND CONCLUSIONS

The first matter which the Arbitrator must address and determine is the appropriate standard against which the Employer's disciplinary action is to be measured. In this regard, the Agreement contains no specific provision mandating that management's decisions with respect to the termination of an employee must be supported by "just cause"; however, the Agreement acknowledges that such a standard exists and is applicable under certain circumstances as indicated in Article X. In Article X, the parties clearly recognize that seniority can be broken by "discharge for just cause." Based on this reference and acknowledgment, the undersigned concluded that absent a clear proviso to the contrary, the "just cause" standard should be implied in the instant Agreement. This is the standard against which the Employer's action will be measured.[12]

The second consideration in this case is not whether the hearsay Report should be admitted, for it was admitted as already indicated, but its criticalness and what, if any, weight or probative value the Arbitrator should give to the Report.[13]

There is no question but that the Report is a critical document in this case; without it, the Employer has no evidence. In fact, the determination of the presence or absence of "just cause" turns on whether the Report of Magee is credited over the direct denial of the Grievant.[14]

As already indicated in the footnote references, there are disagreements in the arbitral ranks as to the admissibility of documents such as the Report in this case, the probative value of such Reports if admitted into evidence, and the balancing of the wieght between such Reports and the testimony of the affected employee, particularly when the balance must resolve a direct conflict on a critical and pivotal fact. Some arbitrators will not even accept the testimony of an undercover agent whose testimony is not corroborated;[15] others will accept the testimony of an undercover agen in credibility conflicts with the testimony of the affected employee.[16] In the instant situation, there was no testimony from the undercover agent; regardless of the reason for this critical witness's absence, the Arbitrator and the Grievant were not afforded an opportunity to evaluate and weigh this person's testimony. The balance in this case is between a Report, which is clearly hearsay, but which is equally relevant as a business record, and the specific and categorical denial of the Grievant.

After carefully considering the approaches by various arbitrators in circumstances somewhat analogous to the instant case, the better and prevailing view appears to give greater weight to direct testimony on pivotal facts than to a document such as the Report in this matter. This is the view which the undersigned adopts in this case; thus, the Employer has failed to meet the burden of proof necessary to establish the presence of "just cause" to support the Grievant's discharge.

ADDENDUM VI-4

In reaching the above conclusion, the Arbitrator carefully considered the arbitral and court decisions which the Employer cited in support of the proposition that the Report should be given weight; however, each of the cases cited had clearly distinguishable facts in critical areas.[17]

Having discredited the Report in favor of the Grievant's direct testimony, any reliance on the Grievant's past disciplinary history as a possible factor in determining the degree of discipline will not be considered. To reach this consideration, the Arbitrator had to first find that the triggering incident was supported in whole or in part by the weight of the credible evidence; this was not the case.

<u>AWARD</u>

Based on the evidence as presented, it is the AWARD of this Arbitrator that:

The Employer violated the Agreement when it terminated Will Gripe.

Will Gripe shall be immediately reinstated with full seniority rights, benefits and all back pay (less any money earned elsewhere).

Grievance Allowed.

Respectfully submitted,

/s/ Joseph F. Gentile
Joseph F. Gentile
Neutral Arbitrator

JFG:ai

March 13, 1980

Los Angeles, California

ADDENDUM VI−4

NOTES

1. Reference in this decision to transcript of record, page 5, line 25, and page 6, lines 1 through 3.

2. Transcript, p. 6.

3. Transcript, p. 7.

4. With respect to the Grievant's personnel file, it indicated a number of prior disciplinary actions. These will not be reiterated herein; however, they were appropriately noted.

5. After Looking Glass's investigation was completed, Magee was assigned to work undercover at another company. As a result of this undercover work, five individuals employed by that company were charged with drug violations and for theft. Magee apparently left the area and is now living in another state under an assumed name. Looking Glass management has been unable to locate Magee.

6. Transcript, p. 30. This Report was received over the Union's hearsay objections. The Arbitrator indicated that he would "weigh it accordingly."

7. In support of this contention, the Employer cited Arbitrator Nathanson's decision in Specialty Paper Box Company, 51 LA 120 (1968), wherein Arbitrator Nathanson upheld the discharge of two persons who were observed by an undercover agent to be drinking alcoholic beverages. In that case, the undercover agent testified and the undercover agent's report was "not materially challenged by the grievants."

8. "Hearsay evidence," as classically defined, "is the report of a statement (written or oral) made by a person who is not a witness in the proceeding and introduced to prove the truth of what is asserted."

   As indicated in note 6, supra., the Report was received into evidence. The nature of the Report was such that it met, as the Employer correctly argued, the business record exception to the hearsay rule in California, though the strict rules of evidence are not applicable in the arbitral forum. Because of the critical nature of this Report to the Employer's case, the relevant portion of the California Evidence Code, Section 2171 will be noted:

   > "Evidence of a writing made as a record of an act, condition, or event is not made inadmissible by the hearsay rule when offered to prove the act, condition, or event if:

a. The writing was made in the regular course of a business;

b. The writing was made at or near the time of the act, condition, or event;

c. The custodian or other qualified witness testifies to its identity and the mode of its preparation; and

d. The sources of information and method and time of preparation were such as to indicate its trustworthiness."

With reference to further amplification as to the balancing of hearsay with direct testimony in the arbitral forum, these texts were reviewed: Elkouri and Elkouri, How Arbitration Works, pp. 269-272 & pp. 279-281 (3rd ed., BNA, 1973), and Fairweather, Practice and Procedure in Labor Arbitration, pp. 214-216 (BNA, 1973).

9. The Court decisions relied on by the Employer were as follows: Taylor v. Centennial Bowl, Inc., 65 Cal. 2d 114 (1966); Rousseau v. West Coast House Movers, 256 Ca. App. 2d 878, 886 (1967); People v. Gambos, 5 Cal. App. 3d 187, 194 (1970), and Fox v. San Francisco Unified School District, 111 Cal. App. 2d 885 (1952). The Employer relied very heavily on the Fox Decision.

10. The following arbitration decisions were either cited to or quoted from by the Employer in support of this proposition:

Los Angeles Transit Lines, 25 LA 740 (Hildebrand, 1955). In this case the Employer relied on the reports of professional "spotters" in discharging bus drivers for violations of the company rules; the "spotters" did not testify during the hearing.

Shenango Valley Transportation Co., 23 LA 362 (Brecht, 1955). The reports of "checkers," who did not testify, were controlling as to the discharge of employees.

Apollo Merchandisers Corp., 70 LA 614 (Roumell, 1978). Customer-written complaints were admissible even where not all of the customers who complained testified.

B.F. Goodrich Company, 69 LA 922 (Klein, 1977). Deposition of clinical psychologist admitted.

New York Telephone Company, 66 LA 1037 (Markowitz, 1976). Company relied on "grapevine" evidence that an employee was intoxicated when it discharged him.

United States Steel Corp., 58 LA 694 (Kreimer, 1972).
 Written statements of employees who witnessed
 attack admissible.

South Haven Rubber Co., 54 LA 653 (Sembower, 1970).
 Affidavit of company's attorney received into
 evidence; he did not testify.

11. The Union cited to Los Angeles Dodgers, Inc., 58 LA 489
 (Jones, 1972).

12. See Cameron Iron Works, Inc., 25 LA 295 (Boles, 1955).
 With respect to the implied "just cause" standard, the
 undersigned has analyzed this before. American Broadcasting
 Companies, Inc., 63 LA 278 (1974).

13. See General Tire & Rubber Co., 68-1 ARB 8186 (Crawford, 1968).

14. Transcript, p. 45 & 46.

15. General Portland, Inc., 62 LA 709 (Autrey, 1974). This
 approach is not the better reasoned view.

16. American Air Filter Company, Inc., Defense Products Group,
 64 LA 404 (Hilpert, 1975).

17. In the Fox Case, note 9, supra., which the Employer relied
 on in great measure, the affected employee had waived his
 right to an adversary hearing during which the hearsay objection as to the performance reviews could have been raised;
 thus, the Court said that "...he is in no position to now
 object on appeal that the testimony was hearsay...."

 In the Apollo Case, note 10, supra., the Arbitrator used
 the customer complaints as corroborating evidence to support
 the three customers who testified and indicated that these
 statements were admitted for the limited purpose of showing
 that the employer was receiving complaints.

 In South Haven Rubber Co., note 10, supra., the Arbitrator,
 after a careful soul searching, admitted an "affidavit," not
 a statement, and rationalized this admission on the nature of
 the arbitral process (and reference to AAA rules re: affidavits)
 and the permissive nature of the Michigan statute."

 In United States Steel Corp., note 10, supra., the Arbitrator
 allowed the statements of the witnesses into evidence because
 the Union had full knowledge of the statements prior to the
 hearing and the "...Union had full opportunity to request
 attendance of witnesses for cross-examination."

In <u>Shenango Valley Transportation Co.</u>, note 10, <u>supra.</u>,
the Arbitrator based his decision to admit and give weight
to the statements of the "checkers" in order not to destroy
the future usefulness of the system and, the Arbitrator went
on to state, "...it is very doubtful whether all the cross-
examination in the world would alter his findings in any
major respect...." Under no circumstances would the undersigned engage in such conjecture on such a fundamental right
of the arbitral process; thus, the rationale in this case was
rejected and given no persuasive value.

In <u>New York Telephone Company</u>, note 10, <u>supra.</u>, the Arbitrator
was addressing a much different factual context; in that case
the evidentiary dispute rested on the Employer's subsequent
(after the discharge) obtaining and use of medical documentation as to the grievant's physical state at the time, which
documentation substantiated the "grapevine" knowledge which
the employer had at the time it effected the grievant's
termination for intoxication.

In <u>B.F. Goodrich Company</u>, note 10, <u>supra.</u>, the Arbitrator was
dealing with a Deposition, not a statement, which was substantiated by other credible evidence; the dispute as to the
use of this document was in the context that it was not raised
in the earlier stages of the grievance procedure. The information, however, was apparently known.

With reference to the <u>Los Angeles Transit Lines Case</u>, note 10,
<u>supra.</u>, the undersigned found it the most factually analogous
case; however, the Arbitrator could not agree with the rationale
of the Arbitrator, as, in the opinion of the undersigned, this
was out of the mainstream of arbitral and court thinking. In
<u>Specialty Paper Box Company</u>, note 7, <u>supra.</u>, Arbitrator
Nathanson noted this case, acknowledged the importance of
"spotters," but also stated that in his case, the employer
supplied the undercover agent to testify as well as his report.

Chapter **VII**

The Arbitrator's Criteria

For many first-line supervisors, the traumatic experience of being the respondent in a grievance action is only exceeded by being the loser at the final step. Granted that management's first priority should be to resolve the problem and preclude its escalation into a full-scale grievance action, certainly the next priority is to prepare management's case and position so thoroughly that success at the final level of review is assured.

It is interesting to note that where management decisions are ultimately overturned by arbitrators and other third-party neutrals, it is frequently for procedural errors rather than the merits of a particular case. For this reason, it is well to review some common criteria used by arbitrators in assessing the grievance and in evaluating management's case.

At this point it would probably be helpful to identify some of the more significant considerations upon which arbitrators base their judgments regarding rule and contract interpretations. These are generally applicable to a third-party consideration of grievances and include:

1. The master agreement, state and federal laws, and agency regulations and rules.
2. Erosion of the master agreement itself.
3. Management rights and prerogatives reserved by the master agreement, laws or regulations.
4. Effect on other employees.
5. Seniority.
6. Other considerations in rule and contract interpretations.

1. The Master Agreement, State and Federal Laws, and Agency Regulations and Rules

These may make the particular complaint nongrievable or nonarbitrable. There is no inherent right to file a grievance concerning a particular matter unless the regulations or contract allows grievances on that subject. In all grievances, it should first be determined whether grievance procedure applies, in other words, whether the subject has been left to management, or must be resolved in the future by negotiations. Many of the subjects noted below may not be grievable under a particular contract or regulation. Many others may be, simply because the grievance clause uses the unlimited term "working conditions." Whether a matter is considered "working conditions" in an organization can also depend on past practices.

The regulations or contract may also be sufficiently specific that they answer completely the factual situation presented by the grievance.

If the matter is covered, the claim will often be made that this fact situation is not specifically covered, so that the person hearing the grievance is asked to "interpret" those contract clauses, laws, or regulations. If the aribtrator finds interpretation necessary, then the following considerations for the particular types of grievance become important.

2. Erosion of the Master Agreement Itself

The temptation to "interpret" clear contract clauses and regulations should be avoided as grievance decisions can erode benefits gained through bargaining or erode a regulation, the meaning and impact of which have been carefully considered before adoption. "Past practices" should not be followed in grievance decisions where these past practices have been abolished by the negotiated contract or regulations. The grievance may even have been filed to gain an advantage or establish a precedent that the employee association did not get at the bargaining table.

After having a clear picture of the facts and the claim, and before deciding the grievance, consultation with higher supervisors, with the personnel department, and even the person who negotiated the contract can give valuable insight into the nature of the grievance. It can also help the supervisor find out similar, applicable practices and similar decisions in other departments of the organization.

3. Management Rights and Prerogatives Reserved by the Master Agreement, Laws or Regulations

These matters should be nongrievable and nonarbitrable. (See Chapter II for types of management rights clauses.) The applicable management rights and the scope of the management's discretion should be known before any decision is made. These rights and discretion should be carefully protected from erosion. Since employee morale can be affected by applying such a denial of the employee's complaint, a careful, sympathetic explanation should be given.

The trend of courts' and arbitrators' reviews of such denials is to subject management rights and management discretion to limitations of nonarbitrary and noncapricious action, reasonableness, and nondiscrimination, rather than allowing unlimited management discretion. These considerations are applied in the context of all the circumstances of the particular grievance or claim. Management should guard against arbitrary, capricious, unreasonable, or discriminatory actions and decisions in all of the types of grievances discussed below. It should also be aware that often the only way an employee can state a case, under the circumstances, is to claim that the action was discriminatory, unreasonable, or arbitrary and capricious.

4. Effect on Other Employees

Though management cannot assert the rights of other employees when there is a recognized bargaining representative, management can legitimately consider the effect of a grievance settlement on other employees who may be affected and subsequently file their own grievances based on the settlement of one employee's complaint.

5. Seniority

Seniority becomes a very significant consideration in many different types of grievances. The negotiated contract and the laws and regulations must first be consulted to see whether seniority is a factor and, if so, how much weight it must be given in each grievance. Management will want to avoid seniority application when there is a less senior employee who can perform better or otherwise better satisfy management's needs. Seniority clauses often raise a conflict with "management rights" and "fitness and ability" clauses.

Where seniority is a factor, it must also be determined whether the grievant's or others' seniority gives them privileges throughout the entire organization or only within a smaller segment of the organization.

Seniority becomes particularly important in the areas of promotions, job assignments, transfers, vacations, work on holidays, overtime, demotions, layoffs, rehiring, reclassifications, reorganizations, scheduling work, emergencies, and to some extent in discipline and discharge.

6. Other Considerations in Rule and Contract Interpretation

The scope of permissible grievances can be limited by agreement to matters contained in the negotiated contract and/or adopted rules and policies. By implication, this type of grievance clause makes all other subjects nongrievable because they are reserved to management's discretion. Whether or not so limited, arbitrators will consider the best source for resolving grievances to be the negotiated contract, rules, and published management policies.

Negotiated agreements override rules and policies unless the legislature or court decisions require management to retain and exercise judgment and responsibility over the subject matter; there are of course statutory decisions prohibiting public agency management from delegating certain responsibilities via bargaining agreements. However, negotiated contracts and rules often specifically change — or incorporate and affirm — past practices. Legal opinion may thus be necessary to determine whether the contract and regulations are valid and enforceable.

In questions concerning the interpretation of language used, the technical, industry-accepted, and legal meanings of the words or provisions are usually followed by arbitrators in preference to any other claimed meaning. For other wording, arbitrators will generally use the common and normal meaning. Specific provisions on a subject are considered to override general provisions in the contract or rules, provided that an interpretation of one provision will not make another provision meaningless, of no effect, unreasonable, or illegal.

If the language in rules or the contract does not solve the fact situation of the grievance, the arbitrator will try to ascertain the intent of the parties. The bargaining history or identification of problems noted when the regulation was adopted may show:

1. What the parties intended to state.
2. That a particular resolution of this grievance would be consistent or inconsistent with the parties' intent.
3. That past practices were intended to be changed or allowed to continue.
4. That one party proposed a provision which the other rejected, and it was thus not incorporated in the agreement.
5. That by the absence of agreement or for other reasons, such as reserving the matter for future negotiations, the subject was left to management's discretion.
6. That other reasonable inferences may be drawn from the bargaining history or conduct of the parties.

If the law, common sense interpretation of language, or the intention of the parties do not suffice for the arbitrator to make a judgment, past practice may be a persuasive consideration. For this reason, it is sound management policy to ascertain whether prior grievances or arbitrations or actions by other departments of the organization have interpreted the applicable provision by virtue of actual practice. Most arbitrators agree that for a "past practice" to be valid, it must have been a common practice, acquiesced in by both labor and management, and not just isolated, sporadic incidents. Management can determine the validity of its past practices by considering the following questions:

1. Is this the first time a question concerning interpretation of this particular rule or policy has been raised?
2. If other questions have been raised, how were they answered and by whom?
3. If this is the first time a question has been raised, what sources are available to assist in making a correct interpretation? Are minutes of a negotiating meeting or a board meeting available which would contain notes regarding the discussion that took place when this contract provision, policy or rule was being considered?
4. How can the intent of the parties at the time this policy was being negotiated be determined?
5. Are there other policies or rules which would assist in interpreting this one?
6. Assuming the policy is interpreted in the way the grievant desires, would it then be legal?

CONCLUSION

This chapter has considered the critical importance of management personnel's understanding the arbitrator's perspective. We have noted that the ingredients for success in arbitration hearings include an appreciation of what criteria are used by aribtrators in reaching judgments, and how arbitrators may be expected to approach a decision. Attention has been given to the importance of management assessing the validity of its past practices prior to arbitration. Where the statutes, common sense, or the parol evidence illustrating the intention of the parties at the table do not provide the arbitrator with a basis for judgment, he/she will turn to the past practice criteria for the determination.

Such appreciation for the arbitrator's decision-making process will enhance management's prospects of being sustained.

Management Training Programs

The emphasis throughout this handbook has been on the critical role of the first-line supervisor in management's successful implementation of a grievance procedure. The importance of the first-line and middle-management administrators' roles cannot be over-emphasized. Both in terms of the early resolution of difficult employee problems, and the maintenance of a sound management position, it is vital that the first-line management be well-versed in the grievance procedure and skilled in its use. We have endeavored in the previous chapters to point out some of the major facets of the grievance process with which first-line administrators should be familiar. However, no manual, however complete it may purport to be, can possibly reflect the "on-hand" and pragmatic value of a sound in-service training program for management personnel. There is just no substitute for the sharing of experiences, establishment of consistent policies and practices, and the contribution of trained experts which such a training program brings to the first-line administrator. Fortunately, most public agencies do not have a large volume of grievances which reach the arbitration level. Probably the principal reason for this is an enlightened management attitude in the early stages in which efforts are directed toward resolution. However, the other side of this coin is that management personnel in the lower levels do not have any exposure to the grievance process until it becomes a reality. At that stage, it is too late for a crash training program to be effective. It is therefore paramount that management establish an ongoing program of training for those key personnel who will be administering the grievance procedure.

This chapter will consider some of the highlights and considerations in the training of middle management to handle grievances. Included will be a number of suggested agenda and training program components to be found in the addenda to the chapters. Obviously, each public agency will want to tailor its program in conformity with the needs, policies and procedures of the respective agency. Since the leadership of public employee unions considers the grievance procedure the life blood of any master agreement, it certainly behooves public management to give the process as much attention. There is a union axiom which states, "What we don't get at the bargaining table, we'll get through grievances." Unfortunately, this axiom often proves a reality because of the ineptitude or lack of experience of the first-level work site administrator. It is not unusual to find that an agency has, through arduous and firm bargaining, refused to relinquish certain prerogatives through negotiations, only to find that their on-site administrators have given it away at the building level. Hence the paramount importance of an effective management training program for all levels of supervision, but particularly the first level.

A few agencies have established formal training programs for management. However, too many agencies have assumed that the supervisors know how to handle grievances, and have not provided any formal training. Many public agencies have found they have been losing arbitrations because their first-level supervisors: 1) didn't understand the agreement, and 2) didn't understand how to process grievances. One agency learned this the hard way when they realized (in front of the arbitrator) that they had processed a grievance which had been filed one year after the time limit for filing! The grievance had expired and should have been rejected. The arbitrator ruled it was too late to bring that up as an issue.

KNOWLEDGE AND SKILLS NEEDED BY MANAGEMENT

If the agencies expect their management teams to handle grievances well, they must equip them with the proper tools. Immediately after an agreement is negotiated between the agency and employee organization, supervisors should be given at least one full day of training on the major features of the new agreement with an emphasis on the art of handling grievances. Addendum VIII−1 offers a checklist and shows the major objectives and goals for such management training. A well-designed training program will enable managers to:

- Become familiar with the major contract changes or features.
- Know and understand the grievance procedure.
- Process and resolve grievances at the first step.

Knowledge for Handling Grievances

All levels of management must be thoroughly familiar with the grievance procedure of the agreement as well as with agency policies and administrative regulations. This is particularly important if obvious misinterpretations of the agreement or of agency rules are to be avoided. The agency should also expect to devote at least a half-day a year to reviewing past grievances and updating information regarding anticipated problems. In addition, supervisors should be encouraged to consult staff resources at the agency level at the first sign of trouble. This is especially important if the agency maintains a staff relations or grievance advisor for management personnel. Managers need to know, from the agency perspective, the frequency and type of grievance complaints with which they will have to deal. For example, it is important for the supervisor to know if most grievances in the agency have been a result of unsatisfactory evaluations, payroll matters, or interpretations of a particular policy.

Skills For Processing Grievances

Once the supervisor knows and understands the grievance procedure, he or she must next develop techniques which will result in the solution of problems at the lowest level and at the earliest possible moment. This, in effect, means a solution at the initial stages of the grievance procedure. As discussed in previous chapters, the longer grievances are left unresolved, the harder it is to get a settlement of any kind. In addition, antagonism between the parties increases; employees gather support for their position among their peers, and supervisors find themselves caught in an increasingly rigid position as time passes and the matter becomes more widely publicized. A minor dispute between an immediate supervisor and employee, if not resolved as early as possible, may become a major issue between the supervisor and all of the employees in the department.

An in-service workshop training program for management on the subject of grievance procedures should include practical suggestions with respect to the first step in the adjustment procedures. Supervisors should be advised, and preferably exposed to (by use of demonstration techniques) effective grievance resolution skills. At the very least, supervisors should be taken through the grievance handling checklist and should be given a thorough understanding of the reason for each step. A typical instructor's subject outline is illustrated in Addendum VIII–2.

The in-service training program should emphasize some of the necessary skills discussed elsewhere in this manual, including:

1. The very real importance of being a good listener.
2. The value of taking time to make decisions and give answers in the initial conference.
3. The need for restrained emotions and the "depersonalization" of the issue from the administrator's standpoint.

Assessing the Role of the Organization Representative

Another important skill that we have discussed in earlier chapters and which must be cultivated by today's public manager is an appreciation for the association representative's role in grievance procedures. In-service training programs for managers should emphasize the importance of dealing effectively with the employee organization representative at the department level. Such training, therefore, should include an awareness of the nature of the representative as a political entity, as well as a personality. Managers need to be reminded that the representative has a quasi-political relationship with fellow employees and with the higher organization levels of the association. It is important to remember that employee representatives must maintain an image with their peers as people who can present their case firmly and competently, who do not cower in the presence of managers, who can get things done that others cannot because of their negotiating skills, and who are respected by management as individuals to be reckoned with.

The organization or union representatives must also appear highly competent and reliable to higher officials if they are to get their support on future issues. The first-level supervisor must recognize that much of the employee representative's behavior is motivated by the need to maintain this position and image with fellow employees. In this regard, the employee representative may very often be "acting out a role" for the benefit of an aggrieved employee. Experienced labor relations representatives in the private sector have found that it is often to their benefit to be supportive of the employee association representative. An in-service training program for public agency managers should include this consideration as an effective technique for resolution of grievances at the lowest possible level.

OTHER RESOURCES FOR HANDLING
EMPLOYEE GRIEVANCES

In addition to training programs, the agency should look at other methods of preventing grievance problems. Many agencies have prepared grievance handbooks for all their supervisors. These handbooks can provide a reminder system for managers who are involved in grievance processing.

Another reference that should be in the supervisor's possession is a contract clause book. In this book, each clause or policy in the agreement should be explained and interpreted from management's point of view. Employee organizations usually conduct training programs for their representatives in which they explain the language in the agreement, particularly where it is ambiguous. In cases where the district does not do the same, first-level supervisors often accept the language interpretation of the employee organization rather than the management interpretation.

Another very effective way of training supervisors is to send each of them copies of any final grievance adjustments, particularly arbitration decisions that have affected other managers. The entire problem of grievance resolution is often an academic subject for supervisors until they see it affect someone they know. At that point, learning about effective resolution of grievances becomes top priority.

The addenda to this chapter are designed as a handy resource for those administrators who are responsible for developing in-service training programs for supervisors. Included are a checklist for grievance training and goals, objectives, and attitudinal considerations in grievance administration (Addendum VIII–1), an Instructors' outline (Addendum VIII–2), basic techniques (Addendum VIII–3), and suggestions for effective conferencing (Addendum VIII–4).

CONCLUSION

All levels of management must have the knowledge and skills that will enable them to take an active role in employee relations. The continuing need for in-service training programs to provide management with such expertise is of critical importance for first-level supervisors, who are the initial points of contact for the aggrieved employee. One of the primary purposes of such in-service training should be to allay the fears and suspicions of immediate supervisors that grievances are somehow a personal reflection upon their professional competence. This can best be accomplished by pointing out some of the more positive goals and purposes of the grievance procedure. An in-service training program for supervisors, coupled with an effective back-up system to support line managers, will ensure the retention of the most positive and worthwhile aspects of the grievance procedures for employees and, at the same time, reduce to a minimum the negative and disruptive features.

The imperative need for management to establish a functional ongoing training program for its management personnel has been emphasized in this chapter. Attention has been given to the highlights and considerations which should be incorporated into such a training program, and the skills that should be refined by those participating in the in-service experience. No public sector agency can expect to perform its function of service to the taxpayers in today's collective bargaining environment without a paramount emphasis on training its management personnel to cope with the challenges inherent in that process. This is particularly important in the critical area of grievance resolution. Well-trained first-level management personnel resolve grievances at the immediate point of contact with the employee. In addition, those grievances which cannot be resolved or have strategic or political considerations and overtones precluding their early resolution, must be resolved in management's favor as often as possible. Here again the key to success lies in well-trained, efficient, management personnel whose processing of the grievance through all the steps reduces or eliminates procedural error and provides the basis for a sound management case at the arbitration level. Such skillful processing is inherently dependent on effective management training programs.

CHECKLIST: MANAGEMENT GRIEVANCE TRAINING

I. Training Objectives

_____ Each manager understands the grievance procedure.

_____ Line administrators understand management's interpretation of potentially grievable clauses, policies and practices.

_____ Management has the skills to deal with employee organization representatives.

_____ Line administrators know whom to call for advice.

II. Training

_____ Agency supervisory training workshops.

_____ External Resource training workshops.

_____ Articles from current publications.

_____ Discussion at management meetings.

_____ Management newsletter.

III. Materials

_____ Each administrator has a copy of:

    _____ the master agreement

    _____ an agreement interpretation book

    _____ an agency grievance handbook

    _____ grievance and arbitration settlements

    _____ agency grievance forms.

MANAGEMENT GRIEVANCE TRAINING: TACTICAL OBJECTIVES

The Management Training Program should strive to accomplish the following tactical objectives:

1. Strengthening of sound management techniques to preclude surrendering management prerogatives unintentionally at the first level.
2. Discouragement of any "mini-negotiations" at the work location on the subject of the master agreement or current negotiations.
3. Discouragement of argumentation between the first-line supervisor and union representatives.
4. Cultivation of an arbitrator-type objective interpretation and implementation of master agreement language.
5. Concerted effort on the part of supervisors to solve problems at the lowest possible level and effect compromise where appropriate.
6. Development of positive techniques in dealing with union representatives.
7. An awareness of pitfalls and errors by management in implementing the master agreement.

MANAGEMENT GRIEVANCE TRAINING: FUNCTIONAL GOALS

Management training programs should achieve the following functional objectives:

1. A thorough and complete knowledge of the master agreement and agency rules, with an emphasis on the grievance procedure.
2. Familiarity with past grievance decisions as a body of precedents.
3. The ability to communicate effectively with union representatives in the resolution of problems in grievances.
4. An ability to interpret consistently the master agreement at the work site in accordance with management policies.
5. An identification for first-line supervisors of the central resource for contract interpretation questions.
6. Maintenance of an ongoing record or log of problems, desirable language changes, and so on for proposals for the successor master agreement in the next bargaining season.
7. Cultivation of necessary skills and procedures to implement the master contracts and policies effectively.
8. Provision for supervisors to have representation and legal advice as needed.
9. Development of skills in written documentation and due process techniques for employee discipline cases.
10. Emphasis on deliberation as prerequisite to decision making on the part of first-line supervisors (i.e., not making an immediate decision).
11. Delineation of successful "preventive medicine" techniques to resolve incipient grievances.

MANAGEMENT GRIEVANCE TRAINING: ATTITUDINAL GOALS

The training program should achieve the following attitudinal goals:

1. Allay apprehensions of first-line management with regard to grievances.
2. Assure first-line supervisors of top-level management support.
3. Cultivate an awareness and use of critical human relations skills and techniques at the initial state of grievance.
4. Accept the imperfections and realities of collective bargaining in the public sector.
5. Recognize that employees do not have as much latitude under collective bargaining as in the past.
6. Accept that policy makers and other management personnel are in an ongoing process of in-service training today.
7. Cultivate a conviction that management represents the public interest.
8. Acknowledge that effective master-contract implementation requires a new order of management skills and attitudes.

INSTRUCTORS' OUTLINE: GRIEVANCE HANDLING FOR SUPERVISORS

I. The Negotiation Process

    A. Legal requirements
    B. Union demands
    C. Management responses
    D. Effect of no agreement (e.g., strikes)
    E. The parts of the Negotiated Agreement

II. Administration of the Negotiated Agreement

    A. Burden of administration falls on management, specifically on first-line Supervisor
    B. First-line Supervisor's relationship sets tone of Labor Management Relations
    C. Labor Management relationship may affect the productivity of the entire organization

III. Understanding the Negotiated Agreement

    A. Vital to *know* Agreement
    B. Equally vital to know what has *not* been agreed to
    C. Supervisors have to participate in negotiation process so that they understand Agreement
    D. Supervisors have to work with Negotiators so that Negotiators understand operation

IV. Past Practice

    A. Definition: All items not specifically covered in the agreement but followed by one of the parties over a period of time and left unchallenged by the other party
    B. It is not advisable to let things happen that may become harmful practices:
        1. Past practices can be used by unions in grievance
        2. Arbitrators will look at past practice in reaching decisions
        3. Past practices may give away items that should be subject to negotiation
        4. Past practices are almost as difficult to change as negotiated agreements
        5. In some cases past practice can be used by management to defend its position

V. Role of the Supervisor

    A. In administering the Agreement, Supervisors have the ability to make commitments which will affect present and future negotiations

B. The Supervisor must understand the Agreement
C. The Supervisor must have access to information regarding the intent of the parts of the Agreement
D. The Supervisor must know the limits of his or her authority to resolve disputes over contract interpretation
E. Higher-level Supervisors must delegate grievance resolution to low-level Supervisors:
    1. Avoids log jamming of grievances at higher levels
    2. Increases employee confidence in first-level supervisor's authority

VI. Handling Grievances at the First Step

A. Preventing grievances – effective employee relations
B. The informal conference
C. First-step grievances
    1. Let the employee tell his or her story
    2. Get the facts
    3. Give a positive response
    4. Follow up
D. Second-step grievances
    1. The second step process
    2. Expect to be overturned
E. The arbitration process
    1. Testifying as a witness
    2. The importance of documentary evidence
    3. Rules arbitrators use
F. Follow up
    1. Evaluation system for feedback on effectiveness of program.

MANAGEMENT GRIEVANCE TRAINING PROGRAM: BASIC TECHNIQUES

The following techniques may be employed effectively to implement the methodology of grievance training programs:

1. Panel of experts: Use resident expertise and outside resource personnel.
2. "Hands on" workshops.
3. Lecture method.
4. Case-study method: Typical grievances using the "what would you do?" approach.
5. Role playing and simulation: Testifying at a hearing, simulated Step 1 conference, and so on.
6. Checklists: Hand-outs on pointers and pitfalls.
7. Samples of effective correspondence: Conference verification, memoranda of reprimand, due process notices, proper completion of evaluations, "ideal" letters of response at Step 1, and so on.
8. Videotapes on closed circuit: Labor relations issues, ground rules, guidelines, demonstrations, and so on.

CONFERENCING SUGGESTIONS:
COMPLAINTS, CONSULTATIONS, AND GRIEVANCES

1. Maintain a calm, objective manner.
2. Do not raise your voice level.
3. Listen attentively before commenting.
4. Avoid trigger words such as "disagree," "foolish," "ignorant," "uninformed."
5. Use questions rather than dogmatic statements.
6. Try to determine the central point the complainant is making and restate it until he or she confirms it.
7. Try to identify and state areas of agreement between you.
8. Thank the employee for bringing the problem or concern to your attention.
9. State your position clearly, firmly, but in a pleasant, conciliatory manner.

Bibliography

Amundson, *Negotiated Grievance Procedures in California Public Employment: Controversy and Confusion*, 6 CAL. PUB. REL. 2 (August 1970).

Begin, *The Private Grievance Model in the Public Sector*, 10 IND. AND LAB. REL. REV. 21 (1971).

Berger, *Grievance Process in the Philadelphia Public Service*, 13 IND. AND LAB. REL. REV. 568 (1960).

Cohen, *Grievance Arbitration in the United States Postal Service*, 28 ARB. J. 258 (1963).

"A Colloquium on the Arbitration Process," LABOR ARBITRATION—PERSPECTIVES AND PROBLEMS 100-102, 106, 109 (BNA Incorporated, 1964).

Conference on Training of Law Students in Labor Relations, VOL. III, TRANSCRIPT OF PROCEEDINGS 669 (1957).

Cowden, *Deferral to Arbitration by the Pennsylvania Labor Relations Board*, 80 DICK. L. REV. 666 (1976).

Cox, *Reflections Upon Labor Arbitration*, 72 HARV. L. REV. 1492, 1508-1509 (1959).

ELKOURI and ELKOURI, HOW ARBITRATION WORKS, Third Edition, Bureau of National Affairs, Washington, D.C. (1973).

FLEMING, THE LABOR ARBITRATION PROCESS, University of Illinois Press, (1965).

Frazier, *Labor Arbitration in the Federal Service*, 45 GEO. WASH. L. REV. 712 (1977).

GORMAN, BASIC TEXT ON LABOR LAW, West Publishing Co., St. Paul, Minn., 394-95 (1976).

Granof and Moe, *Grievance Arbitration in the U. S. Postal Service: The Postal Service View*, 29 ARB. J. 1 (1974).

Grievance Procedure Under Collective Bargaining, 63 MONTHLY LAB. REV. 175 U.S. DEPT. OF LABOR (1946).

The Grievance Process (Mich. State Univ. Lab. and Ind. Rel. Center, 1956).

HILL and HOOK, MANAGEMENT AT THE BARGAINING TABLE 199 (1945).

HOWLETT, ARBITRATION IN THE PUBLIC SECTOR, Proceedings of the Southwestern Legal Foundation 15th Annual Institute on Labor Law 262 (1969).

Jones and Smith, *Management and Labor Appraisals and Criticisms of the Arbitration Process: A Report with Comments*, MICH. L. REV. 1115, 1152-1153 (1964).

Kagel, *Grievance Arbitration in the Federal Service: How Final and Binding?* 51 ORE. L. REV. 134, 146-49 (1971).

Katzman, *Arbitration in Government Contracts: The Ghost at the Banquet*, 24 ARB. J. 133 (1969).

Koretz, *Labor Relations Law*, 22 SYRACUSE L. REV. 133, 136-39 (1971).

Krislor and Schmulowitz, *Grievance Arbitration in State and Local Government Units*, 18 ARB. J. 171 (1963).

LACEY, PROCEEDINGS OF THE CONFERENCE ON IMPROVING THE RELATIONS BETWEEN THE PARTIES, 29 Univ. of Notre Dame Press (1960).

Lewin, *Collective Bargaining Impacts on Personnel Adminstration in the American Public Sector*, 27 LAB. L. J. 426 (1976).

Luskin, "The Presidential Address: Arbitration and Its Critics," in DEVELOPMENTS IN AMERICAN AND FOREIGN ARBITRATION 125, 133 (The Bureau of National Affairs, Inc., 1968).

MAJOR COLLECTIVE BARGAINING AGREEMENTS: GRIEVANCE PROCEDURES, 1 U.S. BUREAU OF LABOR STATISTICS BULL. NO. 1425-1, (1964).

Massey, "Employee Grievance Procedures," in DEVELOPMENTS IN PUBLIC EMPLOYEE RELATIONS 64-65 (1965).

Mosk, "Arbitration in Government," in ARBITRATION AND PUBLIC POLICY 168 (Proceedings of the Fourteenth Annual Meeting, Nat'l Acad. of Arbitrators, BNA ed. 1961).

Negotiation Impasse, Grievance, and Arbitration in Federal Agreements, U. S. BUREAU OF LABOR STATISTICS, BULL. NO. 1661, (1970).

Note, *Arbitration Awards in Federal Sector Public Employment: The Compelling Need Standard of Appellate Review*, B.Y.U. L. REV. 429 (1977).

Note, *Legality and Propriety of Agreements to Arbitrate Major and Minor Disputes in Public Employment*, 54 CORNELL L. REV. 129 (1968).

Note, *Public Sector Grievance Procedures, Due Process, and the Duty of Fair Representation*, 89 HARV. L. REV. 752 (1976).

Preparing a Steward's Manual, 7 U. S. DEPT. OF LABOR, DIV. OF LABOR STANDARDS, BULL. NO. 59 (1943).

The President's National Labor-Management Conference No. 5-30, 1945, U. S. DEPT. OF LABOR, DIV. OF LABOR STANDARDS, BULL. NO. 77 45-46 (1946).

Report of the Committee on the Law of Federal Government Employee Relations, Section of Labor Relations Law, American Bar Association 1972 Committee Reports 144-46 (1972).

Reynard, *Drafting of Grievance and Arbitration Articles of Collective Bargaining Agreements*, 10 VAND. L. REV. 749 (1957).

Rock, "The Role of the Neutral in Grievance Arbitration in Public Employment," in COLLECTIVE BARGAINING IN GOVERMENT 141 (J. Lowewenberg and M. Moskow eds. 1972).

Ross, "Distressed Grievance Procedures and Their Rehabilitation," LABOR ARBITRATION AND INDUSTRIAL CHANGE 104, 107-108 (BNA Incorporated, 1963).

Smith and Jones, *The Supreme Court and Labor Dispute Arbitration: The Emerging Federal Law*, 63 MICH. L. REV. 751, 755-60 (1965).

Somers, *Grievance Settlement in Coal Mining* 43 (W. VA. UNIV. BULL. SERIES 56, No. 12-2, 1956).

Toole, *Judicial Activism in Public Sector Grievance Arbitration: A Study of Recent Developments,* 33 ARB. J. 6 (1978).

The Twentieth Century Fund, *Pickets at City Hall: Report and Recommendations of The Twentieth Century Fund Task Force on Labor Disputes in Public Employment* 17-18 (New York, 1970).

Ullman and Begin, *The Structure and Scope of Appeals Procedures for Public Employees,* 23 IND. AND LAB. REL. REV. 323 (1970).

U.S.C.S.C./O.L.M.R., GRIEVANCE ARBITRATION IN THE FEDERAL SERVICE: PRINCIPLES, PRACTICES AND PRECEDENTS (1977).

WELLINGTON, LABOR AND THE LEGAL PROCESS 97-100, The Yale University Press (1968).

WELLINGTON and WINTER, THE UNIONS AND THE CITIES 162-64 (The Brookings Institution, Washington, D. C., 1971).

Wolf, "Grievance Procedures for School Employees," in EMPLOYER-EMPLOYEE RELATIONS IN THE PUBLIC SCHOOLS 133 (R. Doherty ed. 1967).

ARBITRATION REFERRAL SOURCES

Federal, State, and Territorial Mediation and Conciliation Agencies

Federal Mediation and Conciliation Service

Address: Administrative Offices
2100 K Street, N.W.
Washington, D. C. 20427
Telephone: (202) 653-5290

ALABAMA

Department of Labor
State Administration Building
Suite 600
Montgomery, Alabama 36130

ALASKA

Department of Labor
Post Office Box 1149
Juneau, Alaska 98811

ARIZONA

Industrial Commission
Labor Department
1601 West Jefferson Street
Phoenix, Arizona 85007

ARKANSAS

Department of Labor
Capitol Hill Building
Little Rock, Arkansas 72201

CALIFORNIA

Department of Industrial Relations
State Conciliation Service
State Building Annex
455 Golden State Avenue
San Francisco, California 94102

Mailing Address:
Post Office Box 603
San Francisco, California 94101

COLORADO

Department of Labor and Employment
Division of Labor
251 East 12th Avenue
Denver, Colorado 80203

CONNECTICUT

Labor Department
Board of Mediation & Arbitration
200 Folly Brook Boulevard
Wethersfield, Connecticut 06109

DELAWARE

Department of Labor
State Mediation Service
801 West Street
Wilmington, Delaware 19899

DISTRICT OF COLUMBIA

Federal Mediation & Conciliation
Service
2100 K Street, N.W.
Washington, D. C. 20001

Public Employees:
District of Columbia Board of Labor
Relations
Suite 821
1010 Vermont Avenue, N.W.
Washington, D. C. 20005

FLORIDA

Mediation & Conciliation Service
1321 Executive Center Drive, East
Tallahassee, Florida 32301

GEORGIA

Department of Labor
State Labor Building

54 Washington Street
Atlanta, Georgia 30334

HAWAII
Department of Labor and
Industrial Relations
Honolulu Hawaii 96813

IDAHO
Department of Labor and
Industrial Services
Room 400, Statehouse
317 Main Street
Boise, Idaho 83720

ILLINOIS
Department of Labor
Conciliation & Mediation Service
910 South Michigan Avenue
Chicago, Illinois 60605

Public Employees:
Office of Collective Bargaining
Room 200, 525 West Jefferson Street
Springfield, Illinois 62702

INDIANA
Division of Labor
Department of Mediation &
Conciliation
Indiana State Office Building
Room 1013
100 North Senate Avenue
Indianapolis, Indiana 46260

IOWA
Bureau of Labor
Capitol Complex
Des Moines, Iowa 50319

KANSAS
Department of Human Resources
Division of Labor-Management and
Employment Standards
610 West Tenth Street
Topeka, Kansas 66612

KENTUCKY
Department of Labor
U.S. 127 South
Frankfort, Kentucky 40601

LOUISIANA
Department of Labor
State Land & Natural Resources
Building, 10th Floor, Room 1015
Post Office Box 44094
Baton Rouge, Louisiana 70804

MAINE
Board of Arbitration & Conciliation
State Office Building
Augusta, Maine 04333

MARYLAND
Division of Labor and Industry
Mediation & Conciliation Service
203 East Baltimore Street
Baltimore, Maryland 21202

MASSACHUSETTS
Department of Labor and Industries
Board of Conciliation & Arbitration
Saltonstall Office Building
Government Center
100 Cambridge Street
Boston, Massachusetts 02202

MICHIGAN
Department of Labor
Employment Relations Commission
Leonard Plaza Building
309 North Washington Square
Lansing, Michigan 48909

MINNESOTA
Bureau of Mediation Services
First Floor
Veterans Building
20 West 12th Street
St. Paul, Minnesota 55155

MISSISSIPPI
Has no authorized state agency.

MISSOURI
Department of Labor and Industrial
Relations
State Board of Mediation
421 East Dunklin
Jefferson City, Missouri 65101

MONTANA
Department of Labor and Industry
Capitol Station
Helena, Montana 59601

NEBRASKA
Department of Labor
Post Office Box 94600
550 South 16th Street
Lincoln, Nebraska 68509

NEVADA
Department of Labor
Room 601, 505 East King Street
Carson City, Nevada 89701

Mailing Address:
Capitol Complex
Carson City, Nevada 89701

NEW HAMPSHIRE
Board of Conciliation & Arbitration
62 Congress Street
Plymouth, New Hampshire 03801

Public Employees:
Public Employee Labor Relations
Board
Pine Inn Plaza
117 Manchester Street
Concord, New Hampshire 03301

NEW JERSEY
Department of Labor and Industry
State Board of Mediation
Room 306, 1100 Raymond Boulevard
Newark, New Jersey 07102

NEW MEXICO
Labor and Industrial Bureau
Kennedy Hall, College of Santa Fe
Santa Fe, New Mexico 87501

NEW YORK
Mediation Board
34th Floor
Two World Trade Center
New York, New York 10047

Public Employees:
Office of Collective Bargaining
250 Broadway
New York, New York, 10007

NORTH CAROLINA
Department of Labor
Conciliation & Arbitration Division
4 West Edenton Street
Raleigh, North Carolina 27611

NORTH DAKOTA
Department of Labor
State Capitol
Bismarck, North Dakota 58501

OHIO
Department of Industrial Relations
2323 West Fifth Avenue
Columbus, Ohio 43216

OKLAHOMA
Department of Labor
State Capitol
Oklahoma City, Oklahoma 73105

Public Employees:
Public Employees Relations Board
300 City National Tower
Post Office Box 25715
Oklahoma City, Oklahoma 73102

OREGON
Employment Relations Board
Conciliation Service Division
402 Capitol Tower Building
388 State Street
Salem, Oregon 97310

PENNSYLVANIA
Department of Labor and Industry
Bureau of Mediation

Labor & Industry Building
Harrisburg, Pennsylvania 17120

PUERTO RICO
Department of Labor and Human
  Resources
Bureau of Conciliation & Arbitration
Munoz Rivera Ave., Corner
  Domenech Street
Hato Rey, Puerto Rico 00917

RHODE ISLAND
Department of Labor
220 Elmwood Avenue
Providence, Rhode Island 02907

SOUTH CAROLINA
Department of Labor
Division of Conciliation
3600 Forest Drive
Post Office Box 11329
Columbia, South Carolina 29211

SOUTH DAKOTA
Department of Labor
Division of Labor & Management
  Relations
Foss Building
Pierre, South Dakota 57501

TENNESSEE
Department of Labor
501 Union Building
Nashville, Tennessee 37219

TEXAS
Department of Labor and Standards
Box 12157
Capitol Station
Austin, Texas 78711

UTAH
Industrial Commission
Labor Relations Commission

350 East 500 South
Salt Lake City, Utah 84111

VERMONT
Department of Labor and Industry
State Office Building
Montpelier, Vermont 05602

VIRGINIA
Department of Labor and Industry
Post Office Box 12064
Fourth Street Office Building
Richmond, Virginia 23241

VIRGIN ISLANDS
Department of Labor
Post Office Box 708
Christiansted, St. Croix 00820

WASHINGTON
Department of Labor and Industries
General Administration Building
Olympia, Washington 98504

Public Employees:
State Personnel Board
600 South Franklin Avenue
Olympia, Washington 98504

WEST VIRGINIA
Department of Labor
Capitol Complex
1900 Washington Street
East Charleston, West Virginia 25305

WISCONSIN
Department of Industry, Labor and
  Human Relations
201 East Washington Avenue
Madison, Wisconsin 53702

Wisconsin Employment Relations Commission
Room 906
30 West Mifflin Street
Madison, Wisconsin 53703

American Arbitration Association

Main Office:
140 West 51st Street
New York, New York 10020

ARIZONA
Security Center
Suite 669
222 North Central Avenue
Phoenix, Arizona 85004

CALIFORNIA
443 Shatto Place
Post Office Box 57994
Los Angeles, California 90020

San Diego Trust & Savings Bank
  Building
Suite 909
530 Broadway
San Diego, California 92101

445 Bush Street
5th Floor
San Francisco, California 94108

CONNECTICUT
37 Lewis Street
Room 406
Hartford, Connecticut 06103

DISTRICT OF COLUMBIA
1730 Rhode Island Avenue, N.W.
Suite 509
Washington, D. C. 20036

FLORIDA
2250 S.W. Third Avenue
Miami, Florida 33129

GEORGIA
Equitable Building
100 Peachtree Street, N.W.
Atlanta, Georgia 30303

ILLINOIS
180 North LaSalle Street
Suite 1025
Chicago, Illinois 60601

MASSACHUSETTS
294 Washington Street
Boston, Massachusetts 02108

MICHIGAN
City National Bank Building
Suite 1234
645 Griswold Street
Detroit, Michigan 48226

MINNESOTA
510 Foshay Tower
Suite 1001
821 Marquett Avenue
Minneapolis, Minnesota 55402

NEW JERSEY
One Executive Drive
Somerset, New Jersey 08873

NEW YORK
585 Stewart Avenue
Garden City, New York 11530

109 South Warren Street
720 State Tower
Syracuse, New York 13202

34 South Broadway
White Plains, New York 10601

NORTH CAROLINA
Post Office Box 18591
Charlotte, North Carolina 28218

OHIO
Carew Tower
Suite 2308
441 Vine Street
Cincinnati, Ohio 45202

215 Euclid Avenue
Room 930
Cleveland, Ohio 44114

PENNSYLVANIA
1520 Locust Street
12th Floor
Philadelphia, Pennsylvania 19102

221 Gateway Four
Pittsburgh, Pennsylvania 15222

TEXAS
Praetorian Building
Suite 1115
1607 Main Street
Dallas, Texas 75201

WASHINGTON
Central Building
Room 330
811 First Avenue
Suite 200
Seattle, Washington 98104

Index

SANDHILLS COMMUNITY COLLEGE

3 9884 00090 5846

Fountaindale Public Library District
300 W. Briarcliff Rd.
Bolingbrook, IL 60440

IBRAHIM MOUSTAFA
Writer & Artist

BRAD SIMPSON
Color Artist

HASSAN OTSMANE-ELHAOU
Letterer

IBRAHIM MOUSTAFA
Cover

AMANDA LUCIDO
Assistant Editor

ROB LEVIN
Editor

JERRY FRISSEN
Senior Art Director

MARK WAID
Publisher

Rights and Licensing - licensing@humanoids.com
Press and Social Media - pr@humanoids.com

With overwhelming appreciation for my wife, Janna, for always making it work. My endless thanks to: Fabrice Sapolsky for opening the door to me at Humanoids; to Alex Donoghue for helping me to walk through it; to Mark Waid for championing this book from the start; and to Rob Levin for his expertise and insights.
—Ibrahim

COUNT. First Edition. This title is a publication of Humanoids, Inc. 8033 Sunset Blvd. #628, Los Angeles, CA 90046. Copyright © 2021 Humanoids, Inc., Los Angeles (USA). All rights reserved. Humanoids and its logos are ® and © 2021 Humanoids, Inc. Library of Congress Control Number: 2020942925

The story and characters presented in this publication are fictional. Any similarities to events or persons living or dead are purely coincidental. No portion of this book may be reproduced by any means without the express written consent of the copyright holder except for artwork used for review purposes. Printed in Latvia